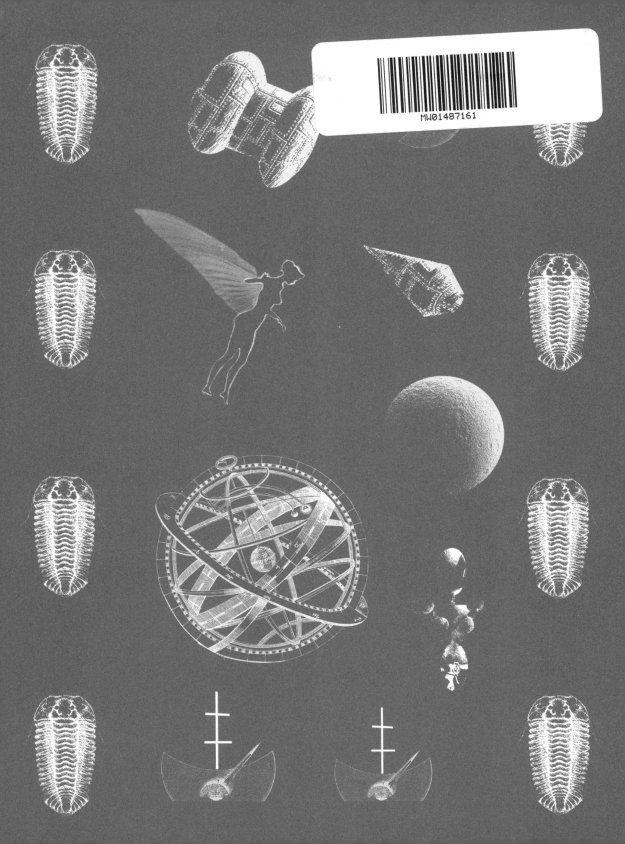

OTHER SPACES, OTHER TIMES

A life spent in the future

Robert Silverberg

Nonstop Press • New York

OTHER SPACES, OTHER TIMES
A LIFE SPENT IN THE FUTURE

First edition

Copyright ©2009 Agberg, Ltd.

Silverberg Bibliography ©2009 Nonstop Press

*For information or a free full-color
newsletter/catalog contact:
nonstop@nonstop-press.com
or: POB 981, Peck Slip Station,
   New York, NY 10272-0981*

*Nonstop Press
www.nonstop-press.com*

*publisher's catalog-in-publication
available upon request*

*Nonstop editor
Luis Ortiz*

*Copy editor
Beret Erway*

Production & Design by Nonstop Ink

*Special thanks to: Mike Ashley, Bob Eggleton,
Alex Eisenstein, Carol Emshwiller, Jane Frank,
Phoebe Gaughan, Peter Griffin, David Hartwell,
Earl Kemp, Jay Kay Klein, Karan Ortiz,
John Picacio, Andrew I. Porter, and Tim White*

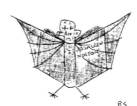

ISBN-13 978-1-933065-12-0

Printed in S. Korea

CONTENTS

INTRODUCTION

BY ROBERT SILVERBERG

Nietzsche once wrote, "My memory says I did this, my pride says I did not. My memory yields." That's sufficient warning, as though we needed it, that the autobiographies of writers are not to be trusted as factual documents.

Writers of fiction make stuff up. That's what the word "fiction" means — it's derived from the Latin verb *fingere*, which means "to imagine," "to invent," "to fabricate." Out of *fingere* comes the noun *fictum*, meaning "that which is invented," and out of fictum comes our English word "fiction."

Those two Latin words have some secondary meanings that are of some relevance here. *Fingere* also means "to arrange," "to put in order." And *fictum* can mean "a lie."

You see where I'm heading here. The fiction-writer makes things up, and also puts the things he has invented into some sort of rational order so that the reader can make sense out of them. This is especially true, alas, when the fiction-writer is talking about his own life. Even people who aren't fiction-writers tend to arrange their own memories in a kind of rational order for the sake of having a coherent view of their past. That involves some editing, which is to say, some revising, and very often some unintentional modification of the facts. (The modifications may not be all that unintentional, either. It isn't at all unusual, of course, for people, writers and non-writers both, to create *ficta* — downright lies — about their pasts.) One special problem for fiction writers in this area is that after having applied their particular inventive gifts to their stock of personal memories during the process of putting it in order, they aren't always sure where a little artistic embellishment may have taken place. We are story-tellers by first nature, and we want to tell good stories. We usually want them to be truthful stories, too, but sometimes, after having told the story of our lives often enough, we lose track of the enhancements we have introduced in the interest of artistic verisimilitude.

I have no doubt I've done something of that sort myself from time to time. I have a very retentive memory, but by now it stores more than three score and ten years' worth of events; so it is altogether likely that some of those events, rolling around in my fiction-writer's mind for all those decades, have undergone some modifications all unbeknownst to their custodian. That doesn't mean I've been telling a lot of lies about my past, but it does mean that I may very well be serving up fictionalized versions of some events, narratives that have been subconsciously tinkered with by my inner editor to turn them into better stories. They aren't lies, because there's been no intention to deceive, but they may not exactly be the truth, either.

I don't like to lie — about my past, or anything else. (Though I will, if forced to a choice between lying and revealing something that might cause injury to someone else.) But if I prefer, on the whole, to tell the truth, I feel under no obligation to tell *all* of it. There are things I have done — especially in my troubled and troublesome childhood — that I would just as soon forget, though I am unable to. I have, however, outlived nearly all the witnesses to those relatively trivial but embarrassing things, and those that remain have almost certainly forgotten them. Fine. I will not, therefore, bring all those sorry episodes back to life by writing about them. (Though I have embedded a good many of them in the lives of characters in my stories and novels.) Jean-Jacques Rousseau wrote a book that among other things tells of all the vile and shameful deeds of his life — it is rightfully called *The Confessions of Jean-Jacques Rousseau* — and though it is a fascinating book that has never lacked for readers in the past two and a half centuries, I don't care to emulate it. (I haven't done very many vile and shameful things, anyway, and I'm probably the only one who would think they're particularly vile.)

So I've never written a formal autobiography, and I have no intention of writing one. This is in part because, for the reasons I've just enumerated, I don't trust myself to get all the facts entirely straight, and also because some of the facts that I would feel obligated to include, about my childhood, for instance, would probably make me look like a nastier little boy than I really was. Then, too, a proper autobiography would, I believe, require me to describe my interactions over the span of a long and complicated life with various people who might not care to have those interactions publicly described. Therefore I have avoided writing anything like a conventional autobiographical book, and I intend to go on avoiding writing one to the end of my days. The closest I've come to it has been the lengthy essay called "Sounding Brass, Tinkling Cymbal," first published in 1975 and updated several times since, but even that leaves out much of the personal data and concentrates mainly on my career as a science-fiction writer.

That career, though, has been a long and busy one. I've been a significant player in the science-fiction field for more than half a century. That can be said of very few sf writers, apart from such phenomenal examples of longevity as Jack Williamson and Frederik Pohl. My timespan as an active writer has already outlasted those of Isaac Asimov, Robert A. Heinlein, and Poul Anderson, to name just a few who maintained notably lengthy and prolific careers, and I'm closing in on that of Arthur C. Clarke.

I've seen a lot of history in all that time. In the course of my six decades of writing, I've witnessed the transition of science-fiction publishing from being a pulp-magazine-centered field to one dominated by mass-market paperback companies, and I've known and dealt with virtually every editor who played a role in that evolution. For much of that time I was close to the center of the field as writer and sometimes as editor, not only deeply involved in its commercial mutations but also privy to all the personal and professional gossip that it generated. All that special knowledge has left me with a sense of my responsibility to the field's historians. I was there, I did this and did that, I worked with this great editor and that one, I knew all but a handful of the major writers on a first-name basis, and all of that will be lost if I don't make some sort of record of it. Therefore it behooves me to set down an account of those experiences for those who will find them of value.

Which I have duly done, piecemeal, in a long series of introductions to many of my published novels and nearly all of my short stories, and the anecdotal data out of which I have built those introductions, based on my extensive correspondence file and my own still pretty exceptional memory, form a kind of collective serial autobiography that will have to do in lieu of a single formally constructed one. Non-Stop Press has brought much of that material together in this book.

As my initial warning should indicate, all memoirs are open to a certain degree of suspicion, including mine. I may not have attained perfect factual accuracy here. My memory is an excellent one but is not infallible; some of my correspondence files and business records were lost or defaced in a fire that wrecked my house in 1968; and there is always the unavoidable tendency of any writer to reshape rough facts into smoothly rounded stories that must be taken into account. But if I have made free with reality in any of the essays that follow, I urge you to believe me when I say that I did none of it intentionally. You will find here the story of my life in science fiction as I remember it and as I have recorded it, and though I may have unknowingly retouched or misinterpreted some of that story, I have, at least, not consciously distorted it. Trust me on that, won't you?

In any case, very few of the people I mention here are still alive to contradict me. As Frederik Pohl said to me long ago, one big advantage of outliving your friends is that your version of the story is the only one that counts. Here's my version, then, of how I spent close to sixty years writing science fiction. It's as close to being the accurate one as I can produce. And from here on, it's the only one that counts.

September, 2008

ONE: BEGINNINGS

A picture of me at summer camp, August 1953, reading what I think is the September 1953 issue of **GALAXY** *with a Sturgeon story in it. —RS*

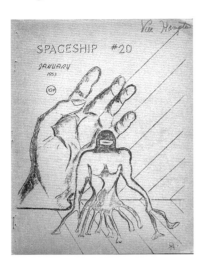

Cover of 20th issue of **SPACESHIP,** *January 1953.*

MEMORIES OF A CURIOUS CHILDHOOD

I am, like some of you, older than I used to be — old enough to remember when science-fiction magazines cost a quarter, and how to change a typewriter ribbon, and what Isaac Asimov looked like before he grew those side-whiskers. I'm old enough, I'm afraid, so that I've outlived most of my childhood schoolteachers, some of my childhood friends, even my college roommate.

But one thing I haven't outlived is my curiosity. Even now, I keep looking ahead, peering around corners, eager to see what's coming next. And it's that quality of restless curiosity, or what remains of it in me, that keeps me (relatively) youthful of spirit. The powerful desire to know what next month will bring, or next year, or next century — to learn *how things are going to turn out* — is a better rejuvenating tonic than Geritol.

Of course, a lot of things that once mattered supremely to me I now don't care about at all. Who wins this year's National League pennant, for example, or even who wins this year's Hugo for Best Science Fiction Novel. Talk to me about baseball next time we're both in 1948, and I'll go on and on about the great new Brooklyn Dodger players like Gil Hodges and Roy Campanella and Duke Snider, and what wonders they'll accomplish next season. But these days the Dodgers play in L.A. and I don't have a clue to who's on first. As for Hugos, well, I still show up at the annual ceremony and I applaud dutifully as my colleagues collect their shiny trophies, and when I win one myself, as happens now and then, I am quite sincerely delighted, but the old summertime fascination of speculating on the probable Labor Day winners no longer seems to be there for me.

It's a natural process, I guess, this ebbing of the curiosity-libido. Most of us past forty can't manage to keep our waistlines where they were twenty years ago, our hair undergoes funny changes of color about the same time, and the mind begins to pull in some of its antennae too, I guess. But I have enough curiosity left in me, even now, to keep myself revved up about things to come.

No matter what time I've gone to sleep the night before, I'm up at six the next morning without benefit of alarm clock, so avid am I to see what the new day will bring. I look forward impatiently to the morning mail, to the day's telephone calls, to the unfolding of my day's writing stint. I find myself wondering where I'll have dinner that night — a Thai restaurant? Ethiopian? Indian? — and what new and unfamiliar things I'll find on the menu.

It goes beyond that, of course. I want to last long enough to find out what it will feel like to date a letter "January 4, 2001." I want to hang in there until the exploration of space starts up again, so I can hear astronauts describing their jaunts across the sands of Mars. I want to be around when the Chinese finally excavate the gigantic mound that covers the tomb of the Emperor Ch'in Shi Huang Ti. And I have all sorts of travel plans in mind — Australia, Portugal, the Galapagos Islands, the heights of Macchu Picchu, the reconstructed museums of reunited Berlin, a list that goes on and on into my dotage.

It's a healthy thing, curiosity. I've had an acute case of it ever since I was a boy.

What an *annoying* little brat I was! When I was in the first grade I discovered by reading the printed warning on its side that one must not, under any circumstances, take the fire extinguisher down from the corridor wall and turn it upside down. Why not? I wondered. What would happen? So I took it down and turned it over. Foam, of course, came shooting out in wondrous abundance, and teachers came running from all directions." Well, I wanted to know what would happen," I told them. If they were amused by my precocious inquisitiveness, they kept it well hidden.

Somehow, a year later, I became fascinated by eels — by the idea that certain fishes looked very much like snakes. Snakes interested me. So did snails, and frogs, and just about everything else. A fish that looked like a snake was irresistible. So I asked Mr. Brenner, the good-natured man who ran the fish market on the corner, to get a live eel for me. (In those days we knew all the local market proprietors by name, the grocer and the baker and the fish man, and we called them "Mr." this and that, not "Sid" or "Jose.") I was much more extroverted and outgoing then than I later became, and a lot of people were charmed by the way I went around poking my nose into their business. Mr. Brenner, God only knows why, promised to get me an eel.

And he did. He called me into the store a few days later and handed me a big whonking brown eel in a huge jar, and I carried it home and (since I had no fish tank) put it in the bathtub. We had only one tub to serve the whole family, and turning it into an eel-tank would very quickly have caused some household inconvenience, but I suppose that when you're seven you're better at expressing curiosity than you are at thinking about consequences.

My mother, a third-grade teacher, came home from school a little while later and found a live eel in our bathtub. This was over fifty years ago and I don't quite recall her reaction — but, though she had had plenty of opportunity to watch me in action by this time, it was probably less calm than a simple, straightforward "Robert, why is there an eel in the bathtub?" I do remember that the eel went back to Mr. Brenner very quickly and that there was a lively discussion when my father got home an hour or two later.

I had a microscope, of course. When I heard that the brine from pickle-barrels contained interesting microorganisms, I went across the street to Mr. Cohen's grocery store and asked for some pickle brine. When I explained why I wanted it, he gave me a pickle too. Coming home with the brine caused less fuss than coming home with the eel had created.

I saw the man who ran the laundry — I don't remember *his* name — reading a Chinese newspaper. I asked him for a copy and he gave me one and I spent an hour trying to figure out how to read Chinese. Languages already interested me: at eight, I had already learned a few words of Spanish and a bit of French. Got nowhere with Chinese, but it was instructive to see how rich and various one planet's languages could be.

In 1944 someone gave me a subscription to the *National Geographic* — I get it to this day — and instantly I yearned to see with my own eyes all the places in those wondrous photographs, where bizarre creatures dwelled, where alien architecture brightened the landscape. I longed to climb the Pyramids and trek the Gobi and stare up at the redwood trees of California. Coral reefs, rain forests, geysers, volcanoes, Mayan jungle temples, the dunes of the Sahara, the cactus forests of Mexico — so long as it was something qualitatively different from Brooklyn, N.Y. , I wanted to see it. It was wartime, then, and nobody went anywhere except

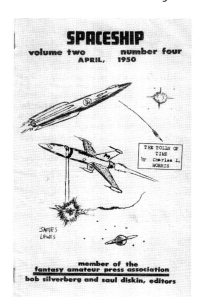

Cover of eighth issue of **SPACESHIP,** *1950.*

with government permission; but I have diligently spent my adult life searching out those myriad places which, back then, I was able to visit only vicariously, via the *National Geographic.*

But the *Geographic* wasn't enough. The same intellectual hunger that led me to turn over fire-extinguishers, bring home eels, peer into microscopes, and ponder the laundryman's incomprehensible newspaper caused me to turn my attention to ever more distant places and eras — other worlds, other epochs. I wanted to make great swooping journeys in space and time. My mind boiled with questions. What were the dinosaurs *really* like? Would we ever go to Mars, and if we did, what would we find there? And the planets of other stars: were they anything like the ones I saw depicted in *Planet Comics* and the Buck Rogers newspaper strips?

Ah, that was frustrating! I could never hope to go on journeys to the Mesozoic; and as for the glorious raygun and spaceship future shown in the comics, I knew even then that I would live to see only a small segment of it, a short way into the 21st century at the very best.

But then I stumbled on science fiction. It was a handy substitute for the fulfillment of those impossible curiosities of mine. John Taine's novel *Before the Dawn* was as good an eye-witness account of the dinosaurs as I could hope to have, and H. G. Wells *The Time Machine* showed me the eons to come in 40,000 astonishing words; and soon I found the sf magazines, too, where writers named Heinlein and Asimov and Williamson and van Vogt who were depicting it for me in fictional form with such vividness and clarity that I could almost believe I was there. Such magazines as *Astounding Science Fiction* and *Startling Stories* became the *National Geographic* of this next phase of my intellectual development.

"He had never seen a humanoid," Jack Williamson wrote, in a classic story published in 1947. "Smaller and slimmer than a man. A shining black, its sleek silicone skin had a changing sheen of bronze and metallic blue. Its graceful oval face wore a fixed look of alert and slightly surprised solicitude. Altogether, it was the most beautiful mechanical he had ever seen."

And a door opened for me, and I was in the rhodomagnetic future of "With Folded Hands," and for the next hour my curiosity about what the world of two or three hundred years hence was going to be like was satisfied. I *knew.* I was *there.* Jack Williamson had taken me there. Science fiction, for the moment, had soothed my need to peer into the impossible-to-attain worlds beyond my own probable lifespan.

You understand. You've had the same experience, or you wouldn't be reading this book.

That overriding curiosity that never lets up — that hunger to get answers to the most audacious questions — I've always had it, and I have it still, though I don't bring live eels home any more. You have it too. And, I'm willing to bet, have eel stories of your own to tell.

1997

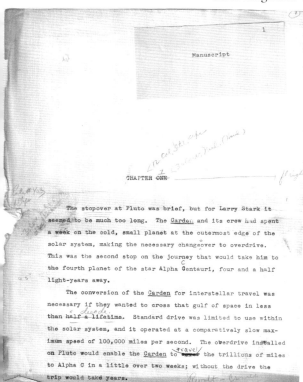

This is the first page of the manuscript for my first novel, **REVOLT ON ALPHA C,** *published in 1955.* — RS

CRIMES OF MY YOUTH

Hear my confession, folks. A career of crime lies buried deep in my past, and I can't keep it concealed any longer. When I was a boy I committed dozens of murders for the sake of what I thought of as "science." My intensive research, as I thought of it then, added not one iota to the sum of human knowledge. It was all brutal folly and nothing more than that, and, thinking of it now, I feel covered with guilt over the loss of all those innocent lives. Mea culpa, mea culpa, mea maxima culpa.

RS with parents, age six months or so.

These lethal depredations of mine took place somewhere around 1945 or 1946. That is, I was ten or eleven years old, bristling with the sort of savagery that I suppose is universal in prepubescent boys. In my case, because I was a *bright* prepubescent boy who was expected by all to achieve wonderful things when he grew up, I could cloak my boyish savagery in an aura of serious purpose. My literary talents had not yet revealed themselves, back then. It was generally assumed, even by me, that I was ultimately going to be a scientist of some kind. And so, during those long-ago summers in the earliest years of the atomic era, what I did was kill a lot of hapless frogs. A *lot* of frogs, indeed.

Looking back now on the cheerfully cold-blooded boy I was then, I feel not only shock but disbelief. How could I have been so cruel? I will swat a mosquito today, under proper provocation, and I will spray poisonous vapors on the hordes of ants that invade our house every winter, and sometimes I will step on a garden snail who's munching on some horticultural rarity of mine, but otherwise I go out of my way not to take life, and I don't feel so good about the necessity of offing those mild-mannered ants and snails. (Mosquitoes are a different story.) Indeed, when it comes to my fellow creatures, I am today a veritable St. Francis of Assisi, at least so far as harming them with my own hands goes. I will carefully gather up spiders who intrude into the household on sheafs of paper and carry them gently outside; I scoop drowning salamanders and even wasps and hornets out of the

*One of my Earliest
Rejection Slips.— RS*

swimming pool; I catch garden moles in tin cans and transport them to woodsy areas nearby, where I not only release them but hover around to defend them from stray cats until they have scurried out of sight.

There is a little inconsistency in my piety, I admit, where the issue of food comes in. Last night's swordfish steak was not synthetically grown in a test tube, nor the veal scaloppini of the night before. I have no illusions about that. I have made a treaty with myself whereby I allow other people to kill on my behalf, yea, even unto innocent lambs and calves, in order to provide me with food. I forgive myself that sin on the grounds that I was created an omnivore without being consulted about it, and thus I look upon meat as an important, even necessary, part of my diet. But if I had to hunt and butcher the animals I eat myself, I have no doubt at all that I'd be a vegetarian.

That's now, though. Let's look at *then*.

The ten-or-eleven-year-old me is quite different from the present-day item, and not simply because I didn't wear a beard in the mid-1940s. There's the matter of that sense of my destiny as a future scientist, something that vanished from me utterly as soon as I realized, somewhere around the age of thirteen, that I was obviously intended to be a writer. There was a component of hearty extroversion in me back then, too, that would disappear also in another few years. And, also, there was a certain blithe amorality about ten-year-old me that now strikes me as altogether alien. That little boy could easily have grown up to be the sort of white-coated villain who coolly hands placebos to dying children or practices vivisection on someone's pet cat or dog captured at dawn in the suburbs in order that some question of medical research can be answered. But something changed in me around the time I turned thirteen and I grew up to be the creator of the gentle, tormented telepath David Selig of *Dying Inside* and that reluctant warrior, the peace-loving Lord Valentine of *Lord Valentine's Castle*.

Here is the beady-eyed, ruthless little Robert Silverberg of fifty-plus years ago, though, stalking through the marshes of a muddy little lake in Ulster County, New York. A city-bred boy, turned loose every year for eight wondrous weeks in the relatively unspoiled world beyond the urban pavement. Watch him go at it:

Catching frogs with ruthless swoops of his unerring right hand. Killing them without a flicker of remorse by a process euphemistically known as *pithing*, which consisted of driving a spike through their little heads. Cutting them open, then, with deft strokes of a keen blade that would have been better employed for its intended purpose, which was carving model airplanes out of balsa wood. Peeling back the froggy integuments; staring with fascination at the tiny internal organs within. And then, I suppose, throwing them away, their purpose served.

But what purpose was that? I told myself, of course, that doing this thing to frogs was part of my scientific education. What was I learning, though? That frogs have curious little organs of various colors inside their soft little abdomens? One frog would have taught me that much. But I kept on catching and dissecting them, frog after frog, spending those carefree summer days marching around in the marshy part of the lake until I spied a small green nose above the water, and then pouncing, pithing, slicing, staring.

I was a skillful frog-hunter. I've always had terrific reflexes. Sometimes I'd put my cupped hand down against the muck and trap the poor frog before it had a chance even to jump; otherwise, I'd grab it in mid-air with a diabolical twist of the wrist as it tried to flee. What a wonderful achievement! Here's the frog, two inches long, minding his own business in the water. Here's the gigantic boy, a full four feet tall or even bigger, descending like the wrath of Jehovah. The deft hand descends. And seizes.

How did I get into this business of dissecting frogs? Why, I must have read about the importance of knowing what was inside frogs' bellies in one of the textbooks of biology that my obliging father, guiding me toward the future laboratory career that never was to be, provided for me. Or maybe there was an account of pithing technique in some issue of *Nature Magazine* or *Natural History*, both of which I read faithfully back then. I must have had some guidance of that sort, because I certainly knew not only the technique of pithing frogs but the term itself, which sticks in my vocabulary decades after my crimes themselves came to an end.

It would be nice to think that I actually learned something of a scientific nature by killing all those frogs. I still have one of those biology texts of long ago — *Biology and Human Welfare*, Peabody and Hunt, 1933 — and on page 441 is a diagram of the internal organs of a frog. I hope that I consulted it as I worked, so that I did in fact discover that this thing here was the frog's liver, this the kidney, these the large intestines, this the bile sac. I might then have gone on to contemplate the functions of these tiny organs, their interrelationships, the ingenious design of them. I could have come away from these boyish exploits, then, not only with some awareness of the nature of metabolic processes in small amphibians, but also — what would have been much more valuable to the writer I would one day become — a sense of the well-nigh miraculous nature of life, of the astounding perfection of design that informs even the humblest of the universe's myriad creatures.

Did any of that cross my mind? Or did I, all the while pretending to be a scientist, simply get a kick out of catching frogs and cutting them open? I can't tell you that, not after more than half a century. I can only plead innocent boyish curiosity as my defense. I didn't know there was anything wrong about killing frogs, and it never occurred to me that frogs might have feelings too, and I really, *really* wanted to know what they looked like inside. That might excuse the first frog, or maybe even the next two or three. The human race has done many a hor-

This was taken at the 1956 Worldcon in N.Y., I know not by whom. A.J. Budrys on the right and a fan named Charles Harris on the left. — RS

rible thing out of sheer curiosity, and some of those horrible things have led eventually to beneficial consequences. Dissecting the little girl next door would have been beyond the bounds of innocent boyish curiosity, but I think a frog or two could be deemed expendable, considering the restless, questing nature of the kid I was.

Nevertheless, I can't find any excuse for continuing to cut up frogs after my first few. Even the infamous Nazi surgeon Joseph Mengele probably was actually learning something from the ghastly experiments on human beings that he conducted in the death camps, whereas I, once I had satisfied my curiosity about the shape and color of the internal organs of frogs, was learning nothing further about them, and should have stopped. But for the fact that Mengele was experimenting with human beings and I was simply fooling around with frogs — and frogs don't have, so far as we know, hopes and dreams and soaring visions — a case could be made out that I was doing something even more evil than he was. Mengele, at least, was carrying out real scientific investigation, however monstrous and loathsome. I was just cutting open frogs: pretending to be studying their internal anatomy, but actually merely killing for the pleasure of killing.

I suppose I figured that out, after a time, and gave up my nefarious frog-hunting ways forever in another summer or two. I know that by the time I entered my teens I had ceased all such stuff forever. My passionate interest in natural history remains with me — the one surviving vestige of my inquisitive boy-scientist youth — but when I spy some small creature today in woods or pond, I feel only pleasure at its beauty and efficiency of design, no yearning whatsoever to lay bare its internal organs.

If I were a biologist instead of a writer, I might feel otherwise. As readers of these columns are probably aware, I am no opponent of legitimate scientific research. Nor can I really condemn the eager, even ravenous, hunger for knowledge that led me to explore the innards of those frogs when I was ten or eleven. Better that, even at the expense of a few innocent little creatures' lives, than mere placid bovine passivity and glassy-eyed lack of interest in the world of natural phenomena. But oh, how I wish that I had stopped after the first two or three!

1998

I justified the pages by typing them all out, rounding off each line with ////, and then inserting the appropriate number of spaces indicated by the /// in the final version when I typed the mimeograph stencils. A pain in the neck, actually.— RS

BACKTALK

THE BIG YEAR

As I write this, on a stormy Sunday before Christmas, the Year of the Jackpot is slowly dying. But 1952--which will be remembered for a long time as science fiction's Big Year--refuses to go with a whimper. Even as the year ends, news comes of still two more prozines, edited by Sam Merwin and by an unnamed fan. Presumably the boom will go roaring on through 1953, until science fiction loses whatever remains of its insular quality, and is a mass fiction field such as detective or western fiction is now.

1952 has been covered adequately enough this issue; let's look to 1953. Here are some thoughts for the new year:

Ziff-Davis will surge to the top rung when Amazing joins the quality ranks. Authors will flock to cash in on the fantastic word-rates dished out by Browne, and by the end of the year either Amz or Fantastic or both will be monthly.

Startling Stories will set a new circulation record at Standard Publications, and publisher Ned Pines will increase his firm's s-f activities, possibly by making TWS a monthly.

TCSAB will fold. The Avon Reader will likewise be short-lived. ASF is about due for some sort of major change. December 1953 will see at least 40 prozines in the U.S. and England. Campbell may bring out an all-fantasy magazine, possibly Unknown, to match Galaxy's new companion.

Basic word-rates will be established at 1½¢ per word rock bottom, with the top magazines paying as much as 6¢ per on occasion.

Many of 1952's top fanzines will fold, and fewer new titles will appear next year. The fanzine field will consolidate, with a smaller number of magazines published, but with higher quality throughout. SPACESHIP will survive the year and publish its Fifth Anniversary Issue in 1954.

Okay, take us up on them in '53. There are nine major predictions up above...we'll pull a Palmer and run a "Fan from Tomorrow" department every time one of them comes true or otherwise.

*   *   *   *   *

One of the most interesting publishing events of the year was Dutton's reprinting of E.R. Eddison's The Worm Ouroboros. This is the legendary fantasy novel which, when available, sells for $20 or $25 a copy. Dutton's new edition sells for $5, which isn't exactly tailored to fit the

--- 24 ---

ALADDIN'S CAVE

You all remember the story of Aladdin's cave, don't you?

The magician who shows Aladdin the marble slab in the desert, with the copper ring set into it, and tells him that if he seizes the ring and raises the slab, a fabulous treasure will be his, for he alone can lift the slab. The staircase of twelve steps, leading down into a great cave in the earth. The four rooms containing gold and silver jars; the fourth room with the door leading into a garden; the trees whose fruits were rubies and emeralds; and above all else the room beyond the garden where a lamp hangs from the ceiling, the lamp of wonders

that can summon the powerful spirits known as the Slaves of the Lamp, who can grant all wishes —

This is the story of my own Aladdin's Cave.

It's an episode more than half a century old that I think will stir some emotion in the bosom of anyone who, like myself of long ago, found it exciting to collect the science fiction magazines of ancient days. The year was 1950. I had just turned fifteen. I was a high-school sophomore, a voracious reader of science fiction ever since I had come upon H. G. Wells' *The Time Machine* and Jules Verne's *20,000 Leagues Under the Sea* when I was about ten. I had branched out, in the previous couple of years, from such classic authors as Wells and Verne to the rather less respectable pulp magazines of the day — first *Weird Tales*, which I discovered early in 1948, and then *Amazing Stories,* the following year, a magazine that I much preferred because I had the illusion that its stories were grounded in scientific speculation. (It would be another year or two before I came to see that dear old *Amazing* was just a trashy adventure-story magazine, whose stories were hardly more scientific in their orientation than the spooky fiction *Weird* traditionally offered.)

I couldn't get enough of the stuff. You know the feeling, because you went through it yourself in those first glorious months after you stumbled into reading sf. I wanted to read every bit of it I could find. There wasn't much science fiction being published then — just a handful of magazines and the *very* infrequent paperback. A few publishers were doing hardcover science fiction also, but of course I couldn't afford those back then ($3 was the cover price), and when I searched for them in the public library (where they were listed under the category of "pseudo-scientific fiction" they were never there, probably always having been checked out by those wiseguy 17-year-olds who had discovered sf a few years ahead of me. So I went hunting for the back issues of *Amazing* and its companion *Fantastic* and the gaudily named *Thrilling Wonder Stories* and the other pulp sf magazines of the era.

New York City, where I lived then, was full of shops that dealt in back-issue magazines. I was already a regular customer of one, a musty place called Jackson's,

RS and Dean Grennell, August, 1955.

in a seedy corner of Brooklyn, where I had gone frequently in 1947 and 1948 to buy old copies of *The National Geographic Magazine* that aided me mightily in my homework. I hustled over there and asked Jackson — a creepy old character with bristly gray stubble all over his face — about science fiction magazines. He pointed the room. There they were, a dime apiece, and I went tottering away with a tall stack of pulps, several dollars' worth, issues going back two or three years.

But all Jackson had were the recent issues. I craved older stuff, four, five, even ten years old, issues that contained the classic stories that veteran readers still were raving about in the magazine letter columns. One day, visiting a friend who also had begun collecting sf magazines, I noticed that the cover of one of his recent acquisitions bore the rubber-stamped address of a shop in downtown Brooklyn. It might be worth investigating, I thought. Surreptitiously — because he and I were very competitive in amassing the old magazines — I jotted down the name of the store.

I think it was called The Curio Shop, though after all this time I'm not entirely sure of that. But graven on my memory forever is its address — 106a Court Street. I hustled down there after school the next day, a short trip by

The first and last page of my first story, written in February or March of 1949 in collaboration with my friend Saul Diskin (with whom I am still in touch, 59 years later.) No way of telling, after all this time, which of us wrote what, but the handwriting is mine. – RS

subway from my home.

106a Court turned out to be a decrepit nineteenth-century building just at the edge of the downtown district, three or four blocks from the county court-house that gives the street its name. I found myself in a long, narrow, dimly lit shop, cluttered from floor to ceiling with junk of all sorts — tables and chairs, pots and pans, bookcases, mismatched dishes, incomplete sets of silverware, and I know not what else. The proprietor, a gaunt, fierce-looking woman with griz-zled gray hair, sat behind a desk just inside the front door. She gave me a quizzi-cal look, as though wondering what a rosy-cheeked lad like me was doing in her bedraggled emporium.

I was pretty terrified. "Old science fiction magazines?" I managed to say.

"Downstairs." She pointed to a staircase dimly visible toward the back of the shop. "Watch your head going down. The light's on your left."

The staircase was a rickety affair, and I had to crouch as I descended it. Some groping and I found the light switch. A faint bulb revealed a dusty realm of floor-to-ceiling odds and ends: more of the same junk as the upstairs room held, all piled higgledy-piggledy, everything crammed closely together, with only one

I know he would have wanted this way, being one of the more outstanding men of science of our time. I can feel the magnamil sinking slowly into a fissure that is developing under my trembling legs. I will have time for only a few more sentences. I wish to make it known that I am not afraid to go to my death after having witnessed this spectacular sight. Gentlemen, I express my deepest regret at the failure of the Western Hemisphere expedition to Saturn. The creatures have surrounded me as I write this, but I shall push myself into the fissure before they can kill me.

MARTIN DAVIES

(DEEP SILENCE IN THE COUNCIL-ROOM AS FISHER FINISHES)
(SILENCE CONTINUES FOR 5 MINUTES)
A NEWSPAPER MAN RISES SLOWLY FROM HIS SEAT AND APPROACHES THE CHAIRMAN

"May I have permission to print this in the SCIENTIFIC GAZETTE?"
"I shall leave it to the delegates to vote upon —"
THE VOTE IS TAKEN
"The decision is unanimous: You may use the printed text of the report, but if one word is used untruthfully to glamourize the account, the Council shall declare your paper out of existence."
"May we fotograph the assembly —"
"You may not, for obvious reasons —"
"I will entertain a motion for adjournment."

FINIS   1,948
THE END   words.
COMPLETED
ALL DONE

narrow passage permitting entry. Cautiously I advanced, squinting in the dimness. And in flimsy bookshelves tucked under the staircase I came upon the rubies and emeralds of my Aladdin's cave: heaps and heaps of science fiction magazines, some fairly recent, but most of them truly ancient ones! Dates like 1934 and 1930 and 1927 leaped out to dazzle my eyes. And not just a few magazines, but dozens — hundreds!

1934 and 1930 and 1927 must seem prehistoric to you — dates out of a time when your grandparents were little children. I assure you that those years seemed every bit as prehistoric to me, back there in 1950. Not only hadn't I been born when those magazines were new, but most of them went back to a time when my parents hadn't yet met. For me anything before around 1941 was pre-historic — practically paleolithic.

I barely knew where to begin. Over here was a stack that turned out to be a nearly complete file, covering the years from 1930 to 1933, of *Astounding Stories of Super-Science*, the remote ancestor of today's *Analog*. In astonishment I pulled forth the incredibly rare first issue, January, 1930. Nearby were scores of copies of *Amazing Stories* — not the shoddy-looking pulp magazine I was familiar with, but its slick jumbo-sized forebear, founded in 1926 by the legendary Hugo Gernsback for whom today's Hugo awards are named. Back of them were many issues of *Science Wonder Stories* and *Air Wonder Stories*, the successor magazines that Gernsback had started when a bankruptcy suit cost him control of *Amazing*, and beyond them were dozens of his later title, *Wonder Stories*, in both its pulp and slick formats. Everything was in splendid condition; some looked as though they had come straight from the newsstand. Somebody back there in the 1930s had collected science fiction magazines with zeal and had preserved them with great care, and then, perhaps, had gone off to war and never returned, and his family had sold the whole batch to The Curio Shop, where they had slumbered quiet-ly down here until I came upon them.

Even now, seeing my teenage self darting from shelf to shelf in that congest-ed cellar, I can feel my pulse-rate rising. How I had coveted these ancient, fabled magazines! But I had never seriously expected to own them, or even just to hold

(bottom)
L to R: Theodore Cogswell, Damon Knight, James Blish, RS, and Katherine MacLean. Photo taken by Ed Emshwiller at the first Milford Science Fiction Conference, 1956.

them in my hands. Could I afford to buy them, I wondered? There were hundreds of them. My allowance was perhaps two dollars a week. A month or so before I had purchased, for fifty cents, a 1929 copy of *Science Wonder Stories* missing its front and back covers, from a mail-order dealer on Staten Island. How much would these magazines, in practically perfect condition, cost me? Whatever it was, it was surely going to be beyond my reach.

I rushed upstairs. I must have been a wild-eyed figure, flushed, perspiring, covered with dust. Trying to be cool, I inquired after the price of the magazines downstairs.

"Some are half a dollar, some a quarter," the proprietor said. "Depends on what mood I'm in when you ask."

Reader, I bought them all.

And I still have them, somewhat the worse for wear after fifty-seven years that have taken me from one end of the country to the other, but most of them still in pretty nice shape. I didn't buy them all at once, you understand. But very quickly I came to an understanding with the fierce-looking proprietor — Virginia Mushkin was her name — and her more gentle-looking husband David. They saw in me, correctly, a bright kid for whom those magazines were tremendously important — someone who was passionately in love with them, in fact — and they agreed to sell me the whole kaboodle at whatever pace I could pay for it. After all this time I have no recollection of how I raised the money — probably through advances on my allowance — or how long it took, but in the course of time I transferred those hundreds of unthinkably rare sf magazines, two paper-bag loads at a time, from 106a Court Street to my own apartment in another part of Brooklyn. The Mushkins and I became good friends; I was a sort of adopted son to them, and they looked on with interest as I began to write my own first science fiction stories a year or so later. They are both long dead, now, but they did live on to see me become a published author.

I read those magazines, one by one. I *studied* them. Sometimes I look at them even today, though not to read, because most of the stories they contain are crude, practically unreadable things. No matter. The mere sight of them gets my heart beating faster. For me they contained the whole history of science fiction in magazine form, and I cherished them for that, and I still do. I hope you who collect old sf magazines have Aladdin's Cave stories like that, but I know you can't have any to equal this one, the discovery of long runs of 1930 *Astoundings* and 1927 *Amazings* in the basement of a cluttered, dusty old junkshop, for sale at a pittance.

Oh — one little twist. Among the magazines I acquired there was two 1946 *Astoundings* that contained a serialized novel by the utterly forgotten writer Arthur Leo Zagat with an Aladdin angle of its own — "Slaves of the Lamp."

2008

THE BOOKS OF CHILDHOOD: ONE

In recent years I've been reassembling the books I loved in my childhood some fifty years ago — an enterprise born not simply of nostalgia but from deep curiosity about the narrative material that went into the forming of Robert Silverberg, writer. For surely what we read in childhood makes the strongest impressions on us, leaving ineradicable imprints that, so I believe, recur in the work

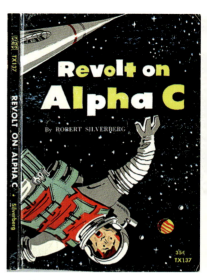

(opposite top & above) Art by William Meyerriecks for the 1960s Scholastic edition of REVOLT ON ALPHA C.

One thing I remember about the book's original reception back in 1955. The Sunday New York Times *reviewed it in its "Spaceman's Realm" column, bracketing it with a new Heinlein juvenile. The* Times *reviewer's conclusion was that Heinlein's book was better. Somehow, since I suspected a priori that that might be the case, I was less wounded by the comparison than an older writer might have been. I was 20 years old and not ready to stack myself up against Heinlein.*

Most or maybe all the characters in REVOLT ON ALPHA C *were named for friends of mine — Larry Stark, Harl Ellison, and (I think) Redd Boggs and Dean Grennell, maybe more. It was a common thing for young fans to do in that era. I outgrew it pretty fast.— RS*

STARMAN'S QUEST

Robert Silverberg

The original publisher of **STARMAN'S QUEST** *(Gnome Press) never bothered to copyright the 1958 edition. (Gnome was a one-man operation that cut corners wherever it could. I wonder if such other Gnome titles as the Foundation novels and the Conan series went uncopyrighted also!) In 1986, the woman who was handling my renewals for me informed me of this and offered to file a belated registration for me, but I replied, "In this case, the entire book was rewritten about 1969, and the newer version is protected by copyright, so I think it's safe to let the 1958 text go into public domain, no one is likely to go after it, and the substantially altered later version remains protected."*

Underlying all this is the basic fact that I have no intention of authorizing a new edition of even the later version of this novel, since it follows the story line of the original, which I wrote when I was about 19, and is of purely antiquarian interest nowadays despite the revisions I made in 1968. —RS

of any creative artist throughout his life. And now, with hundreds of stories and an uncountable number of books behind me, I'm trying to learn something about the source from which that seemingly inexhaustible flow of narrative has come.

So I've been prowling the rare-book dealers, and consulting catalogs, and cudgeling my own memory to try to reconstruct my reading preferences of the late 1930's and early 1940's. A ferociously retentive person like me would be expected to have the books of his childhood still on hand, I suppose, but in fact many of them were books I never owned in the first place, because I was such a dedicated user of the Brooklyn Public Library. (When I returned to Brooklyn a few years ago I revisited my ancient library branch, naively thinking some of those books would still be on the shelves, but of course they had been read to tatters long ago and replaced by the favorites of a newer generation.) As for the books I did own, some are still in my possession but most were destroyed in the fire that swept through my house in 1968. I made notes at the time on what was lost (and in some instances kept the charred copies) and that has helped me greatly in this job of reclaiming the past.

I'm not talking, incidentally, of the standard children's books that everyone in my era read — *Tom Sawyer, Huckleberry Finn, Alice in Wonderland, Through the Looking Glass, Lamb's Tales from Shakespeare, Peter Pan, Just So Stories, The Arabian Nights*, and such. I read all of those, of course — read them dozens of times — but what I've been looking for are the more esoteric things, the ones that went particularly into the shaping of the science fiction writer that I was to become.

In fact I should have become a fantasy writer, I guess, because what particularly preoccupied me in those early years were books of myths and legends. I have some of them on the desk before me now: Padraic Colum's *The Children of Odin*, a retelling of the Norse myths, and an obscure little pamphlet called *The Heroes of Asgard* by A. and E. Keary dealing with the same body of material (my original copy, water-stained but intact) and Colum's *The Adventures of Odysseus and the Tale of Troy*. And also, a really esoteric one, Helen Zimmern's *The Epic of Kings*, which draws on the great Persian epic of Firdausi, and which after years of searching I have only recently managed to find again. How they filled my mind with wonders, those books! Loki and the Fenris wolf, Audhumla the primordial cow, Odin at Mimir's well, the tale of the Volsungs, of Sohrab and Rustem, of the injudicious Kai Kaous and the noble Kai Khosrau, the death of Achilles, the wanderings of Odysseus — I dreamed of them, I embroidered on their plots in my mind, I longed to enter their world in actuality. Images from those Norse and Greek myths still course vividly through my mind and I can find their correlatives in my own writing; but I have transmuted them all to science fiction instead of producing new adventures of the Aesir or the heroes of Troy. Most likely the primary reason for that is that I came to maturity at a time when fantasy was an unpublishable category and science fiction a thriving and expanding operation, and I wanted what I wrote to see print.

But there is another reason. I was exposed at the same early age to the sf virus, which had the same mythic power for me, and which, apparently, affected me even more deeply.

For instance, here is my copy of *The Complete Works of Lewis Carroll*, the Modern Library edition, which I see from my father's inscription was given to me when I was not quite eight years old. The first 271 pages of this 1293-page volume are given over, of course, to the two Alice novels, which show signs of having been read and read and read. But the trail of fingerprints and eyetracks indicates that I went right on to the next two novels, *Sylvie and Bruno* and *Sylvie and Bruno Concluded*, books that no one else I know has ever mentioned reading. I don't know what category they fall into: not quite fantasy, not really science fiction; but there is a weird logic to them that makes them seem almost like parallel-world stories, since they take place in a sort of England, but not any England we would recognize. What Lewis Carroll achieved in these two little-known books was a variation on the free play of fantasy that we see in *Alice* or *Looking Glass*, but it is a down-to-earth kind of fantasy that has more resonance with science fiction. Beyond them in the huge volume is "The Hunting of the Snark," and some other poems, and then, in the back, an astonishing bunch of conundrums in logic and other mystifications that had a profound effect on my childish mind although I was unable even to begin understanding what their author was talking about. It was Lewis Carroll's rigorous, orderly, and logical exploration of the utterly incomprehensible, I think, that helped me to understand what science fiction (as opposed to fantasy) is all about.

A couple of other discoveries about the same time pushed me toward science fiction. The Buck Rogers comic strip, for one — I dimly remember a Sunday page, circa 1941, in which aliens with red puckered faces came swarming over a sea-wall while Buck and his companions tried to push them back. And then, in 1942, *Planet Comics* — embodying a glorious vision of the spectacular interplanetary future that left me hungry for more of the same, and led me on and on until at last by the age of ten I had found H. G. Wells and Jules Verne and my destiny was set in stone forever. (I tried, a couple of years ago while attending a convention of comic-book collectors, to find the issue of *Planet* that had so spun my mind into orbit. I was willing to pay the staggering sum being asked for issues of that vintage. But I couldn't seem to recognize, in the crudely drawn pages of the issues I saw, the particular splendors that had illuminated my mind nearly half a century before. Perhaps the ink had faded; or perhaps I was looking at the wrong issue.

Here is another book of my childhood that sent me in still another direction as a writer: Walter de la Mare's marvelous fantasy *The Three Mulla-Mulgars,* a curious tale of the adventures of three highly intelligent monkeys who set out across the heart of a fantastic Africa to find the golden land from which their father had come. (It's a wonderful book, and I say so not merely because I see it through the eyes of the child who loved it: I re-read it yet again a few months ago and was as profoundly moved by its beauty and mystery as I had been when I was nine.) Images out of that remarkable book have been turning up in my own science fiction books for decades; I usually recognize them for what they are after the fact, and smile, and leave them there as an homage. There are passages in my novel, *Kingdoms of the Wall*, that owe their power to my decades-old recollections of *The Three Mulla-Mulgars.* So be it. No writer invents everything from scratch; our imaginations are billion-piece mosaics fashioned from everything we have ever experienced, including all that we have ever read. But also de la Mare led me circuitously to write an immense historical novel; for his monkeys encounter, midway through their jungle odyssey, a stranded Englishman named Andrew Battell, with whom they become involved for two or three chapters. About 1965 I discovered quite by accident that Andrew Battell

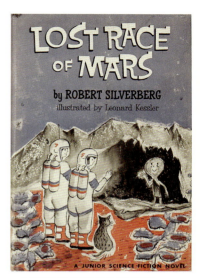

LOST RACE OF MARS
1960, Scholastic Books.

An early (1953) rejection slip from Horace Gold, this one for his magazine **BEYOND FANTASY FICTION.** *Horace would go on to send me some very harsh rejection slips for* **GALAXY,** *but I learned a great deal from them and was never offended by his tough letters. — RS*

From the desk of: 1953
H. L. GOLD

Dear Mr. Silverberg:

   Aside from a tendency to be over-explicit in spots and repeat in dialogu something already stated in narrative, you've told your story well.

   Trouble is that you don't have an ending. Not, at any rate, one that fantasy readers would be happy with. Anyone who buys a fantasy magazine naturally expects a fantasy payoff, and is understandably put out when he fails to get one. The trick is to find a conclusion that startles. You can argue that this isn't always true of BEYOND, but it's not because I want it that way.

   Let's see more. And type your name where you now have the wordage; that you can put at the top.

                              Cordially,

galaxy publishing corporation

had really lived; and, stumbling upon the text of Battell's own journal, which surely de la Mare had used in writing his novel, I resolved to retell his story myself, and eventually did so in my immense historical novel, *Lord of Darkness*, which is nothing else than my imagined version of Andrew Battell's autobiography. I tip my hat to Walter de la Mare again and again throughout its 559 pages, but only someone who has read *The Three Mulla-Mulgars* would know that, and I have never met anyone else who has.

I am pleasantly aware, as I forage through the reconstituted library of my childhood, that books I have written are part of other people's store of images and recollections. Again and again I hear that someone's first novel was one of my early books for young readers — *Revolt on Alpha C,* say, or *Lost Race of Mars.* So the cycle goes round and round. We read, we absorb, we transmute, and we offer new stories for new readers, who will eventually recycle our own work into tales for the readers of generations to follow.

In darker moments I wonder whether today's young readers — brought up on *Teenage Mutant Ninja Turtles* instead of *Heroes of Asgard* and *The Children of Odin* — will produce fables and fantasies of their own with any value whatever. Garbage in, garbage out, as they say. But I want to think that I'm wrong: that the myth-making function of mankind is eternal, and that there will always be powerful new stories growing out of powerful ancient ones, no matter what debasements of popular culture may thrive in the marketplace. In any case, it's not my problem. I won't be around to see what the writers born in 1985 will be writing forty years from now. And if I don't care for what has been produced in the interim, well, I can always go back and re-read *The Three Mulla-Mulgars* or *Sylvie and Bruno* or *The Epic of Kings* one more time.

1992

FUTURE SCIENCE FICTION, Feb. 1959, contains "You Do Something To Me" RS writing as Calvin M. Knox.

THE BOOKS OF CHILDHOOD: TWO

Graham Greene, again: I have long found his essays and novels a source of wisdom and inspiration. This comes from his autobiographical essay, "The Lost Childhood":

> "Perhaps it is only in childhood that books have any deep influence on our lives.... In childhood all books are books of divination, telling us about the future, and like the fortune teller who sees a long journey in the cards or death by water they influence the future."

Greene was speaking in particular of how the books he had read in his own distant childhood in Edwardian England had sent him on the path toward becoming a writer, and had even shaped the *kind* of fiction he would choose to write. But not only writers, he says, are set on their paths by their early reading.

"I was safe as long as I could not read," Greene tells us. "The wheels had not begun to turn — but now the future stood around on bookshelves everywhere waiting for the child to choose — the life of a chartered accountant, perhaps, a colonial civil servant, a planter in China, a steady job in a bank, happiness and misery...." We are stamped irrevocably in our childhoods, he says; the impressions

we receive then determine the years ahead. And he offers as one epitome of that idea the startling lines from AE's poem "Germinal":

> In ancient shadows and twilights
> Where childhood had strayed,
> The world's great sorrows were born
> And its heroes were made.
> In the lost boyhood of Judas
> Christ was betrayed.

Photo of attendees at the Metrocon (Metropolitan Science Fiction Conference) Hotel Empire, New York, Oct. 23-25, 1954. Including a nineteen-year old RS at 5F. Other attendees include: Phyllis Economou (14A), Isaac Asimov (14D), Edmond Hamilton (14L), Leigh Brackett (14O), Julius Schwartz (11N), Evelyn Gold (14H), Judith Merril (8J), Barbara Brown (later to become Mrs. Silverberg) (5D). 4th Row, center: James Blish (7G) (Photo by Ben Jason) (Identification provided by George C. Willick and Robert Silverberg)

Exactly so. In every childhood there is a moment when a door opens and lets the future in — and very often it is a book that provides that moment. Previously, I spoke of the books in my own childhood that did that for me — retellings of Norse and Persian legends and the poems of Homer, an obscure novel by Lewis Carroll, and a wonderful fantasy by Walter de La Mare, among others. But I didn't speak in any particular way about the science fiction books that I stumbled upon some forty-five years ago that sent me spiraling off into the orbit that has defined my life's career. I mentioned some Jules Verne and H. G. Wells, yes, but only in passing.

I have the actual books on my desk before me now — five of them, treasured artifacts of my childhood. Here is Verne's *Twenty Thousand Leagues Under the Sea*, in an undated and virtually anonymous edition published by "Books, Inc." I suspect it was given to me in 1943 or 1944. I had no idea, of course, that it was science fiction; I was not to hear that phrase itself for another couple of years. But I knew, as I read it over and over, that it was a magical tale of adventure that relied not on witchcraft and the supernatural but on a clear-eyed comprehension of the real world. Verne's crisp technical descriptions ("Besides other things the nets-brought up, were several flabellariae and graceful polypi, that are peculiar to that

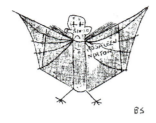

BS

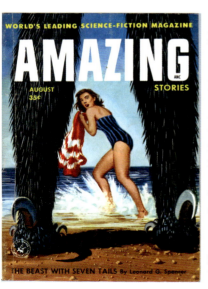

part of the ocean. The direction of the Nautilus was still to the southeast. It crossed the equator December 1, in 142 degrees latitude; and on the fourth of the same month we sighted the Marquesas group. . .") provided so plausible a texture of verisimilitude to my science-oriented mind that I took it quite for granted when Captain Nemo made a side trip to visit the sunken ruins of Atlantis in his submarine. Verne's underwater tour of the world showed me our planet as a place of marvels populated by hordes of extraordinary creatures. Somehow, unawares, I learned the distinction between fantasy and science fiction even then, and my mode of writing was determined in that moment, years before I even knew I was going to be a writer.

Then here is Donald A. Wollheim's *The Pocket Book of Science Fiction,* first of all paperback sf anthologies. The copyright date is 1943, but my edition is a 1947 printing, and that must be when I discovered it and eagerly paid my twenty-five cents. Ten stories, here; one of them was by H. G. Wells, whom I had already discovered in the public library. (I had read *The Time Machine,* at least, by 1946, though it would be years before I owned a copy myself.) I knew Wells's name was a mark of quality in this peculiar kind of literature for which I already knew I had a predilection; but I discovered other writers in Wollheim's anthology, too, someone named Theodore Sturgeon, and Stanley G. Weinbaum, and Robert Heinlein. I wasn't sure how to pronounce Heinlein's name, but his whacky fourth-dimensional story, "—And He Built a Crooked House," gave me immense pleasure. So did Sturgeon's powerful "Microcosmic God," and Weinbaum's joyous "A Martian Odyssey." And then there was T. S. Stribling's long, mysterious "The Green Splotches," which I now know to be a classic early sf story by a once-famous mainstream writer.

My head reeled with wonders. I was thrown into a fever of excitement. My yearning for the world of the distant future was so powerful that I could taste and touch and smell it. Off I went to the book department at Macy's, and stumbled at once into *Portable Novels of Science,* edited by — Wollheim again! In it was Wells' *First Men in the Moon,* and John Taine's epic of time-travel and dinosaurs, *Before the Dawn,* and Lovecraft's spooky *The Shadow Out of Time,* and above all Olaf Stapledon's tale of super-children, *Odd John,* which seemed to speak directly to lonely, maladjusted, high-I.Q. twelve-year-old me.

The damage was completely done. Not content to read these stories, I had to recreate them in my own words. I started writing imitations of the stories that had most moved me in Wollheim's second book: fragmentary Lovecraftian visions of the far future, time-machine epics replete with Mesozoic scenery, moody tales of the emotional problems of young supermen. I have no idea where any of these things are today — no doubt they would enliven somebody's doctoral thesis on my life and works. But I scribbled away with enormous energy, reliving the stories I had come to love by paying them the sincerest form of flattery.

I had thought all along that I was going to be a scientist when I grew up, by the way. A paleontologist, most likely, or perhaps a botanist. And so I was startled, one day in 1948, when a school adviser who had spoken recently to my father said, "Your parents seem to think you're going to be a writer. Do you think that's so?"

I was astounded. A writer? It had never crossed my mind! "I'm planning to go into science," I told her in bewilderment. But apparently I was the only one who hadn't seen the obvious. That day was a pivotal one in my life — one of those profound Greenian moments when the future reaches toward a child and engulfs him. I have never forgotten the confusion in which I said to myself, "They think I'm going to be a writer? Are they serious? *Could* I be a writer? Am I a writer already? Maybe I am." And the mechanism began to tick in me. Paleontology's loss was science fiction's gain, that day in 1948 — for, now that the suggestion had been openly made, I embraced it as though it was what I had had in mind all along. Which very likely I had.

The next two books confirmed the addiction and thrust me further along the path. One was Groff Conklin's *A Treasury of Science Fiction*, with stories by Heinlein, Arthur C. Clarke, L. Sprague de Camp, Murray Leinster, Jack Williamson, and a good many more of my future demigods. (And one great story, "Vintage Season" by the pseudonymous "Lawrence O'Donnell," to which I would write a sequel, forty years later.) Hardly had I plumbed the depths of the Conklin anthology when I found another and even more astonishing book, the classic Healy-McComas *Adventures in Time and Space*, which dazzled me beyond repair with Heinlein's "By His Bootstraps" and del Rey's "Nerves" and Hasse's "He Who Shrank" and van Vogt's "Black Destroyer" and de Camp's "The Blue Giraffe" and a passel of others that I read until I knew them virtually by heart. (Among them was one called "Nightfall," by someone with the odd name of Asimov. I lived long enough to help turn that one into a novel. You live long enough and the strangest things happen to you.)

What those two anthologies told me, other than renewing my belief that science fiction was a wondrous thing that expanded my fledgling mind toward the infinite, was that there was such a thing as science fiction magazines. Cannily I looked at the copyright lines of the stories in the books and found their names: *Amazing Stories, Planet Stories, Thrilling Wonder Stories*, and above all *Astounding Science Fiction*, where perhaps 75% of all the stories I had most admired had originated. I rushed out and bought them — and began to buy back issues too — and neglected my homework to read them late at night — and sent the editors my crude and pitiful little stories —

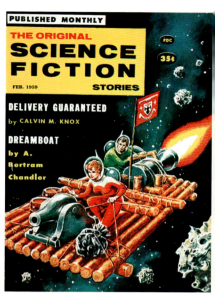

Cover story by RS, writing as Calvin M. Knox, for **THE ORIGINAL SF STORIES,** *Feb, 1959. I did stories written around covers for a number of editors, though more of them for Bob Lowndes than anyone else. (I did some for Larry Shaw of INFINITY and Howard Browne of AMAZING and FANTASTIC, one or two for Fred Pohl at GALAXY, and probably some others I don't remember now.) Most of the Lowndes covers I did were by Ed Emshwiller, but that was because he was doing most of Lowndes's covers; the covers I wrote around for Shaw and Browne were by other people. But in those years Ed did more covers than any other artist and any time a painting was assigned to a writer the chances were that it would be an Emsh. His wife Carol was often the model for them — I saw many women in those paintings with her distinctive facial structure.— RS*

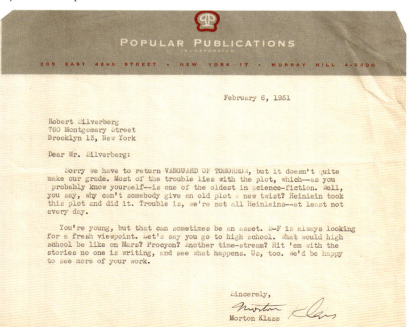

German edition (1959) of novella "Shadow on the Stars," published by Ace as STEPSONS OF TERRA.

STEPSONS OF TERRA (1958) was an intricate time-paradox novel with a certain van Vogtian intensity.—RS

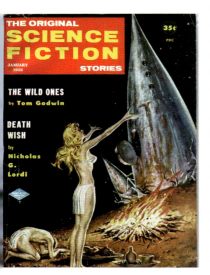

And — well — my parents were right. Evidently I was thinking of becoming a writer. Before me on my desk are the five books that did it to me. As Graham Greene put it, the future had been standing around on bookshelves everywhere waiting for this child to choose. And choose it I did, in a double sense of the word. Once I had those five books in my possession my future was determined, and it was to be a future of science fiction writing.

The process never stops. Books did it for Graham Greene; books and sf magazines did it for me. Somewhere, right now, someone as young and impressionable and alert-minded as I was in 1947 is picking up a glossy issue of *Amazing* and staring at it in growing excitement and curiosity. And in that moment of mounting wonder was the winner of the Hugo Award for 2032 A. D. decided.

1992

A MATTER OF DEFINITIONS

You'd think that making the transition from amateur to pro would be a fairly clean-cut on-off change of state, not much unlike losing your virginity; but it isn't hard to see that even losing your virginity can be carried out in a series of imperceptible shifts that carry you from angelic purity to a condition of eternal damnation without sharp boundaries between states. It's a matter of definitions.

You can define loss of virginity any way you like, from getting to first base on around to going all the way, with all the little conceptual variations in between. But it ought to be simple to know when you're turning into a professional writer. It's when some publication gives you money for something you've written. Right? And on that basis I made my first sale some time in 1951 or very early 1952, when a publication called *The Avalonian* gave me $5 (or was it $10) for a short story called "The Sacred River."

Already the problems are surfacing. For a writer not to remember the exact date of his first sale, or the amount he received down to the penny, is very much like forgetting when you lost your cherry, and with whom. So obviously I didn't consider the sale to *The Avalonian* as a "real" sale — it was just a little adolescent smooching, so to speak. Although I keep my file copy of *The Avalonian* on the same shelf as the one where my professionally published magazine stories live, there is no entry for the sale in the ledger that I've been keeping throughout my entire career; I remember that I got paid for it, and that it wasn't very much, but I'm not sure of the amount.

And in fact *The Avalonian* was a kind of fringe fanzine. It was an outgrowth of a slender fanzine-sized printed magazine called *Different*, which was dedicated largely to poetry of a particularly dreadful post-Tennysonian rumpteetum kind, but which also published an occasional fantasy short story. The editor and publisher was a woman named Lilith Lorraine, who had sold a few stories to Hugo Gernsback and had had one in the fifth issue of *Astounding*, back in 1930. Somehow I had begun receiving her magazine, perhaps in trade for the fanzine I had started publishing in 1949, and when I was about fifteen I must have sent her some of the fiction I was writing then. I recall that she was kindly and encouraging. (I met her once or twice at New York conventions in that era; I recall a woman in the elaborately ornate costume one would expect a venerable poetess to wear. She was very nice to me.)

And in 1951 or maybe very early 1952 she actually sent me a small check for my story "The Sacred River," which was a feeble pulpy space opera about a fugitive on Venus sending thought-messages to Samuel Taylor Coleridge that were transformed into the poem "Kubla Khan." In synopsis the story sounds far less absurd than it actually is; the prose is by Richard S. Shaver out of Rog Phillips, vintage Ray Palmer *Amazing*, and I would not look kindly on having the thing reprinted by some historical-minded smartass. By the time she published it, Lilith Lorraine had transformed *Different* into a neatly printed annual called *The Avalonian*, and there I am on page 37. The issue also includes a story by James McKimmey, Jr., who had some science fiction published in the 1950's, and poetry by Stanton A. Coblentz and a lot of other people — Betty Jean Twieg, Etta Josephean Murfey, Margilea Stonestreet, and so on.

So was that my first professional sale? A sale, beyond doubt, but not exactly professional: it was a magazine that circulated only among amateur poets and writers, I think. And I never quite counted it.

The next stop is the summer of 1953, when Harry Harrison, then editor of a short-lived but excellent magazine called *Science Fiction Adventures*, invited me to do an essay explaining fandom as the inaugural of a column he meant to institute called Fanmag. I visited his office several times — it was the start of a friendship that still endures — and did a 3000-word piece, which he accepted, and for which I was paid $30, cash in hand, at the worldcon in Philadelphia that September. (I later learned that Harry had laid the money out of his own pocket, and didn't collect from his own fly-by-night employer for over a year.) My piece was published a few months later. It was unquestionably professional in all the important ways, since it appeared in a nationally distributed newsstand magazine and I got paid for it. And indeed I carry it right in the top entry of my ledger, sale number one. But it was *journalism*, wasn't it? It wasn't fiction. And I wanted to be an sf pro.

So, then, I had one story sale that didn't seem professional enough to count, and one non-fiction sale, professional but not fiction. My literary virginity was starting to get a bit frayed, but in my own mind I didn't yet think

(opposite bottom)
THE ORIGINAL SCIENCE FICTION STORIES, *January, 1958, cover art by Ed Emshwiller for "Prime Commandment" by RS writing as Calvin M. Knox.*

(bottom)
The first piece of fiction anyone ever paid me for – "The Sacred River," from the semi-pro magazine THE AVALONIAN, 1952 edition. I think my fee was $5. —RS

The Sacred River

Bob Silverberg

"In Xanadu did Kubla Khan
A stately pleasure-dome decree
Where Alph, the sacred river, ran
Through caverns measureless to man
    Down to a sunless sea."
                    —Coleridge

A beam of red light glinted on the rocks of the cavern. Stretching out for untold miles, a rippling river flowed, strange blind fish playing in its inky, bottomless depths. The torch flickered once, twice in Mara's hand, casting an eery glow in the dark cavern. A serpent rose up, questioningly, to pass before Mara, and slithered back to its watery home. Struggling through the dim light, he walked on.

He strode forward into the darkness, standing on the mold-encrusted banks of rock bordering the river. Al'p-he, the Sacred River, the great underground mystery of Venus. Mara battled forward

thoughts across the millions of miles of void to Venus' sister-world, Earth. The greatest scientific minds of the Venusian nobility had been unable to solve the problem of the interplanetary band—but it remained for Mara, a vaguely discontented member of the ruling elite, to make that discovery.

And that discovery had resulted in Mara's imprisonment in the caverns, with sure death waiting at either entrance—for at one end was the Land of Monsters, a place famed more in fable than in fact.

The Monsters were results of unsuccessful experiments by the more scientific of the nobles. Twelve-foot children born of commoners treated with rays; beast-men with skins of slime, who had once been farmers in the lush fields of Venus; and certain other monsters of which no one but Kai-ebla dare think—all these were

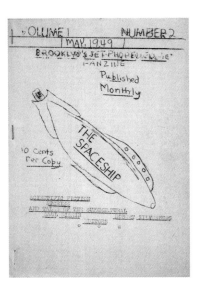

(above)
Front cover of second issue of my fanzine
SPACESHIP, *1949.* – RS

I was really a pro.

A few weeks after the Harry Harrison sale I sold a novel. An honest-to-Gernsback novel, *Revolt on Alpha C*, which is still in print all these years later and earned me something like $483 in royalties a few months ago. I submitted some chapters and an outline in the summer of 1953, and in September or October the publisher told me to go ahead and write the book. Beyond anybody's doubts that was a pro sale, and I suppose I should date the start of my career from the autumn of 1953, with one novel and one non-fiction piece sold almost simultaneously. In fact, I generally do date my career from that point, which means I should have paid more attention to my silver jubilee anniversary in the fall of 1978.

But I can be very technical about these things. Thomas Y. Crowell gave me an acceptance on *Revolt on Alpha C* in the fall of 1953, but no money and no contract, and for a while it was touch and go as to whether they really would publish the book; the original "acceptance" was actually merely encouragement to produce a complete manuscript. Which I did in short order, but they didn't like it a whole lot, and asked for revisions. Which I gave them. But they wanted more revisions. However, this time they did give me a contract. Word of formal and binding acceptance came by telegram on January 2, 1954 — that much I remember with fair accuracy — and soon I had a contract calling for a $250 advance. Even if none of the previous events counted as the beginning of my career, certainly that did. (Except that I still wasn't certain of publication. I had a contract and I even had some of the money, but I wouldn't have a book in print unless I revised the manuscript to the point where they'd publish it. And there was still more work to be done in 1954 before they reached that point. Publication came in the summer of 1955.)

And I still hadn't sold a story to a science-fiction magazine. Not until February of 1954, when the Scottish prozine *Nebula* found my little tale "Gorgon Planet" worthy of print and sent me a check for $12.60. Of course, that wasn't an American prozine, so none of my old high-school buddies would yet be aware that I had made good on my boyhood ambitions, but that last detail was taken care of in August when Bob Lowndes bought my short-short "The Silent Colony" for *Future* for a nifty $13.50. And at that point I could consider myself thoroughly deflowered. Which of my three 1954 sales finally made it clear in my mind that I was a Pro, I can't tell you; but I think that perhaps I should have done something-or-other of a hype nature in 1979 to let the world know that this was my twenty-fifth year as a professional writer.

I didn't do it. The main reason, I guess, is that I didn't think of it; it doesn't seem really awesome to me to have a career stretching back 25 years, when we have a Jack Williamson or a Cliff Simak around with careers going back before the time of my birth, or even a young fella like Fred Pohl who's been in the business more than forty years and is still going off and doing fan guest of honor gigs. But also there was the doubt in my mind about the precise starting point that I ought to commemorate. Because my career didn't start with a single spectacular big bang, such as the sale of a serial to *Astounding Science Fiction*, I've never been anniversary-oriented in that way, though I've always kept track of the fact that I entered FAPA (Fantasy Amateur Press Association) in August of 1949 and got my first mailing, the 49th, that November.

But then a young whippersnapper named Harlan Ellison, who didn't begin selling stories until 1955, began talking up a lot of silver-anniversary stuff for himself this year (1980), and even went so far to have a specialty publisher put out a commemorative volume, with essays by a lot of folks, including me. I wish I had thought of that. And then last month Elinor Mavor, the editor of *Amazing Stories*, invited me to choose a story of mine to be reprinted in a department called The Amazing Stories Hall of Fame, and when I looked back for my first story in *Amazing* I discovered that it was exactly 25 years since I had sold it. (And it will be reprinted in the January 1981 issue, 25 years after its first appearance.) So I've managed an anniversary celebration of sorts after all.

The next anniversary I have to worry about comes in 1982. That's when my 1954 stories are 28 years old and I need to begin the red tape of renewing copyrights. That's when a writer begins to feel he's been around for a while, I guess.

1980

July 1953 issue of RS' fanzine SPACESHIP.

IT WASN'T ALL THAT EASY

I've been a professional science fiction writer for something like 55 years now, have had so many books and stories published that I long ago lost count of how many there are, and never have any trouble finding publishers to pay me for what I write. To a modern-day would-be writer, all that sounds pretty enviable, right? How splendid to be Robert Silverberg, you must think! All he has to do is move his fingers over the keyboard and salable fiction comes tumbling out! Well, let me tell you: I was once a would-be writer just like you, who looked at famous professional writers like Theodore Sturgeon and Robert Sheckley and L. Sprague de Camp with the same sort of envy, thinking that they had somehow been born with an innate ability to write stories that any editor would want to publish, and merely had to sit down and start typing in order to produce something splendid. I was wrong about that, as I discovered when I got to know those writers later on. Nothing had been magically easy for them. They had struggled to break in, and then, having made the grade, they had struggled to stay there. So had all the other writers I idolized, the one exception being Robert A. Heinlein, who seems to have begun his career at full velocity and kept right on going for the next forty years. And I struggled plenty too. I know I did, because the other week, while looking for something else, I came upon a file folder full of ancient rejection slips, and I was reminded yet again of that anguished period in my middle and late teens when I wanted desperately to sell a story to a science fiction magazine, any magazine, and had everything I wrote sent back to me with a nasty little "sorry, can't use it" note clipped to it.

Of course, I *was* only in my teens then. Not only hadn't I mastered the skills that a professional storyteller needs to know, I didn't know a whole lot about the world, either, and so the best I could hope to do was to recycle ideas that older writers had turned into stories, and do it not nearly as well as they had. If I had been 32 years old and worldly-wise, as Heinlein had been in 1939 when he wrote and sold his first sf story, I might have begun my career as effortlessly as Heinlein had. But I wasn't 32, and I wasn't Heinlein. (And even Heinlein got a story rejected once in a while, though such events were few and far between.)

Instead I was 14 or thereabouts, and pretty wet behind the ears, when I began mailing stories to the science fiction editors of the day.

They came back with amazing rapidity. I don't seem to have kept the earliest rejection slips I got, which dated from early in 1949 and came from the premiere editor of the era, John W. Campbell, Jr., of what was then called *Astounding Science Fiction* and is now *Analog*. I remember them as crisp postcard-sized printed forms explaining that the story that had been submitted did not meet the magazine's present needs, and perhaps they were signed with the distinctive bold scrawl that was Campbell's signature, and why I didn't keep them I have no idea. What looks like the oldest survivor in the file comes from *Amazing Stories*, the first sf magazine that I read regularly, and it must date from 1949, because it bears a Chicago address and at the end of that year *Amazing* moved to New York. It simply says, "Sorry overstocked," written by hand and signed, "H. Browne, editor." Overstocked, all right: what I didn't know was that *Amazing* was completely staff-written and that Howard Browne, the editor, never read *any* unsolicited story. (Six years later I would become a member of Howard Browne's New York staff and sell dozens of stories to *Amazing*, but not even in my dreams could I have expected that in 1949!)

Here's another early one, from Fiction House, Inc., which published the grand old pulpy mag *Planet Stories*. It dates from April, 1950, and was earned by my story "Where Alph, the Sacred River, Ran . . ." which I wrote that month and sold for $5, a year later, to a semi-pro magazine called *The Avalonian*. "Dear Contributor," it begins. "We regret that your manuscript does not meet our editorial requirements. In general, we want well-plotted stories with emphasis on swift, colorful action. To get a clear idea of our specific needs we suggest that you read and analyze recent copies of the magazine." Sure. But I *had been* reading and analyzing recent copies of the magazine, staring intently at every word. The problem was that I wasn't capable of moving from analysis to creation, any more than the baseball fan who carefully analyzes the home-run swing of his favorite slugger is able to hit one out of the park himself.

But that *Planet Stories* rejection slip came with something special attached: a personal note from the magazine's young editor, Jerome Bixby, to whom I had been writing letters about the stories in his magazine: "Right back at you with a bilious Fiction House rejection slip for your collection." (And a bilious green it was, very unappealing.) "'Where Alph, the Sacred River Ran . . .' is one of the best fan jobs I've seen in a long time. Keep it up. . . you're bound to connect sooner or later. Probably later, though, when your collection has grown some."

I was thrilled. Before long, I sent Bixby another story, certain that he would accept it. But he had moved along to another magazine by then, and from his successor at *Planet* came a cruel postcard, not even a rejection slip, dated January 2, 1951: "We are holding your manuscript, 'Introduction,' for pickup or $.06 return postage." Not even "does not fit our needs"!

Another from 1950, from the low and slow-paying *Weird Tales*, thanks me "for the privilege of reading your manuscript. Its return does not necessarily imply lack of merit, but means that it does not fit in with our needs." Another from *Amazing* in Chicago — "Sorry overstocked," again. It refers to a story called "Homeward Retreat," of which I have not the slightest recollection. From *Future Science Fiction*'s Robert W. Lowndes, to whom I would sell a host of stories years later: "We are sorry that your manuscript is not for us, and that we could not return it with an individual letter. We realize that a cold, printed rejection slip does not tell you whether your submission approached our requirements — but we receive such a large volume of manuscripts every day that. . . ."

I didn't give up hope. Not completely, anyway. Certainly I was downcast by these rejections — I have cited here only these few out of more than a dozen from 1949 and 1950 — but I was driven by that peculiar madness that afflicts young would-be writers, and I sent my stories out again and again. Bea Majaffey of *Other Worlds Science Stories* sent me a form that included about thirty reasons for turning a story down ("Logic is faulty". . . . "Science is inaccurate". . . . "Too dull and factual. . . .") The two items that were checked for my story were "Not convincingly written" and "Poorly plotted." Well, I was only fifteen. But I urged myself to write more convincingly next time.

One of the pivotal rejection slips of my young life arrived in February 1951 from Morton Klass — the younger brother of Phil Klass, better known as the sf writer "William Tenn"— of *Super Science Stories*. (I'm not making that one up!) Addressing me as "Mr. Silverberg," he said, "Sorry we have to return 'Vanguard of Tomorrow, ' but it doesn't quite make our grade. Most of the trouble lies with the plot, which — as you probably know yourself — is one of the oldest in science fiction. Well, you say, why can't somebody give an old plot a new twist? Heinlein took this plot and did it. Trouble is, we're not all Heinleins — at least not every day.

"You're young, but that can sometimes be an asset. Sf is always looking for a fresh viewpoint. Let's say you go to high school. What would high school be like on Mars? Procyon? Another time-stream? Hit 'em with the stories no one is writing, and see what happens. Us, too. We'd be happy to see more of your work."

I was, of course, disappointed to see "Vanguard of Tomorrow" come bouncing back — I had written it one sweltering week in September 1950, using a punchy, high-powered short-paragraph style that I borrowed from Clifford D. Simak, and I thought it was great stuff. (I still have the manuscript. It isn't great stuff.) But Mort Klass's encouraging letter sank in deeply, and just two years later I began a book for young readers on just the theme he suggested that became my first published novel, *Revolt on Alpha C.*

Published novels seemed infinitely far in my future back there in 1951, and 1952, too. From William Hamling's *Imagination* came three printed rejection slips, and then a fourth with a scrawled note from Hamling in the margin: "Sorry, Bob, this doesn't quite make it. But keep plugging!" I kept plugging. Eventually I would sell him dozens of stories. From H. L. Gold of *Galaxy* came a typed note dated May 8, 1953: "Sorry we can't use 'The Cure.' However, we like your style and hope you'll try us again." (He likes my style? Really, or was that just boilerplate? Apparently he did. Further stories brought longer notes from Gold, some of them encouraging, some of them vitriolic, but all of them useful.) ("Aside from a tendency to be over-explicit in spots and repeat in dialogue something already stated in narrative, you've told your story well. Trouble is that you don't have an ending. . . . !") Gold beat me about the head and shoulders with many such notes, but eventually he beat me into shape and bought a goodly number of stories from me for his prestigious magazine, starting in 1956. (As soon as I got "The

Another encouraging rejection slip, this one from Larry Shaw, just a few months before I would make my first professional sale of fiction.— RS

WORLDS OF SCIENCE FICTION
KINGSTON · NEW YORK

May 12, 1953

Mr. Bob Silverberg
760 Montgomery Street
Brooklyn 13, New York

Dear Bob:

There's nothing wrong with the writing in QUEST, and I think it's safe to predict you won't have too much trouble in joining the professional ranks. But it seems to me this kind of pessimism about man's fitness to inhabit the universe has been overdone; it was all right the first few times but the possible variations on it are very limited.

Try again, by all means, and best wishes.

Cordially,

Larry

Larry T. Shaw
Associate Editor

LTS/do

1960 Italian edition of my first novel, REVOLT ON ALPHA C.— RS

Cure" back from Gold I sent it to Sam Moskowitz of Hugo Gernsback's *Science Fiction Plus*, who turned it down in June as "well-written, smooth & clever. Good dialogue. The ending is very weak, but some of the background is interesting. Too long for the extent of the ideas." I have no idea today what that story was about.)

I've got a sheaf of others from the early 1950s: a two-inch file of them. The most significant of them came from the now-forgotten Peter Hamilton, editor of the now-forgotten *Nebula Science Fiction*, published in Scotland. I had sent him "Vanguard of Tomorrow," and he returned it in April 1953 with a lengthy note telling me he was turning it down because "it is very complicated for nonfans (who make up the vast majority of my readers) and... it seems to pack no punch or realism." But, he added, he was anxious to help young authors on the way up, and advised me "to do a spaceship-alien planet theme, keeping the plot simple and the writing taught [sic!] and send it to me again. I'll do all I can to show you where you go wrong and suggest how to put it right, and I believe, with a little perseverance, you will make quite a promising writer."

I took the advice to heart and wrote a 3000-worder called "Gorgon Planet," which Hamilton accepted in January 1954, paying me $12.60. It was my first sale of fiction to any professional sf magazine, and I was on my way. Before long I had sold stories to Bob Lowndes and Bill Hamling, and then, in 1955, to Howard Browne of *Amazing* and the formidable John W. Campbell of *Astounding*, and after that I would be able to sell just about any story I wrote.

But not always to the first editor I showed it to. Even after my career was launched, occasional rejection slips still showed up. (John Campbell, 1963: "Glad to hear from you again . . . but I'm afraid this one really isn't a story." Larry T. Shaw, same year: "I'm sure someone will buy it, but what we need is something more intellectually slanted and strongly plotted." Damon Knight, 1969: "This one is ingenious, but I could not persuade myself that I cared what happened to either of the characters." And so on, every now and then, especially after I began writing stories for the very hard to please Alice K. Turner of *Playboy* in 1981. She bought a lot from me, but she turned plenty down, too.)

Yes, I did get to have a long and rewarding career despite all those early rejections, and no, it wasn't easy to get started, however it might look in hindsight. Many a time back in 1952 and 1953 I was just about ready to give up trying to sell my stories altogether, even as you sometimes are. For me that would have been a mistake. Perhaps it would be for you also. Some people, however keen their ambitions might be, simply will never learn the knack of writing stories people will want to read. If you have what it takes, though, you'll keep right on jogging down that bumpy road until you get where you want to go.

2008

THE WHEEL KEEPS TURNING

Last week I had dinner with a new sf writer, one who has sold about half a dozen stories, and she asked me if I would mind taking a look at a manuscript of hers that was collecting rejection slips. Something evidently was wrong with the story, she said, because the editors kept sending it back, but she couldn't see where the problem lay and the editors who had nixed it hadn't been particularly explicit in stating their objections. Perhaps, she said, I could put my finger on the story's weakness. And the request took me back to an extraordinary moment early in my own career — all the way back to March of 1956, in fact.

Do you remember March of 1956?

Probably not. The demographic surveys of the sf audience show that most of the readership of sf magazines belongs to the baby-boom generation, the people who came swarming into the world between 1945 and 1963 or so, and my guess is that the birth-dates of most of you fall into the 1950-60 slot. So the events of 1956 aren't going to be very clear in your mind.

They certainly are in mine, though. I was 21 years old that year. 1956 was one of the most significant years of my life and I have bright and vivid memories of much that was happening then.

I began that year as a senior in college, living in a furnished room on West 114th Street in New York with Harlan Ellison in the room next door. In June I graduated and in August I got married, rented an apartment all my very own, and began buying actual adult furniture. (Some of which I still use, 43 years later.) My career as a writer was just hitting full stride. At the World SF Convention in New York in September I collected my first Hugo.

There were some notable world events that year too — rather apocalyptic stuff, in fact. We conducted the first open-air test explosion of an H-bomb at Bikini Atoll in May. A month later, there was an uprising in Poland against Soviet rule. It was crushed by Russian troops. In July, the government of Egypt seized the Suez Canal and threatened to close it to Western shipping, touching off a world economic crisis. A summer of fruitless negotiation led to the invasion of Egypt by the armies of Israel, Great Britain, and France in October in what proved to be an abortive attempt to return the canal to international control. More or less at the same time, an anti-Communist rebellion broke out in Hungary and this, too, was squelched by the Soviets. In the middle of all these startling things, the United States held a presidential election in which the incumbent, Dwight D. Eisenhower, easily defeated his challenger, Adlai Stevenson, even though Eisenhower had had a serious heart attack the previous year: it was not a time when the country wanted to change leaders.

And there I was, a college boy from Brooklyn just getting ready to take his first steps into real-world life — if you call setting yourself up in business as a full-time science fiction writer an entry into "real-world life."

What I had been doing, all through my senior year at Columbia, was writing stories as fast as I could turn them out and bringing them downtown to the editors of the half a dozen or so sf magazines that existed then. Randall Garrett, a well-known writer of the era who also was living in the residential hotel where Harlan and I had rooms, had introduced me to these editors — John W. Campbell, Howard Browne, Robert Lowndes, and others — and every Monday I would make the rounds of the editorial offices, dropping off the stories of the previous week and picking up anything that hadn't sold. (Just about all of my stories of that period did sell, but not always on the first try!)

The big editor, in more ways than one, was John Campbell. Since 1937 he had guided the fortunes of *Astounding Science Fiction*, the predecessor of today's *Analog*; it was Campbell who had launched the careers of such great writers as Isaac Asimov, Robert A. Heinlein, A. E. van Vogt, Theodore Sturgeon, and Arthur

C. Clarke. To me and my whole generation of science fiction readers and writers he was a legendary figure, though now he was in the twilight of his long career. A massive man with a powerful voice and a commanding no-nonsense manner, Campbell seemed intimidating indeed to a youngster like myself, but, shoved forward by the ebullient Randall Garrett, I had managed (to my own amazement) to sell him half a dozen stories in the six months between August of 1955 and February of 1956. By March, it was part of my regular routine to stop off every other Monday at Campbell's small, cluttered office in a drab old building on East 45th Street with my latest opus.

Often, on these Mondays, I would encounter other writers or artists who also had dropped in to see Campbell. One week it might be Kelly Freas, and the next Algis Budrys, or Ted Sturgeon, or even Isaac Asimov. I found all that pretty awesome too. But on the particular March day in 1956 that I have in mind, Campbell was being visited by no less a person than Will F. Jenkins, himself a legend of the field, the author of such cherished classics as "First Contact," "Sidewise in Time," and "The Mad Planet." His effortlessly told stories, most of them pub-

Rejection slip from Peter Hamilton of the Scottish magazine NEBULA, which would give me my first professional sale a few months later with "Gorgon Planet." — RS

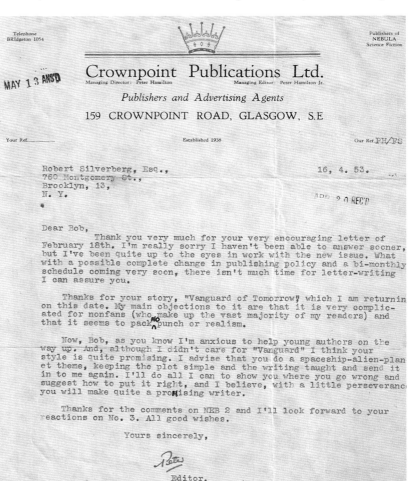

lished under his pseudonym of "Murray Leinster," had been admired by editors and readers for forty years.

Jenkins was a smallish, dark-haired man with a soft, lovely Virginia accent. I had met him before, though he hardly would have remembered it. It was at a little convention six years before in a squalid meeting-hall in Manhattan; I had asked him to sign the first thing I could lay my hands on, which was that month's issue of *Astounding*, and he had scrawled his name in pencil on the contents page. John Campbell had signed right below — in ink. The magazine is still in my possession today.

That day in 1956, Will Jenkins was 60 years old. John Campbell was 46. I was 21. So we represented three different generations of science fiction writing.

One thing we had in common was our precocity. Will Jenkins began selling stories at 17, in 1913. Campbell had sold his first story in 1929, when he was 19. I had made my own first sale in 1953, at 18. I realize now that these two titans of the field, the grand old man and the legendary editor, must have felt a touch of kinship with the pink-cheeked beardless boy who now sat with them, presumably as a colleague, in that messy little office.

Well, and there I was, with my latest story — a fourteen-page effort called "Sourdough," something about a prospector who was using a dowsing rod to find uranium ore in the South Dakota hill country. Even as my early stories go, it wasn't very much of anything. I had carefully constructed the basic idea to fit John Campbell's big obsession of the moment, which was the reality of psionic powers. (Campbell was ever an obsessive, and his writers quickly learned to keep up with his whims and fads.) Jauntily I took a seat next to Will Jenkins at John Campbell's desk, was duly introduced, shook hands, and slipped into my new mode of calm acceptance of my professional status. I could not allow myself to think I was mingling with demigods. Here we were, right? — just Will and John and Bob, three science fiction people.

"Bob's one of our new writers," Campbell said casually to Jenkins. —"Do you have anything today, Bob?"

"As a matter of fact, John" — I had lately begun calling him "John," and the heavens had not fallen upon me — "I do." And I opened my briefcase and took out the manuscript of "Sourdough."

"Well, let's see," Campbell said. I assumed he would slip the manuscript into *his* briefcase, read it at home that night, and give me his verdict the following week. But to my utter horror he began to read the story then and there.

It doesn't take long for an experienced editor to read a fourteen-page manuscript. For me it was an anguished eternity, though. I sat there studying Campbell's every flicker of expression at a distance of perhaps five feet while he methodically leafed through my story, scowling occasionally, tugging at the tip of his nose, stroking his chin. I had $120 at stake, aside from the prestige, vast at the time, that accrued to anyone who sold a story to *Astounding*. That $120 fee was non-trivial: perhaps $1500 in modern purchasing power, and remember that I was still in college, living in a furnished room that cost $10 a week: this one sale represented three months' rent.

At last John looked up and said casually, "Something's wrong with the ending of this, but I'm not sure what. Will, would you mind taking a look?" And he flipped my story across the desk to Will Jenkins.

L to R: RS, Barbara Silverberg, Katie MacLean, unknown, Cyril Kornbluth, and Evelyn del Rey. Photo taken by Ed Emshwiller at the first Milford Science Fiction Conference, 1956.

So I had to endure a second in-my-presence reading of "Sourdough," and this time by the senior figure of the field, a man who had been a well-known professional when Calvin Coolidge was in the White House. Jenkins, the cagy old pro, skimmed swiftly through the story, nodded, indicated page twelve. "I see the problem," he said — to Campbell, not to me. And offered a dazzling rewrite suggestion, with which Campbell concurred. John pointed to the typewriter on his secretary's desk and instructed me to sit down and write a couple of new paragraphs right on the spot.

Which I did, in a state of high astonishment; and Campbell bought the story ten minutes later.

All this was a long time ago. Jenkins and Campbell have been dead for decades. My own career has stretched across 45 years, now, which means I have been a professional writer longer, as of 1999, than Will Jenkins had been that day in 1956. The Eisenhower presidency is farther away in time from Bill Clinton's than Warren Harding's was from Eisenhower. And now one of today's new writers has asked me to locate the place where a story of hers goes off the tracks.

The wheel keeps turning; and we are swept along with it, boys and girls turning into men and women, green new writers becoming eminences grises. I was a kid just starting out, that day when John Campbell and Will Jenkins read my story before my very eyes and Jenkins told Campbell how I ought to fix it. Long, long ago … and how bright the memory of that strange hour remains in my mind.

1999

TWO: ON WRITING SF

JAN • 67 •

ROAD TO NIGHTFALL (1954)

I was in my late teens, a sophomore at Columbia University, when I began sketching this story in the fall of 1953. I had, I recall, been reading "Crossing Paris," a story by the French writer Marcel Ayme, in an old issue of *Partisan Review* — a literary magazine that I followed avidly in those days. It opened this way:

"The victim, already dismembered, lay in a corner of the cellar under wrappings of stained canvas. Jamblier, a little man with graying hair, a sharp profile, and feverish eyes, his belly girdled with a kitchen apron which came down to his feet, was shuffling across the concrete floor. At times he stopped short in his tracks to gaze with faintly flushed cheeks and uneasy eyes at the latch of the door. To relieve the tension of waiting, he took a mop which was soaking in an enameled bucket, and for the third time he washed the damp surface of the concrete to efface from it any last traces of blood which his butchery might have left there. . . ."

It sounds like the beginning of a murder mystery, or a horror story. But in fact "Crossing Paris" is about the task of transporting black-market pork by suitcase through the Nazi-occupied city. The grim, bleak atmosphere and the situational–ethics anguish of the characters affected me profoundly, and almost at once I found myself translating the story's mood into science fictional terms. What if I were to take Ayme's trick opening paragraph literally? That is, assume that the "victim" is not a pig but a man, as I had thought until the story's second page, and have the city suffering privations far more intense even than those of the war, so that cannibalism is being practiced and the illicit meat being smuggled by night through the streets is the most illicit meat of all.

I wrote the story in odd moments stolen from classwork over the next couple of months, intending to submit it to a contest one of the science fiction magazines was running that year. A thousand-dollar prize (roughly ten thousand in modern purchasing power) was being offered for the best story of life in twenty-first century America written by a college undergraduate. For some reason I never entered the contest — missed the deadline, perhaps, but in the spring of 1954 I started sending my manuscript around to the science fiction magazines. I was nobody at all then, an unpublished writer (although, somewhat to my own amazement, I had just had my first novel, *Revolt on Alpha C*, accepted and scheduled for publication in the summer of 1955.) Back the story came with great speed, just as all the fifteen or twenty other stories I had sent out over the previous six years had done. (I was about thirteen when I began submitting my stories to magazines.) When it had been to all seven or eight of the magazines that existed then, and every editor had told me how depressing, morbid, negative, and impossible to publish it was, I put it aside and wrote it off as a mistake.

A couple of years passed. I started selling my stories at a rapid clip and became, before I turned twenty-one, a well-known science fiction writer. I was earning a nice living from my writing while still an undergraduate at. Columbia.

Meanwhile, a young would-be writer from Cleveland had come to New York and moved in next door to me. His name was Harlan Ellison, and I have maintained a warm, turbulent, and indissoluble friendship with him ever since, despite enormous differences of opinion on almost everything on which it's possible to have differing opinions. One day in 1956 I mentioned to him that I had managed to sell every story I had written except one, which no editor would touch, and he demanded to see it. Harlan read it on the spot. "Brilliant!" he said, "Magnificent!" Or words to that effect. He was indignant that such a dark masterpiece should meet with universal rejection, and he vowed to find a publisher for it. Around that time, the gentle and unworldly Hans Stefan Santesson took over the editorship of a struggling magazine called *Fantastic Universe*, and Harlan, telling him I had written a story too daring for any of his rivals, essentially defied him not to buy it. Hans asked for the manuscript, commented in his mild way that the story was pretty strong stuff, and, after some hesitation, ran it in the July 1958 issue of his magazine.

After all these years I find it hard to see what was so hot to handle about "Road to Nightfall." Its theme — that the stress of life in a post-nuclear society could lead even to cannibalism — seemed to upset many of the editors who turned it down, but there was no taboo per se on the theme. (*Cf.* Damon Knight's 1950 classic, "To Serve Man," just to name one.) Most likely the protagonist's moral collapse at the end was the problem, for most sf editors of the time preferred stories in which the central figure transcends all challenges and arrives at a triumphant conclusion to his travail. That I had never published anything at the time was a further drawback. Theodore Sturgeon or Fritz Leiber, say, might have persuaded an editor to buy a story about cannibalism, or one with a downbeat ending- but a long downbeat cannibal story by an unknown author simply had too much going against it, and even after my name had become established it still required the full force of the Ellison juggernaut to win it a home.

To me it still seems like a pretty good job, especially for a writer who was a considerable distance short of his twentieth birthday. It moves along, it creates character and action and something of a plot, it gets its not-extremely original point across effectively. If I had been an editor looking at this manuscript back then, I would certainly have thought its writer showed some promise.

2004

RS writing as Calvin M. Knox. Cover story "Prime Commandment" for **The ORIGINAL SCIENCE FICTION STORIE**S, *January, 1958.*

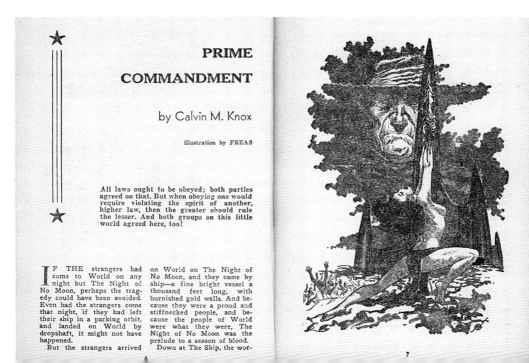

PRIME COMMANDMENT

by Calvin M. Knox

illustration by FREAS

All laws ought to be obeyed; both parties agreed on that. But when obeying one would require violating the spirit of another, higher law, then the greater should rule the lesser. And both groups on this little world agreed here, too!

IF THE strangers had come to World on any night but The Night of No Moon, perhaps the tragedy could have been avoided. Even had the strangers come that night, if they had left their ship in a parking orbit, and landed on World by dropshaft, it might not have happened.

But the strangers arrived on World on The Night of No Moon, and they came by ship—a fine bright vessel a thousand feet long, with burnished gold walls. And because they were a proud and stiffnecked people, and because the people of World were what they were, The Night of No Moon was the prelude to a season of blood.

Down at The Ship, the wor-

6

7

(Above) An early French translation — GALAXIE from January 1959.

(Opposite) The novella version of HAWKSBILL STATION in a 1966 Dutch edition of GALAXY. Cover art by Milton Davis.

YOKEL WITH PORTFOLIO (1955)

All through my adolescence I dreamed of becoming a science fiction writer. Feverishly I wrote stories, typed them up, sent them off to the magazines of the day (*Astounding Science Fiction, Amazing Stories, Startling Stories*, and so forth.) They all came back.

But then, in 1953, when I was 18 and a sophomore at Columbia, I began to make my first sales — an article about science fiction fandom, then a novel for teenage readers only a few years younger than myself, and then a short story. On the strength of these credentials I was able to get myself a literary agent — Scott Meredith, one of the pre-eminent science fiction specialists of that era, who represented such notable clients as Arthur C. Clarke, Poul Anderson, Philip K. Dick, and Jack Vance.

My hope was that under the aegis of so powerful an agent my stories would get faster and more sympathetic attention from the editors than they had been getting when I sent them in myself. It didn't quite work that way — maybe I got faster readings, sure, but my stuff was still competing with the stories of Messrs. Clarke, Anderson, Dick, and Vance for space in those editors' magazines. Still, during the course of the next year or so Scott did manage to make a few tiny sales for me to a couple of minor sf magazines. The first, in June, 1954, was a 1500-worder called "The Silent Colony." Eight tense months later, in February of 1955, he produced a second one: "The Martian," 3000 words, which Scott sold to William L. Hamling's *Imagination*, an unpretentious little penny-a-word market that filled its pages with stories that various top-level writers (Gordon R. Dickson, Robert Sheckley, Philip K. Dick, Damon Knight) had been unable to sell to better-paying magazines. I was pleased to be joining their company. Even though these two sales had netted me a grand total of $40.50, I felt I was on my way toward the start of a career. And I was still only a junior in college, twenty years old, after all. There would be time later on to consider whether I could actually earn a living this way.

Three more months went by before my next sale: a second one to Hamling, "Yokel with Portfolio." Looking at it now, I suppose that I wrote it with Horace Gold's *Galaxy Science Fiction* in mind, or Anthony Boucher's *Fantasy & Science Fiction*, since those two top-of-the-field editors were particularly fond of the sort of light, slick science fiction that I imagined "Yokel with Portfolio" to be. But the Meredith agency obviously didn't think I was quite ready for prime time yet, for I see from the agency records that they sent it straight to *Imagination* in March of 1955 and that on May 8 Hamling bought it for $55. It was published in the November, 1955 issue of *Imagination*'s new companion magazine, *Imaginative Tales* — my third published short story, no classic but, I think, a decent enough job for the lad of twenty that I was at the time I wrote it.

2005

THE MACAULEY CIRCUIT (1955)

"The Macauley Circuit" was written in June of 1955, right on the eve of the real beginning of my career as a professional science fiction writer. I was still a Columbia undergraduate then, having just finished my junior year, but I had managed to meet most of the magazine editors and had received considerable encouragement from them, and in just another few weeks would be making my first flurry of consistent story sales, enough to convince me that I would be able to sustain a career as a full-time writer.

Like most of my stories at that time this one made its modest way from editor to editor, descending from the top-paying markets to those further down the pecking order, and early in 1956 was bought, for a glorious $40, by Leo Margulies, the publisher of *Fantastic Universe*, who was beginning to accept my work with some regularity. He ran it in the August 1956 issue. It's not a masterpiece, no: I wasn't really up to turning out a lot of masterpieces when I was twenty years old. But it stands up pretty well, I think — an intelligent consideration of some of the problems that the still virtually unborn computer age was likely to bring. If you ever get the chance to read it, please bear in mind that computers, in 1955, were still considered experimental technology — "thinking machines" or "electronic brains" is what they were generally called then — and musical synthesizers existed only in the pages of science fiction.

There's a nice irony — one of the many pleasures of having had a long career — in this story's later history. I have survived to see the cumbersome "electronic brains" of 1955 evolve into the ubiquitous personal computers of our own era, and to see the publishing industry begin to migrate from the print media to the various electronic formats. In 1997, one of the pioneering electronic-publishing companies asked me for the rights to some of my stories for Internet distribution. I included "The Macauley Circuit" in the package, not without some misgivings about how today's computer-savvy readers, most of whom had not even been born when I wrote the story, would react to its quaintly archaic view of how computers and synthesizers would work. Evidently the story wasn't as quaint as I thought. Through all the years since it first became available to on-line readers, it has been one of the top three bestselling stories on that web site.

2004

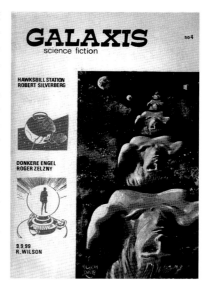

LONG LIVE THE KEJWA (1956)

A great deal happened to me, professionally, between the publication of "Yokel With Portfolio" in the autumn of 1955 and the appearance of "Long Live the Kejwa" seven months later. The most important development was the arrival in New York City, where I was living then, of one Randall Garrett.

Garrett, a charming, roguish fellow seven or eight years older than I was, came from Texas but had been living in the Midwest, working as a chemist and writing science fiction on the side, in the early 1950s. He was a natural storyteller and had a good grasp both of science and of the traditions of science fiction, and very quickly he sold a dozen stories or so to most of the major markets, including two excellent novelets ("The Waiting Game," 1951, and "The Hunting Lodge," 1954) to John W. Campbell's *Astounding*, one of the leading magazines of the field. But like too many science fiction writers Garrett had an unfortunate weakness for the bottle, which led early in 1955 to the end of his marriage and the loss of his job; and then the friends in Illinois with whom he had taken refuge

I don't have a complete file of my own work — there are plenty of foreign editions I've never seen — but the ones I do have fill a good-sized cottage back of the main house, and overflow in all directions. Finding any particular item now is often a tough job. Harlan Ellison has the same problem. Isaac Asimov didn't keep the magazines his work appeared in — just tore out his own contribution and threw the rest away, which I found horrifying.— RS wearied of his wayward ways and suggested he move along. That spring he packed up his few possessions and a box of unfinished manuscripts and headed for New York to establish himself as a full-time science fiction writer.

One of the few people he knew in New York was Harlan Ellison, who had come from the Midwest a year before Garrett with the same goal in mind. Harlan and I were close friends, and at my suggestion he had taken a room next door to me in the seedy Manhattan residence hotel where I was living during my college years, on West 114th Street, a couple of blocks from the Columbia campus. It was a place inhabited by a sprinkling of undergraduates, an assortment of aging graduate students, a few aspiring writers like Harlan and me, some very aged ladies living on pensions, and an odd collection of down-on-their-luck characters of no apparent profession. When he reached New York, Garrett phoned Ellison, who was still meeting only frustration in his attempts to break into print. Harlan told him about our hotel, and very suddenly we had him living down the hall from us. Almost immediately thereafter Garrett and I went into partnership as a sort of fiction factory.

He and I could scarcely have been more different in temperament. Randall was lazy, undisciplined, untidy, untrustworthy, and alcoholic. I was a ferociously hard worker, ambitious, orderly, boringly respectable and dignified, and, though I did (and do) have a fondness for the occasional alcoholic beverage, I was (and am) constitutionally unable to drink very much without getting sick. But we did have one big thing in common: we both were deeply versed in the tropes of science fiction and intended to earn our livings entirely by writing science fiction. We had the same agent, too. Furthermore, we had complementary sets of skills: Garrett's education had been scientific, mine literary. He was good at the technological side of sf, and also was a skillful constructor of story plots. I, though still a beginning writer, was already showing superior stylistic abilities and the knack of creating interesting characters. I was tremendously productive, too, able to turn out a short story in a single sitting, several times a week. Garrett was a swift writer

Illustration by Jack Gaughan for "Blaze of Glory" **GALAXY,** *August, 1957.*

too, but only when he could stay sober long enough to get anything done. It occurred to him that if we became collaborators, my discipline and ambition would be strong enough to drive both of us to get a great deal of work done, and his more experienced hand as a writer would help me overcome the neophyte's flaws in my storytelling technique that had kept me from selling stories to any but the minor magazines. And so we set up in business together. (Harlan, having not yet reached a professional level of writing ability, remained on the outside, somewhat to his displeasure.)

Garrett was a man of grandiose ideas, and so he and I aimed for the top right away: we meant to sell a novel to Campbell's *Astounding.* As soon as my third year of college was over that June, he and I began plotting a three-part serial built around one of Campbell's favorite formulas, the superior Earthman who helps benighted alien beings improve their lot in life. Since Campbell was of Scottish ancestry, Garrett suggested that we make our hero a Scot, one Duncan MacLeod. I cheerfully agreed. We worked it all out in great detail, and then, to my surprise, Garrett told me that we were going downtown to Campbell's office to pitch the idea in person.

I had never expected anything like that. I thought we would let our agent handle the marketing of the project. But Garrett, a supremely gregarious man, believed in personal contact with his editors; and so one summer morning he swept me off to Campbell's office, where I was introduced as a brilliant new talent with whom he would be collaborating thenceforth. We pitched our story; Randall did most of the talking, but I added a thoughtful bit of Ivy League eloquence every now and then. Campbell loved the idea. He had a few improvements to suggest, though — in fact, by lunchtime he had transformed our story beyond all recognition. Then he told us to go home and write, not a novel, but a series of novelets, first, and then a novel. I went back to West 114th Street in a daze.

Of course, I never thought anything was going to come out of this. Me, not even old enough to vote yet, selling a series of novelets to John W. Campbell? But we sat down and wrote the first in our series almost instantly, sticking the joint pseudonym "Robert Randall" on it, and Campbell bought it on the spot, reading it in his office before our eyes, in August, 1955. I was so stunned at the idea that I had sold something to *Astounding* that I couldn't sleep that night.

Garrett didn't want us to stop there. It was the personal touch that did it, he was convinced. Editors wanted to put faces behind the manuscripts. So we needed to visit all the other editors, too — Howard Browne of *Amazing*, Bob Lowndes of *Future*, Larry Shaw of the new magazine *Infinity*, etc. Later in August, Garrett and I attended the World Science Fiction Convention in Cleveland, where I met William L. Hamling, who had bought two stories from me that year and let me know now that he'd like me to send him some others. Garrett was right: in the small world that was science fiction in 1955, the personal touch did do it. On the strength of my collaborative sale to Campbell's *Astounding*, coming on top of my scattering of sales to a few lesser magazines, I had acquired enough professional plausibility to find the doors of the editorial offices opening for me, and Garrett's prodding had brought me inside.

Bob Lowndes, who had already bought a story from me the year before, seemed glad to meet me, and by way of our shared love of classical music struck up a friendship right away. He had high tastes in science fiction, and would buy many more stories from me, usually the ones I had tried and failed to sell to the better-paying magazines. Browne, about whom I will have more to say a little further on, also gave me a ready welcome. He ran a different sort of magazine, featuring simple action tales staff-written by a little stable of insiders — Milton Lesser, Paul W. Fairman, and a couple of others. It happened that in the summer of 1955 Browne had two vacancies in his stable, and he offered the jobs to Garrett and me the day we showed up in his office. So long as we brought him stories every month and maintained a reasonable level of competence he would buy everything we wrote, sight unseen.

That struck me as almost as improbable as my selling novelets to John Campbell. Here I was, a kid still in college who had sold less than a dozen stories, and a cagey old pro like Howard Browne was offering me what amounted to a job, with a guaranteed rate of pay, to keep his science fiction magazine supplied with copy!

I didn't hesitate. I had a story called "Hole in the Air" that Scott Meredith had returned to me because he didn't think he could sell it to anyone. I handed the manuscript to Howard Browne on an August day and he bought it. The following week Garrett and I batted out a novelet, "Gambler's Planet," and he bought that too. We did another for him in September, "Catch a Thief," and I sold two stories to Bob Lowndes, too, and another novelet to Campbell, and then more to Browne, and so on. In the first five months of the Garrett partnership I made a phenomenal 26 story sales — some of them collaborations, but many of them solo stories, for with Randall's help I had acquired the momentum for a career of my own.

One thing I did, as I grew more confident of my relationship with Howard Browne, was to feed him some of the unsold stories that I had written in the pre-Garrett days, when I was simply sending them off to Scott Meredith and hoping that he would find a market for them somewhere. In June of 1955 I had written "Long Live the Kejwa," built around a classic theme that I had encountered in my anthropology class. Toward the end of the year, since it was still unsold, I asked Scott to send it over to Browne as part of my quota of stories for the month. It was published in the July, 1956 issue of *Amazing Stories* under Howard's title, "Run of Luck," which was, perhaps, a better title than mine. But I restored it in my short story collection *Tales from the Pulp Era*; after five decades in limbo I preferred the original title for it.

That July 1956 *Amazing* provided another milestone for me in that dizzying year, because "Run of Luck" was one of three stories that I had in the issue. Its companions were "Stay Out of My Grave," another early unsold story that I had salvaged by selling to Browne, and "Catch a Thief," a Garrett collaboration published under the byline of "Gordon Aghill." Fifteen months earlier it was an awesome thing for me to get any story published, and now here they were showing up in threes in a single issue!

2005

SUNRISE ON MERCURY (1956)

That curious ancient custom — now extinct, I think — of having writers construct stories around cover paintings, rather than having covers painted to illustrate scenes in stories that had already been written — brought "Sunrise on Mercury" into existence in the hyperactive November of 1956, when I was beginning to enter my most prolific years as a writer. In that vanished era, the pulp-magazine chains liked to print their covers in batches of four, which meant that there was usually no time to go through the process of buying a story, sending it out to an artist to be illustrated, making plates from the artist's painting, etc. Instead the artists thought up ideas for illustrations — a scene conceived for its qualities of vivid and dramatic visual excitement, but not necessarily embodying any sort of plausibility — and it went to press right away, while some reliable writer was hired to work it, by hook or by crook, into a story that could be published to accompany it. It's a measure of how quickly thing had changed for me at this point that I was already being given such assignments, here in the second year of my career. But the editors had come to see that I could be depended on to utilize the illustration in some relatively plausible way and to turn my cover story in on time.

So Bob Lowndes, the editor of *Science Fiction Stories* and *Future Science Fiction*, would hand me two or three covers at once, and I would go home and write stories of five or six thousand words to accompany each one. The money wasn't much — a cent or maybe a cent and a half a word, cut-rate stuff even in those days — but it was a guaranteed sale, and so speedy was I at turning out the stories that even at $60 for 6000 words, which is what I was paid for "Sunrise on Mercury," I did all right. (I could write a short story in a day, four a week with the fifth day reserved for visiting editors, back then. $60 for a day's pay was nothing contemptible in 1956, when annual salaries in the mid-four-figure range were the norm.)

The cover that inspired this one, by Ed Emshwiller, showed the bleak landscape of Mercury with the sun rising ominously in the upper left-hand corner, a transparent plastic dome melting in Daliesque fashion in the upper right, and two harassed-looking men in spacesuits running for their lives below. Obviously something unexpected was going on, like sunrise happening a week ahead of schedule; so all I had to do was figure out a reason why that might occur, and I had my sixty bucks. The result, all things considered, wasn't half bad; and the story, which Lowndes used in the May, 1957 *Science Fiction Stories,* has been frequently anthologized over the past forty years.

2004

Author's bio from inside front cover of **FANTASTIC,** *Aug. 1956.*

GUARDIAN OF THE CRYSTAL GATE (1956)

*A*mazing Stories and its companion magazine, *Fantastic Adventures*, were big, shaggy pulps published by Ziff-Davis of Chicago. They featured fast-paced adventure stories aimed at adolescent boys, a group to which I belonged when I started reading them in 1948. I loved nearly everything I read, had fantasies of writing for them some day, and had no idea that the two books were staff-written by a dozen or so regular contributors whose work was bought without prior editorial reading and who worked mainly under pseudonyms that the editor, Ray Palmer, would stick on their material at random. (About fifteen different writers were responsible over the years for the stories bylined "Alexander Blade," who was one of my special favorites when I was about 14.)

While I was still an Alexander Blade fan Ziff-Davis moved its operations to New York. Editor Palmer preferred to stay behind in Chicago. The new editor was a big, burly, good-natured man named Howard Browne, who had been one of Palmer's stable of regulars, producing undistinguished stories for him in the mode of Robert E. Howard and Edgar Rice Burroughs under an assortment of names. Indeed, Browne thought that science fiction and fantasy was pretty silly stuff. What he preferred was detective stories. His own favorite writer

THEY WRITE...

ROBERT SILVERBERG

I can't write the usual sort of autobiography because I haven't had the usual sort of writer's life. I've recently of working at filling stations and roadside cafes and such places, I went into writing after leaving college and thus can't list a long string of occupations.

Like so many other professionals from Ray Palmer through Bradbury to Algis Budrys, I served my apprenticeship in the fan ranks first, and for a number of years was active in the world of fans and fanzines while learning my craft. (In fact, my first pro sale, to a now defunct magazine, was an article about fandom.)

I sold my first story in 1953, after four solid years of trying, to *Nebula,* a Scottish s-f magazine. Sales to the American markets followed, slowly at first, then picking up with gratifying rapidity. At first the checks would show up about three months apart; after a while, they started coming more often, and I'm now happily employed as a full-time writer, specializing in science fiction. (I've sold westerns, sports, and detective stories too, but s-f is the type of fiction I most enjoy doing.)

My first novel, *Revolt on Alhpa C,* was published last summer. I've recently completed a second, with another on the horizon for '57. Readers of *Amazing* and *Fantastic* first saw my name on a short story in last January's *Amazing,* but I hope to be appearing in these magazines more often in the future.

Like Isaac Asinov, I got my college education at Columbia, and like Isaac I began writing while still an undergraduate. (The resemblance ends there.) I'll be getting married, shortly, to a lovely and intelligent young lady who won't read any s-f but mine. *That ought to prove how smart she is!*

FANTASTIC, Vol. 5, No. 4, August 1956 is published bi-monthly by Ziff-Davis Publishing Company, William B. Ziff, Chairman of the Board (1946-1953), at 64 E. Lake St., Chicago 1, Illinois. Entered as second-class matter at Post Office at Chicago, Illinois. Subscription rates: U. S. and possessions and Canada $4.00 for 12 issues; Pan American Union Countries $4.50; all other foreign countries $5.00.

was Raymond Chandler and he had written a number of creditable mysteries in the Chandler vein. Gossip had it that he had taken over Palmer's job mainly in the hope, never realized, of talking Ziff-Davis into letting him edit a mystery magazine as well.

By the time Browne had been on the job a couple of years my own tastes in reading had grown more mature, and I was no longer very enamored of the work of Alexander Blade and his pseudonymous colleagues. Truth to tell, I had come to think of *Amazing* and *Fantastic Adventures* as pretty awful magazines, and, with the high-minded fastidiousness common to young men in their mid-teens, said so very bluntly in a 1952 article that I wrote for an amateur magazine of sf commentary named *Fantastic Worlds*. They were, I said, "the two poorest professional magazines of the field," magazines of "drab degeneracy" that were devoted to "a formula of adventure and 'cops and robbers on the moon.'" I said a lot of other things too, some of them fairly foolish. *Fantastic Worlds* allowed Browne to reply to my diatribe, and he did so quite graciously, under the circumstances, defending himself by pointing out that "magazines, like bean soup and bicycles, are put out to make money." He offered reasoned and reasonable arguments for his editorial policies and in general resisted matching my intemperate tone. He did call my piece "unrealistic and irresponsible" but added that "it is axiomatic that only the very young and very old know everything," and obviously I belonged to one of those two categories.

We now jump three years. It is the summer of 1955, and, thanks to Randall Garrett, I have unexpectedly become part of Howard Browne's stable of writers myself, turning in a monthly quota of formula fiction. I would deliver a story on Tuesday or Wednesday, Howard would let the accounting department know, and the following Monday my payment would go out. He rarely bothered to read them. Now and then he would check to see that I was maintaining the minimal level of competence that the magazines required, but he understood that I was, by and large, capable of consistently giving him the right stuff. In fact, after I had been part of his staff for six months or so, he paid me the considerable compliment of asking me to write a story around a cover painting that Ed Valigursky, one of his best artists, had just brought in.

The painting showed two attractive young ladies in short tunics fiercely wrestling atop a huge diamond. I produced a 10,000-word story called "Guardian of the Crystal Gate," which Howard published in the August 1956 issue of *Fantastic*, the successor to the old *Fantastic Adventures*. My name was prominently featured on the front cover and an autobiographical sketch of me, along with a lovely drawing of me as the beardless young man I still was, went on the second page of the issue.

During one of my visits to the Ziff-Davis office about this time, Howard Browne greeted me with a sly grin and pulled a small white magazine from his desk drawer. "Does this look familiar?" he said, or words to that effect. It was that 1952 issue of *Fantastic Worlds*, with my blistering attack on the magazines he edited. He had known all along that the bright young man he had hired for his staff in 1955 was the author of that overheated polemic of three years before, and finally he could no longer resist letting me in on that. He had, of course, calculated how old I must have been when I wrote that piece, and had gallantly chosen not to hold my youthful indiscretion against me.

FUTURE SCIENCE FICTION #36. *Cover art by Ed Emshwiller.*

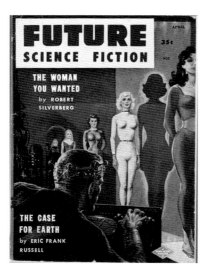

That August 1956 *Fantastic* was pretty much an all-Silverberg issue, by the way. I had broken my personal record of the month before, because I was the author or co-author of four of the six stories it contained. Besides "Guardian of the Crystal Gate," there was a collaborative novelet called "The Slow and the Dead," under the "Robert Randall" byline, and I appeared as "Ralph Burke" with a short entitled "Revolt of the Synthetics." The fourth story, "O Captain My Captain," was one that I had written while still an unknown freelancer back in 1954; unable to sell it the normal way, I had eventually fobbed it off on Browne as part of my regular quota. The interesting thing here is that Browne published it under the byline of "Ivar Jorgensen" — a writer who had been one of my early favorites in the days before I knew that the Ziff-Davis magazines were entirely written by staff insiders using pseudonyms. "Jorgensen" had originally been the pen name of Paul W. Fairman, Browne's associate editor, but now the name was being spread around to the other contributors. So after having been an Ivar Jorgensen fan in my mid-teens, I had, four or five years later, been transformed into Jorgensen myself! It would not be long before I could lay claim to "Alexander Blade" as well.

2005

CHOKE CHAIN (1956)

It was the busy month of February 1956. I was four months away from graduation at Columbia, but by now I was selling stories all over the place, and I was going to classes only when absolutely necessary, spending most of my time holed up in my little room on West 114th St. turning out new material, singly or in collaboration with Randall Garrett. We had sold a second and then a third "Robert Randall" novelet in our series to John Campbell, I had placed stories of my own with Campbell, Bob Lowndes, Larry Shaw, and several other editors, and there was the monthly task of meeting my quota for Howard Browne's two magazines.

Hardly had I finished "Guardian of the Crystal Gate" for Howard and sold him the "Ralph Burke" story "Stay Out of My Grave," but I was at work on an 8000-worder that I called "The Price of Air" for him. It saw print in the December 1956 issue of *Fantastic*. By then Howard Browne had resigned from Ziff-Davis so he could return to writing mystery novels, and the new editor was Howard's former associate, Paul Fairman, a much less jovial man with whom I never attained much of a rapport. Fairman kept me on as a staff writer, but it was strictly a business matter, whereas I think the amiable Howard Browne had regarded me as something of an office mascot.

When he published "The Price of Air," Fairman changed the title to "Choke Chain," which puzzled me, because I didn't know what the term meant. Later I discovered that it's a dog-owner thing. I am a cat-owning sort of person. It is, I suppose, an appropriate enough title for this story, and I have left it in place for later reprintings.

2005

CITADEL OF DARKNESS (1957)

As 1956 moved along, my new career as a science fiction writer, and all the rest of my life as well, began to expand in ways that I would scarcely have dared to fantasize only a couple of years previously. I continued selling stories at the same torrid pace, and in May succeeded in placing one with the prestigious magazine *Galaxy*, edited by the exceedingly difficult, tough-minded Horace Gold. Selling one to him was a big step forward for me. In June I got my Columbia degree and set up shop as a full-time writer. Randall Garrett and I spent two weeks that summer writing the novel for John W. Campbell that we had so grandly imagined selling him the year before — *The Dawning Light*, it was called — and he bought it in August. Later that month I married my college girlfriend, Barbara Brown, and we found a splendid five-room apartment on Manhattan's elegant West End Avenue, a short walk from the Columbia campus but light-years distant from the squalid hotel room where I had been living for the past three years. About ten days later I attended the World Science Fiction Convention, where I was greeted as a colleague by science fiction writers like Edmond Hamilton and Jack Williamson who were old enough to be my father, and where to my amazement I was given the Hugo award as that year's most promising new author.

It was all pretty startling. I was getting published all up and down the spectrum of science fiction magazines, from *Astounding* and *Galaxy* at one end to *Amazing* and *Fantastic* at the other, and soon after the convention I had deals with two book publishers, Ace (for an original novel) and Gnome (for a two-volume reprint of the "Robert Randall" series from *Astounding*.) Everything was happening at once.

In the midst of it all I plugged away at my Ziff-Davis obligations, visiting Paul Fairman's midtown office two or three times a month to bring him new stories. He used "Citadel of Darkness," which I wrote in June 1956 a couple of days after my Columbia graduation ceremony, in *Fantastic* for March 1957. Once more I turned the four-stories-in-an-issue trick, for "Citadel," a "Ralph Burke" story, was accompanied by a story under my own name, one as "Calvin Knox," and one as "Hall Thornton." I wasn't taking anything for granted, but it was pretty clear to me by this time that what was going on wasn't likely to stop, and that, improbable as it had once seemed, I really was going to be able to earn my living as a writer.

2005

COSMIC KILL (1957)

In the 1950s magazine covers were printed well ahead of the interiors of the magazines, done in batches of, I think, four at a time. This was a matter of economics — using one large plate to print four covers at once was much cheaper than printing them one by one. But sometimes the practice created problems.

For example, the April 1957 cover of *Amazing Stories* was printed in the fall of 1956 with a group of others, well ahead of its publication date, bearing this announcement above the name of the magazine: BEGINNING—COSMIC KILL—2-part serial of thundering impact

"Cosmic Kill" was supposed to be a sequel to a short novel that *Amazing* had published six years before — "Empire of Evil," by Robert Arnette. The readers had supposedly been clamoring for a follow-up to that great story all that time, and now, finally, it was going to be published.

The trouble was that the actual author behind the "Arnette" pseudonym on "Empire of Evil" was Paul W. Fairman, and Fairman, having recently become the editor of *Amazing* and *Fantastic*, suddenly found that he didn't have time to write a two-part serial of thundering impact. By December 1956 publication day was nearing, though, for the April issue, due out in February, and a serial had to be found for it. So Paul Fairman phoned me one December morning and asked if I would mind very much writing a two-part serial called "Cosmic Kill," a sequel to something of his from 1951—and deliver it the following week, because it had to be on the newsstands two months from then.

Sure, I said. Nothing to it.

That night I dug out the January, 1951 *Amazing* and read "Empire of Evil," which turned out to be a wild and woolly thing starring blue Mercurians with green blood, savage Martian hill men that had nasty tusks, and Venusians with big black tails. Even back then we knew that there weren't any Mercurians, Martians, or Venusians, of course. That didn't really matter to me at the moment. What did matter was that I had to put together a story of some sort, more or less overnight, that was in some way connected to its predecessor, and Fairman had either killed off or married off nearly all the characters in the original piece.

Well, never mind that, either. He had left one or two surviving villains, and I invented a couple of new characters to set out after them, and in short order I had put together a plot. It wasn't going to be a literary masterpiece; it was just going to be a sequel, written to order, to Fairman's slapdash space-opera, which had been goofy to the point of incoherence. But — what the hell — no one was going to know I had written it, after all. And I reminded myself that plenty of my illustrious colleagues had written pulp-magazine extravaganzas just as goofy in their younger days. Here was my revered Henry Kuttner's novelet from *Marvel Science Stories* of 1939, "The Time Trap," with this contents-page description: "Unleashed atomic force hurled Kent Mason into civilization's dawn-era, to be wooed by the Silver Princess who'd journeyed from 2150 A. D. , and to become the laboratory pawn of Greddar Klon—who'd been projected from five hundred centuries beyond Mason's time sector!" Kuttner had put his own name on that one. And here in the same issue was future Grand Master Jack Williamson with "The Dead Spot" — "With his sigma-field that speeded evolution to the limit imposed by actual destruction of germ cells, plus his technique of building synthetic life, Dr. Clyburt Hope set out to create a new race — and return America's golden harvest land into a gray cancer of leprous doom!"

The reputations of Kuttner and Williamson had survived their writing such silly stories. So would mine. But would I survive writing a 20,000-word novella in two days, which is what Fairman was expecting me to do?

Here my collaborator Randall Garrett came to my aid. I have never been much of a user of stimulants — I don't even drink coffee. Garrett, though, said that my predicament could be solved with the help of something called benzedrine — we would call it "speed" today — which he happened to take to control his weight. A little Benzedrine would hop up my metabolism to the point

THE ORIGINAL SCIENCE FICTION STORIES, *Nov. 1959, with cover art by Ed Emshwiller for "The Impossible Intelligence" by RS.*

where writing 40 pages in a one-day sitting would be no problem at all.

So he came over to my West End Avenue place and gave me a few little green pills, and the next day I wrote the first half of "Cosmic Kill," and the day after that I wrote the second half. I went out of my way to mimic the style of the original story, using all sorts of substitutes for "he said" that were never part of my own style —"he snapped," "he wheezed," "she wailed" and peppering the pages with adverbial modifiers — "he continued inexorably," "he said appreciatively," "he remarked casually." The next day I took the whole 80-page shebang down to Paul Fairman's office and it went straight to the printer. It was just in time for serialization in the April and May, 1957 issues of *Amazing*, my one and only appearance under the byline of Robert Arnette. And on the seventh day I rested, you betcha.

The funny thing is that "Cosmic Kill" isn't really so bad. I had to read it for the first time in 48 years for *Tales from the Pulp Era*, and I was impressed with the way it zips swiftly along from one dire situation to another without pausing for breath, exactly as its author did back there in December 1956. It is the one and only example of Silverberg writing a story on speed.

2005

NEW YEAR'S EVE—2000 A. D. (1957)

(opposite)
THE DAWNING LIGHT *and* **THE SHROUDED PLANET** *both written with Randall Garrett under the name Robert Randall. Cover art by Richard Powers.*

We worked out the plots of those two books together; then one of us would begin writing a first draft (often that would be Garrett) and the other one would revise and type up the final draft. Sometimes we had two typewriters going at once. But Garrett liked to work late at night, and I didn't; sometimes I'd go to sleep and find a bunch of new pages waiting for me in the morning, which I would revise while he slept. In stylistic matters I generally had the last word; on issues of plotting, I usually deferred to his greater story-telling experience.— RS

My meeting with William L. Hamling of *Imagination* and *Imaginative Tales* at the 1955 Cleveland sf convention had led almost immediately to yet another steady writing contract for me. Hamling, a dapper, youthful-looking Chicagoan who, like me, had loved science fiction since his teens, had been Ray Palmer's managing editor for the Ziff-Davis science fiction magazines in the late 1940s, and when the Ziff-Davis company moved its editorial offices to New York in 1950 Hamling remained in Chicago, starting his own Chicago-based publishing outfit. Imagination, his first title, was a decent enough lower-echelon sf magazine, but not even such major names as Robert A. Heinlein and James Blish could get its sales figures up much beyond the break-even point, and in the summer of 1955 Hamling decided to emulate his friend Howard Browne of *Amazing* and revert to the tried-and-true Ziff-Davis formula of uncomplicated action fiction written to order by a team of staffers. The lead stories for the book would be done by such veteran pulp-magazine stars as Edmond Hamilton and Dwight V. Swain. For the shorter material he turned to the same quartet that was producing most of Browne's fiction: Lesser, Fairman, Garrett, and Silverberg. Evidently he figured that our capacity for turning out sf adventure stories to order was infinitely expandable, and, as it happened, he was right. On January 16, 1956, I got this note from my agent, Scott Meredith:

"We sent one of your yarns to Bill Hamling. While he couldn't use this yarn, he's going to write you directly to tell you what he wants in the way of plotting, etc. He does like your stuff and will want to see a lot more of it in the future. You'll know better what to expect when you get his letter, and then you can get right to work."

Hamling's letter followed a month or so later. What he wanted was short, punchy stories with strong conflicts, lots of color and action, and straightforward resolutions. And he made a very explicit offer: the Garrett–Silverberg team was invited to deliver 50,000 words of fiction a month, all lengths from short-shorts up to 7500 words or so, and we would be paid $500 for each monthly package.

At that point we were each writing a couple of stories a month for Browne and doing our novelet series for Campbell, and I was sending out solo stories to such editors as Lowndes, Shaw, and Gold as well. And I was still a Columbia undergraduate, starting the second half of my senior year. But college would soon be behind me and by this time I had dauntless confidence in my own prolifici-ty. We accepted the deal. The first package, six stories, went off to Hamling in June 1956. Early in July we sent him five more, and toward the end of that month another six, and seven in August before I took time off to get married. And so it went, month after month. The $500 checks — $5000 or thereabouts in modern purchasing power — arrived punctually and we split them fifty-fifty regardless of who had written the stories in each package.

I could not tell you, this long after the fact, which of us actually wrote most of these stories. As I look at them now, some seem to be entirely Randall's work, some appear to be exclusively mine, and others must have been true collaborations, begun by one of us and finished later the same day by the other. The names under which the stories appeared provide no clue, because Hamling ignored the pseudo-nyms we put on the manuscripts ("T. H. Ryders," "William Leigh," "Eric

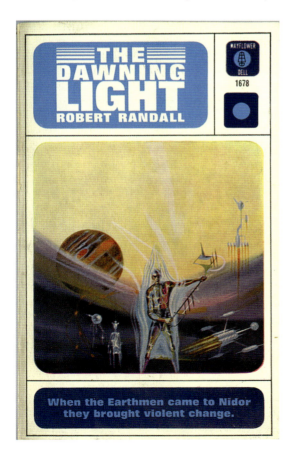

When the Earthmen came to Nidor they brought violent change.

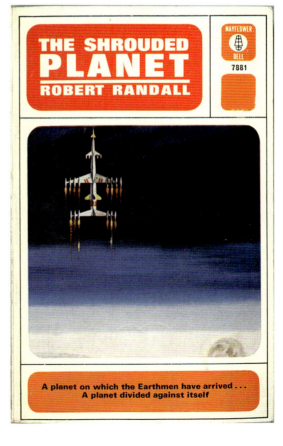

A planet on which the Earthmen have arrived . . . A planet divided against itself

Rodman," "Ray McKenzie," etc.) and randomly stuck bylines of his own choosing on them — "Warren Kastel," "S. M. Tenneshaw," "Ivar Jorgensen," and many another. Sometimes he would put my own name on a story, and sometimes Garrett's, and in several cases stories written entirely by Garrett appeared under my name and stories written entirely by me appeared under his. Some of these switched stories I can still identify: I know my own stylistic touches, and I also know the areas where Garrett's superior knowledge of chemistry and physics figured in the plot of a "Silverberg" story that I could not possibly have written then. But it's a hopeless job to correct the Silverberg and Garrett bibliographies now to indicate that on occasions we found ourselves using each other's names as pseudonyms.

The little story, "New Year's Eve—2000 A. D.," from the September 1957 issue of *Imaginative Tales* — came out under the "Ivar Jorgensen" name. That byline was originally the property of Paul W. Fairman but was transformed by Browne and then Hamling into a communal pseudonym. This one was wholly my work.

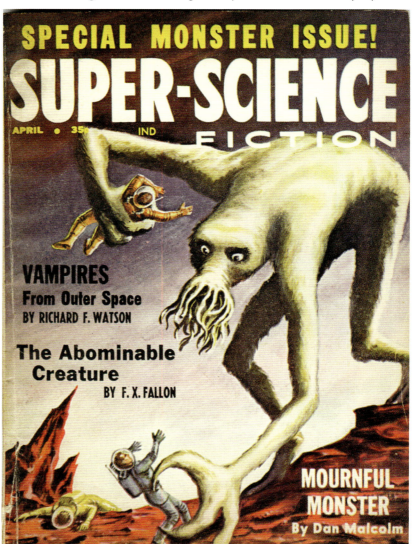

SUPER SCIENCE FICTION, *April 1959, cover art by Ed Emshwiller. Both Richard F. Watson and Dan Malcolm are RS.*

I know that not only because such very short stories as these were almost always written by one or the other of us, not both, but also because I am the sort of pedantic guy who believed that the twenty-first century would not begin until January 1, 2001, as one poor sap tries to argue in this story. (I knew better, when the twenty-first century really did come around a few years ago, than to waste breath voicing that point of view.) I think the story is an amusing artifact. I was wrong about the date of the first lunar voyage by 31 years, but I was right on the nose about the premature celebration of the new century at the dawning of Y2K.

2005

THE ANDROID KILL (1957)

"The Android Kill," from the November, 1957 *Imaginative Tales,* is one of the stories from the batch that Garrett and I sent to Bill Hamling in October 1956. This is another one that I'm pretty sure I wrote entirely on my own.

It's an okay little chase story, but its big significance for me is that Hamling published it under the byline of "Alexander Blade," the first time one of my stories had appeared that way. As I mentioned in the introduction to "Guardian of the Crystal Gate," such powerful Alexander Blade stories as "The Brain" (*Amazing*, October 1948) and "Dynasty of the Devil" (*Amazing*, June 1949) had wowed me back when I was still too young to shave. Now, a mere nine years later, right around the time I was contemplating growing the beard that has been my trademark for the past forty-some years, I had become Alexander Blade myself!

2005

THE HUNTERS OF CUTWOLD (1957)

Harlan Ellison, who had been living next door to me in the summer of 1955 as my writing career suddenly and spectacularly took off, had a somewhat slower start himself, but by the middle of 1956 he, too, was selling stories about as fast as he could write them. Just as I had been, he was an avid science fiction reader who longed to have his own stories published in the magazines he had read in his teens, and very quickly he joined Howard Browne's team of staffers at *Amazing* and placed material with three or four other titles.

But he had a knack for writing crime stories too — tales of juvenile-delinquent kid-gangs were a specialty of his — and in the summer of 1956 he struck up a relationship with two new magazines that published that sort of thing, *Trapped* and *Guilty*. They paid an extravagant two cents a word, twice as much as what most of the science fiction magazines we were selling to then would pay, and their editor, one W. W. Scott, seemed willing to buy as many stories as Harlan could bring them. Harlan was good enough to let me in on this bonanza, and, busy as I was meeting my monthly quota at *Amazing* and *Imagination*, I started doing crime stories too. My records show the sale of "Get Out and Stay Out" to *Guilty* in June 1956, and "Clinging Vine" to *Trapped* a couple of weeks later.

And then W. W. Scott announced that he had been asked to edit a science

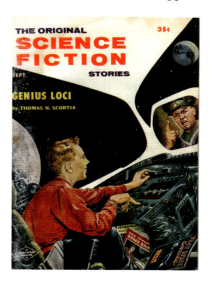

(opposite)
*Art by Ed Emshwiller
for "Sunrise on Mercury";
cover of* **SCIENCE
FICTION STORIES.**

*A who's who gathering
of some of the best science
fiction writers of the 20th
Century. RS is in back row
center, wearing plaid short-
sleeve shirt. To his immediate left are James Blish
(seated in a chair), Jane
Roberts and A.J. Budrys.
Cyril Kornbluth is seated
directly in front of
Silverberg. To RS's right,
back row, are Lester del Rey
(black shirt), Ted Sturgeon,
Fritz Leiber, Carol
Emshwiller (partially
obscured), and Damon
Knight and Arthur C.
Clarke (both seated in
chairs). Hans Santesson is
seated directly in front of
Clarke. Harlan Ellison is
lying on the grass wearing
plaid shorts at center of picture. Judith Merril is seated
with her back to the camera
to the right of Ellison.
Photo taken by Ed
Emshwiller at the first
Milford Science Fiction
Conference, 1956.*

fiction magazine too, *Super-Science Fiction*, and Harlan and I suddenly had the inside track on a lucrative new market.

Scott — "Scottie," everybody called him, except a few who called him "Bill" — was a short, cheerfully cantankerous old guy who would have fit right into a 1930s Hollywood movie about newspapermen, which was what I think he had been before he drifted into magazine editing. His office was tiny and crammed with weary-looking manuscripts that such agents as Scott Meredith, delighted to find a possible new market for ancient stuff that had been rejected everywhere, sent over by the ton. His voice was a high-pitched cackle; he had a full set of top and bottom dentures, which he didn't always bother to wear; and I never saw him without his green eyeshade, which evidently he regarded as an essential part of the editorial costume. To us — and we both were barely past 21 — he looked to be seventy or eighty years old, but probably he was 55 or thereabouts. He freely admitted to us that he knew next to nothing about science fiction and cared even less, and invited us to bring him as much material as we could manage.

We certainly did. Getting an open invitation like that from a two-cents-a-word market was like being handed the key to Fort Knox. In late June I wrote "Collecting Team" for him, which he published as "Catch 'em All Alive" in the first issue — December, 1956 of *Super-Science*. (Under its original title it has been reprinted dozens of times in school readers.) I also did a batch of science fillers for Scottie to use in rounding off blank pages — little essays on space exploration, computer research, and an interesting new drug called LSD. Harlan had a story in that first issue, too, and two in the second one. (I was too busy to do anything but science fillers for that issue.) The third issue had one Ellison and one Silverberg story; the fourth, two of mine, one of his. And so it went, month after month. As I got into the swing of it, I began doing longer pieces for the maga-zine. A 12,000-word story — and I was writing at least one for almost every issue from the fifth number on — paid $240, more than the monthly rent on my West End Avenue apartment, and I could turn one out in two working days.

By 1957, Harlan had moved along to an army base, having been careless enough to let himself get drafted, and the job of filling the pages of *Super-Science Fiction*, *Trapped*, and *Guilty* devolved almost entirely on me. Just as well, too, because I didn't have good personal chemistry with Paul Fairman of *Amazing* and *Fantastic*

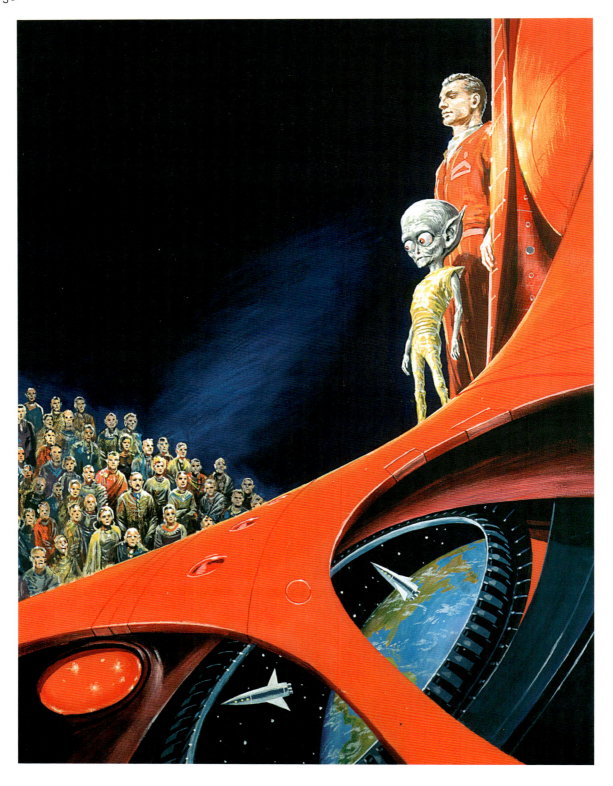

and he had begun to cut back on buying stories from me. Around the same time, Bill Hamling found that the sales figures of *Imagination* and *Imaginative Tales* were trending sharply downward, leading him to buy fewer stories from his staff and soon afterward to kill both magazines. My writing partnership with Randall Garrett had ended, too, at the urging of my wife, Barbara, who disliked Garrett intensely and didn't want him coming around to see me. Faced with the loss of my two most reliable markets and the separation from my collaborator, I needed to be fast on my feet if I wanted to go on earning a decent living as a writer, and so I made myself very useful to W. W. Scott indeed. For *Trapped* and *Guilty* I wrote bushels of crime stories ("Mobster on the Make," "Russian Roulette," "Murder for Money," etc., etc., etc.) and for *Super-Science Fiction* I did two or three stories an issue under a wide assortment of pseudonyms. At two cents a word for lots and lots of words I could support myself very nicely from that one market.

"The Hunters of Cutwold," which I wrote in April, 1957 for the December 1957 *Super-Science Fiction* under the pseudonym of Calvin M. Knox, is typical of the many novelets I did for Scottie: stories set on alien planets with vivid scenery, involving hard-bitten characters who sometimes arrived at bleak ends. I suspect I derived the manner and some of the content from the South Sea stories of Joseph Conrad and W. Somerset Maugham, both favorite writers of mine. Scholars who have been writing theses on such Conrad-influenced novels of mine as *Downward to the Earth* and *Hot Sky at Midnight*, published at much later stages of my career, please take note.

2005

WARM MAN (1957)

My ledger entry for January 1957 shows business as usual for those days — seventeen stories, 85,000 words, and I was still just warming up for the really productive times a couple of years ahead. How I did it, God only knows. By the time we reach the 1990s I will be happy to manage three or four stories

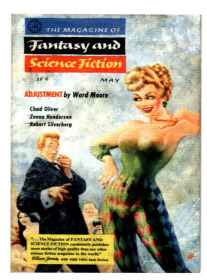

(opposite)
Art by Ed Emshwiller
for REGAN'S PLANET.

(top)
I loved this May 1957 cover, with the hot chick wearing the spray-on bra. It was my debut in **MAGAZINE OF FANTASY & SCIENCE FICTION** *and for some reason I never got tired of looking at that issue.— RS*

Cover art by Freas.

(bottom)
RS and artist Ed Emshwiller c. 1962.

I knew Ed Emshwiller ("Emsh") very well in the 1950s and 60s, and also his wife, still with us, Carol Emshwiller. Ed was a fine abstract painter and one of his 1950's abstracts is hanging about five feet from my left shoulder as I sit here typing this.— RS

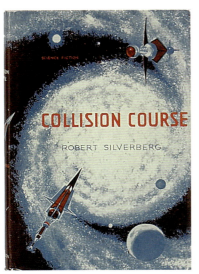

COLLISION COURSE.
Avalon Books, 1961, cover art by Ed Emshwiller.

I wrote **COLLISION COURSE** *somewhere around 1957, when I was 22 years old. I thought it was a pretty good book at the time, and perhaps it was, but it's a very early work of mine indeed.— RS*

(below)
FANTASTIC, *Aug. 1956. RS had four stories in this issue under his own name and various pseudonyms. Cover art by Ed Valigursky.*

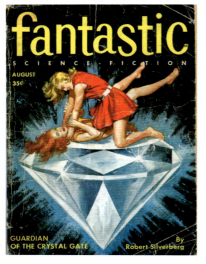

a year; that was a week's work for me in 1957.

A phenomenon, I was. And one who took notice was Anthony Boucher, the urbane, sophisticated editor of *Fantasy & Science Fiction*. He was a collector at heart, who wanted one of everything for his superb magazine — including a story by this hypermanic kid from New York who seemed able to turn one out every hour. (If he could have discovered giants, infants, Siamese twins, Martians, or cats who wrote science fiction, I think he would have solicited their work, too.) But Boucher's desire to add me to his roster of contributors did not mean he would relax his high standards simply for the sake of putting my name on his contents page, and so, though he let me know he'd be delighted to publish something of mine, he turned down the first few stories I sent him, offering great regrets and hope for the future. What I had to do in order to sell one to him, I saw, was to break free of the pulp-magazine formulas that I had taken such trouble to master, and write something about and for adults. (Not so easy, when I was only twenty-two myself!)

The specific genesis of "Warm Man" came at the famous Milford Writers' Conference of September, 1956, where I was the youngest author, surrounded by some of the most illustrious people in the sf field. During one workshop session Cyril Kornbluth had some sort of epiphany about his writing, and suddenly cried out in a very loud voice, "Cold!" Or so it seemed to me, though my colleague Algis Budrys, who was also there, tells me that what Cyril actually said was "Gold!", the name of an important editor of the time. What his outburst signified to him, be it "Cold!" or "Gold!", I never knew, but it seemed to me that his sudden insight must certainly have been a very powerful one. It set something working in me which must not have had anything at all to do with whatever had passed through Cyril's mind — "'Cold,'" I thought, "then why not 'Warm!?'" and out came, a few months later, this tale of psychic vampirism. I sent it to Boucher (who had been present at Milford also, I think) and by return mail across the continent came his expression of delight that I had broken the ice at last with him. It was an exciting moment for me, bringing me the sense of having qualified for a very exclusive club. He ran the story a few months later — May 1957 — and put my name on the cover, a signal honor. Boucher was the best kind of editor — a demanding one, yes, but also the kind who is as pleased as you are that you have produced something he wants to publish. He (and a few others back then) helped to teach me the difficult lesson that quantity isn't as effective, in the long run, as quality. Which is demonstrated by this story's frequent reappearance in print over the span of more than four decades since it was written.

2004

COME INTO MY BRAIN (1958)

This was practically the last story I wrote under my monthly contract deal for Bill Hamling's *Imagination*. I turned it in in March 1957 — it was called "Into the Unknown" then, and the byline I put on it was "Ray McKenzie" — but Hamling, who was gradually working off his inventory all through 1957 as he wound down his magazines, didn't find a slot for it until the June 1958 number, the third issue from the end. It was Hamling who gave it the title it bears

MOURNFUL MONSTER

by DAN MALCOLM

NOVELETTE   *illustrated by* EMSH

It was huge, massive, with a hide of scales, legs like tree trunks and a fanged mouth of utter horror. Yet it was unmistakably intelligent — and filled with sadness

IT was almost time for the regular midweek flight to leave. On the airstrip, the technicians were g i v i n g the two-engine jet a last-minute checkdown. In fifteen minutes, according to the chalked announcement on the bulletin board, the flight would depart—making the two thousand mile voyage across the trackless, unexplored wilderness that lay between the two Terran colonies of Marleyville and New Lisbon, on the recently-s e t t l e d planet of Loki in the Procyon system.

In the Marleyville airport building, David Marshall was having one last drink for the road, and trying unsuccessful-ly to catch the attention of the strikingly beautiful girl in the violet synthofab dress. Marshall, an anthropologist specializing in non-human cultures, was on his way to New Lisbon to interview a few wrinkled old hunters who claimed to have valuable information for him. He was trying to prove that an intelligent non-human race still existed somewhere on Loki, and he had been told at Marleyville that several veteran hunters in New Lisbon had insisted they knew where the hidden race lived.

"Now b o a r d i n g for the flight to New Lisbon," came the tinny announcement from

2

3

here, and he replaced my "McKenzie" pseudonym with the time-honored mon-icker of "Alexander Blade."

2005

CASTAWAYS OF SPACE (1958)

"Castaways of Space" is typical W. W. Scott material: an exotic world, some disreputable characters engaged in interstellar hanky-panky, a bit of a twist ending. I wrote it in January 1958 and gave it the rather flat-footed title of "Pursuit," which Scottie changed to the more vivid "Castaways of Space," and so be it. It ran in the October 1958 issue of *Super-Science Fiction* under the byline of "Dan Malcolm," which I had begun using frequently for Scottie now. There were two other items of mine in the same issue, one under my more familiar pseudonym, "Calvin M. Knox," and the other under my own name. That one was "Gorgon Planet," the very first short story I had ever sold (to the Scottish magazine, Nebula, in 1954), which I dug out now and sold again to Scottie for five times as much as Nebula had paid. He didn't like my title and put what he thought was a much better one on it: "The Fight With the Gorgon." Sometimes Scottie was right about title changes, and sometimes, well, not.

2005

What surprises me, as I reread my early stories for new collections, is how quickly I learned the basic craft of story-writing. There are no classics among those early stories, but they're all assembled out of pretty much the proper mix of dia-log and exposition, and the plots do hold together all the way. I find it hard to believe that writing stories is an innate gift, but I did, at least, pick up the technique by the time I was midway through my teens.— RS

EXILED FROM EARTH (1958)

Though most of the stories I wrote for *Super-Science* were done to order and formula, sometimes I used W. W. Scott as a salvage market for material I had originally aimed at one of the upper-level magazines. He didn't mind that it didn't fit his usual action-adventure mode, so long as I didn't do it too often and the story had, at least, some science fictional color. He and I were pretty much dependent on each other now, he for the material I supplied so effortlessly, I for those resonant two-cents-a-word checks. March 1958 alone saw me sell him two sf stories, "The Traders" and "The Aliens Were Haters," and five crime pieces, "Doublecrosser's Daughter," "Deadly Widow," "Rollercoaster Ride," "Let Him Sweat," and "The Ace of Spades Means Death," plus some batches of science fillers. The pay came to over a thousand dollars, a regal sum in pre-inflation 1958 money. How I thought up all the story ideas, God alone knows: I can only tell you that when I sat down each morning and put paper in the typewriter, a story would be there waiting to be written.

In this case the story that had been waiting to be written, in mid-October of 1957, involved an old actor out in the stars who wanted to go back to Earth and play Hamlet one last time — something that I thought Horace Gold of *Galaxy* might be interested in, for a cent a word more than Scottie would pay. I called it "You Can't Go Back." Horace didn't fancy it. Neither did Bob Mills,

RS writing as Richard F. Watson for SUPER SCIENCE FICTION, April 1959,

VAMPIRES
FROM OUTER SPACE

by RICHARD F. WATSON

NOVELETTE   *illustrated by* EMSH

The weird seven-foot purple bats had come to Earth to stay. Terror ran wild over the land when rumors spread that they were vampires who killed to suck human blood

THE first report of what was quickly to become known as the Vampire Menace reached the central office of the Terran Security Agency half an hour after the attack had taken place. The date was June 11, 2104. Agency Sub-chief Neil Harriman was busy with routine matters when the courier burst into his office, carrying a message pellet gaudy with the red-and-yellow wrapping that meant Top Level Emergency.

Harriman reached one big hand out for the message pellet. "Where's it from?"

"San Francisco. It just came in by simultaneous visitape. Marked special for your office, with all the emergency labels."

"Okay," Harriman said. He flipped the switch that darkened the office and brought the viewing screen down from its niche in the ceiling. As Harriman unwrapped the message pellet and began to slip it into the viewer, he glanced up at the courier, who was standing by with expectant curiosity. Harriman scowled darkly. No words were necessary. The courier gulped, moistened his lips, and backed out of the of-who had replaced Tony Boucher as the editor of *Fantasy & Science Fiction*. So early in April of 1958, I took it down to Scottie. He bought it unhesitatingly, changed its title on the spot to "Exiled from Earth," and ran it under the byline of "Richard F. Watson" in the December, 1958 issue of *Super-Science*, where it kept company with my other two recent submissions, "The Aliens Were Haters" (under my own name) and "The Traders" (as Calvin M. Knox). Scottie renamed the latter story "The Unique and Terrible Compulsion." As I said earlier, some of his title changes were improvements, but not all.

2005

SECOND START (1959)

"Second Start" is the most interesting discovery I made while choosing material for *Tales from the Pulp Era*. As usual, W. W. Scott retitled it for publication — he called it "Re-Conditioned Human." But when I leafed through the magazine, I needed to read only the first paragraph to realize what I had stumbled upon:

"The name they gave me at the Rehabilitation Center was Paul Macy. It was as good as any other, I guess. The name I was born with was Nat Hamlin, but when you become a Rehab you have to give up your name."

Paul Macy, who was called Nat Hamlin before being sentenced to rehabilitation for his crimes, is the protagonist of a novel of mine called *The Second Trip*, which was first published in 1972. I wrote it in November 1970, one of the strongest periods of my writing career. *The Second Trip* is one of my best books. (The novel just preceding it was the Nebula-winning *A Time of Changes*; the one just after it was *The Book of Skulls*.) I rarely re-read my own books, but I happened to read *The Second Trip* a few months ago, in connection with a new edition, for the first time in more than three decades. Coming to it after so many years, I had forgotten most of its details and I was able to read it almost as an outsider, caught up in the narrative as though encountering it for the first time. I have to tell you that I was quite impressed.

Another thing that I had forgotten over the years, it seems, is that back there in 1970 I had based *The Second Trip* on an earlier story, already twelve years old, that I had written one busy morning for *Super-Science Fiction*. Not only had I forgotten that *The Second Trip* had grown out of the earlier story, I had entirely forgotten the whole existence of the earlier story itself, and great was my astonishment when I encountered Paul Macy/Nat Hamlin in that 1959 magazine.

Anyone interested in studying the evolution of a writer would do well to compare the story and the novel that grew out of it. The story is set in a universe of easy travel between stars, many centuries from now. The novel is set on Earth in the year 2011. The former identity of the Macy of the story is an interstellar jewel thief and smuggler, whose old confederates in crime want to force him back into their syndicate. The former identity of the Macy of the novel is a brilliant sculptor who happens also to be a psychopath, and who struggles to regain control of his body after it has been given to a newly created personality. In concept, in handling, in everything, the two works could not have been more different — and yet one plainly grew out of the other, twelve years later. The evidence of the characters' names is there to prove that. The story is the work of a young man of 23, turning out material as fast as possible to fill the pages of a minor science fiction magazine. The novel is the work of a mature writer of 35, who was devoting all the skill and energy at his command to the creation of a group of novels that would establish him as one of the leading sf writers of his day. Reading the two works just a few months apart, as I did last year, was an extraordinary revelatory experience for me.

2005

MOURNFUL MONSTER (1959)

1958 was a bad year for the science fiction magazines. Their sales had been dropping ever since the peak year of 1953, when an all-time record 39 different titles were published (and helped to kill each other off by overcrowding the newsstands.) In 1958 the American News Company, the main magazine distributor, abruptly went out of business, taking with it a lot of magazines that it had been financing through advances against earnings. And the continued boom in paperback publishing was squeezing the surviving all-fiction magazines into a marginal existence.

Many of the sf magazines I had been writing for in the previous four years began to shut up shop or to cut back drastically on frequency of publication, and I was beginning to feel uneasy about my ability to earn a living through the sort of mass production of stories that had carried me through those years. In particular I worried about W. W. Scott's *Super-Science*, which had become my mainstay. It was a poky little magazine at best, which probably had never shown much of a profit, and I wondered how much longer I was going to be able to sell it all those $240 novelets.

Against this gloomy background the sudden upsurge of monster fiction provided one commercial bright spot. In the late 1950s a magazine called *Famous Monsters of Filmland*, which specialized in photo-essays on classic Hollywood horror movies of the "Frankenstein" and "Wolf-Man" sort, had shot up overnight to a huge circulation. A couple of the science fiction editors, desperately trying to

L to R: back row, Harlan Ellison, RS, Barbara Silverberg, Lester de Rey, Philip Klass. Front, Randall Garrett (with bottle), Martin Graetz (sitting on floor in front of Klass). Photo taken by Ed Emshwiller at the first Milford Science Fiction Conference, 1956.

find something that worked, experimented with converting their magazines to vehicles for horror fiction. Thus Larry Shaw's *Infinity* and *Science Fiction Adventures*, for which I had been a steady contributor, vanished and were replaced by two titles called *Monster Parade* and *Monsters and Things*. (I wrote for them too.) And over at *Super-Science Fiction*, Scottie concluded that the only way to save his magazine was to convert it to a book of monster stories also. Word went out to all the regular contributors, of whom I was the most productive, that all material purchased thenceforth would have to have some monster angle in it. I didn't find that difficult, since most of the stories I was doing for him were space adventures featuring fearsome alien beings, and I would simply need to make the aliens a little bigger and more fearsome.

Strangely, Scottie didn't change the title of the magazine. This was odd, because the presence of "Science" in it wasn't something likely to appeal to horror fans. Instead he plastered the words SPECIAL MONSTER ISSUE! in big yellow letters above the name of the magazine on the April 1959 issue, commissioned a painting that featured a gigantic and notably hideous creature sweeping a couple of space-suited humans up in its claws, and retitled every story in inventory to give it a monster-oriented twist: "The Huge and Hideous Beasts," for example, or "The Abominable Creature." (His gift for the utterly flat-footed title may have stood him in good stead here.)

The lead story for the issue was one that I was writing in July 1958, just as the change in policy went into effect. Evidently I found it necessary to restructure the story midway through for the sake of monsterizing it, because on my frayed and tattered carbon copy of the manuscript I find a penciled note in my own handwriting indicating a switch in the plot as of page 26: "They are continuing along when they see a huge monster looming ahead. They lay low, but the monster pursues them. They hear it crackling along behind them. They trip it, but it claws its way out of the trap and comes at them." And so on to the end of the story as you will see it here. Whatever non-monster denouement I might originally have had in mind is lost forever in the mists of time.

I turned the story in with the title I had originally given it, "Five Against the Jungle," a nice old-fashioned pulp title which of course was not right for the revamped *Super-Science*, so Scottie changed it to "Mournful Monster." By so doing, he gave away, to some extent, the fact that it wasn't really a horror story — that the monster, while appropriately monstrous, was actually a sympathetic figure. But so, after all, was Frankenstein's monster, and that didn't harm the commercial appeal of the movie. The prime subtext of the whole monster genre, I decided, must really be existential alienation.

2005

RS and Fred Pohl at the Tricon Worldcon 1966. Photo by Jay Kay Klein

VAMPIRES FROM OUTER SPACE (1959)

Three of the five stories in *Super-Science Fiction*'s glorious SPECIAL MONSTER ISSUE! of April 1959 were my work: the lead novelet, "Mournful Monster," under the Dan Malcolm pseudonym, a short called "A Cry for Help" bylined Eric Rodman, and this one, the second lead, which ran under the name of Richard F. Watson.

I wrote it in September 1958, right after my first visit to San Francisco, which is why the story is set there. (I lived in New York then, the city of my birth, and had not the slightest inkling, then, that thirteen years later I was going to move to the San Francisco area.) The title on the manuscript when I turned it in was simply "Vampires from Space," but the meaningless phrase "outer space" was just then establishing itself as a cliché, and Scottie stuck it right in. It is, I think, the only place the phrase can be found in all my millions of words of science fiction.

2005

THE INSIDIOUS INVADERS (1959)

Super-Science Stories, which by now was my only surviving market for action-oriented science fiction (Bill Hamling had closed his magazines and the Ziff-Davis pair, under the new editorship of Cele Goldsmith, had ceased to be a haven for staff-written formula fiction), continued to make with the monsters as circulation went on dipping. The June 1959 number was the glamorous SECOND MONSTER ISSUE!, to which I contributed "The Day the Monsters Broke Loose" and "Beasts of Nightmare Horror," though other hands than mine were responsible for "Creatures of Green Slime" and "Terror of the Undead Corpses." August 1959 was the gaudy THIRD MONSTER ISSUE!, with no less than four pseudonymous Silverberg offerings ("Monsters That Once Were Men," "Planet of the Angry Giants," "The Horror in the Attic," and "Which was the Monster?"). Then Scottie stopped numbering them: the October 1959 issue, with three more of mine, was labeled simply WEIRD MONSTER ISSUE! That one was the last in the sequence: when I turned those three stories in in March of 1959, Scottie sadly notified me that he would need no more science fiction stories from me after that. Though *Trapped* and *Guilty* were going to continue (for the time being), *Super-Science* had walked the plank.

I would miss it. It had supported me in grand style for three years, and the income from it would be hard to replace.

"The Insidious Invaders" appeared in that final issue under the pseudonym of Eric Rodman. The attentive reader will detect at once the fine hand of W. W. Scott in the story's title. I called it "The Imitator," not exactly an inspired title

Silverberg c. 1970.

either. The story's theme — a predatory absorptive alien — is not one for which I can claim any particular originality, but it has, at least, been one that I've dealt with in a number of interesting ways over the decades, most notably in my short stories "Passengers" of 1969 and "Amanda and the Alien" of 1983. So "The Insidious Invaders" can be considered an early draft of those two rather more accomplished pieces.

One oddity that jumped to my attention here, when I dug the story out for *Tales from the Pulp Era,* involves the names of the characters — Ted Kennedy and his sister and brother-in-law Marge and Dave Spalding. It's not the use of "Ted Kennedy" as a character that I'm referring to, for in 1959 John F. Kennedy himself was only then beginning to make himself conspicuous on the national stage and the existence of his kid brother Teddy was unknown to me. But the protagonist of my novel *Invaders from Earth*, written in the autumn of 1957, was named Ted Kennedy too; his wife's name was Marge; and there was also a character named Dave Spalding, unrelated to Marge, in the book. There is no other link between the story and the book. The Ted Kennedy of the story is a spaceman; the one of the novel is a public-relations man, as is the Dave Spalding of the novel. Why I used the same names for these two sets of characters, two-and-a-half years apart, is something I can't explain, nearly fifty years later. Some sort of private joke? Mere coincidence? I have no idea.

At any rate, with this story I was just about at the end of the phase of my career that had been devoted to writing quick, uncomplicated stories for the low-end science fiction magazines. All the magazines that published that kind of story had folded, by the middle of 1959, or else had shifted their policies in the direction of the more sophisticated kind of sf that *Astounding* and *Galaxy* were publishing. Since I was committed, by that time, to a life as a full-time writer who depended for his income on high-volume production, I needed to change markets, and I did. My records for the second half of 1959 show that I had begun to write fiction and articles for such slick men's magazines of the era as *Exotic Adventures, Real Men*, and *Man's Life*, and that I had found another new slot for my immense productivity in the suddenly hyperactive genre of soft-core erotic paperbacks, where I began turning out two and even three books a month — *Suburban Wife, Love Thieves, Summertime Affair*, and an almost infinite number of others of that ilk. I was still writing the occasional story for the top-of-the-line sf magazines, too. Just ahead for me lay an entirely new career as a writer of popular books on archaeological subjects (*Lost Cities and Vanished Civilizations, Empires in the Dust,* etc.) and then, in the mid-1960s, a return to science fiction with the novels (*The Time Hoppers, To Open the Sky, Thorns*) that laid the foundation for my present reputation in the field.

I have no regrets over having written those reams and reams of space-adventure stories back in the 1950s for *Amazing, Super-Science*, and their competitors. The more of them I wrote, the greater my technical facility as a writer became, something that would stand me in good stead later on. They provided me, also, with the economic stability that a young married man just out of college had to have. Nor was I wasting creative energy that might better have been devoted to writing more ambitious fiction. You would be wrong if you thought that I had stories of the level of "Sundance" or "Enter a Soldier" or "The Secret Sharer" in me in 1957. I may have been a prodigy, but that prodigious I was not, not in my

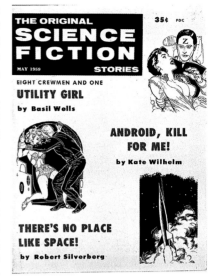

THE ORIGINAL
SCIENCE FICTION
STORIES, *May 1959.
Cover art by Emshwiller.*

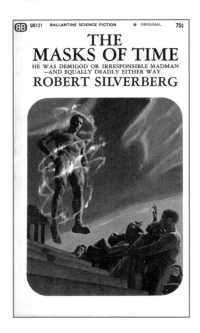

THE MASKS OF TIME,
Ballantine Books, NY; May 1968. Cover art by Robert Foster.

early twenties. Beyond a doubt, though, I was capable back then of "Cosmic Kill" and "Mournful Monster."

2005

TO SEE THE INVISIBLE MAN (1962)

There is a big break in the continuity of the record here. Between 1955 and 1958, most of what I wrote, and I wrote quite a lot in those years, was science fiction. In the following five years I wrote hardly any science fiction at all.

I have never made any secret of the fact that my primary (though not only) concern as a writer in the 1950s was to earn money. I was out of college and on my own in the adult world; I had an apartment to furnish, rent to pay, and all sorts of other new real-world expenses to meet. But after 1958, my fourth year as a full-time writer, making money began to be very difficult to do, if your specialty happened to be science fiction. Midway through that year the American News Company, the vast, omnipotent, and (I think) mob-controlled distribution company that was responsible for getting most of the nation's fiction magazines to the newsstands, abruptly went under as a result of some miscarried financial manipulation, and its collapse brought down dozens of small publishers who depended on advance payments from American News to stay afloat. Among them were most of the science fiction magazines to which I was a regular contributor.

The best ones — John Campbell's *Astounding*, Horace Gold's *Galaxy*, Tony Boucher's *Fantasy & Science Fiction* — were able to survive the debacle. But selling stories to those editors was always an iffy business for any writer this side of Heinlein or Asimov. Most of my mainstays, the risk-free ones who cheerfully bought all the copy I could provide at a cent or two a word, vanished right away or else entered a stage of obvious terminal decline. Larry Shaw's *Infinity* and its companion *Science Fiction Adventures* disappeared, W. W. Scott's *Super Science Fiction* (for which I wrote 36 of the 120 stories it published in four years) did likewise, Bob Lowndes' *Future* and *Science Fiction Stories* began to totter toward their doom, and so forth. I was still free to take my chances with the demanding Boucher, Campbell, and Gold, of course, but the salvage markets that I depended on to accept the stories which those three editors rejected were no longer there, and with the same number of writers competing for space in ever fewer magazines I was faced with the prospect of writing material that would find no publisher whatever. And in any case the magazines that remained had become cautious, bland, unadventurous, their editors preoccupied with the problem of surviving rather than looking for new horizons to explore. So by late 1958 I began to disappear from science fiction myself — the first of several such withdrawals from the field that I would stage.

I was accustomed by now to a pretty good standard of living, and so, fast on my feet as ever, I found a bunch of new markets outside the science fiction sphere for whom I wrote just about anything and everything. Some typical examples from my ledger: a piece called "Stalin's Slave Barracks" for a magazine called *Sir* in March 1959, "Cures for Sleepless Nights" in the January 1960 issue of *Living For Young Homemakers*, "Wolf Children of India" written for *Exotic Adventures* in May, 1959, and so on and on in a really astonishing fashion, reams of stuff that I have completely forgotten doing. I did continue to appear regularly in the science fiction magazines all through 1959, but these were mostly stories that I had written the year before, or even earlier. 1960 saw just four short sf stories of mine published — what would have been a week's work a couple of years before — and the little novel for young readers, *Lost Race of Mars,* which proved very popular and remained in print for decades. In 1961 I wrote just one sf story, and expanded an old magazine novella into a hardcover book for a lending-library publisher. In 1962, no sf short stories of mine appeared, just the novel *The Seed of Earth,* another expansion, based on a story from 1957.

But the veteran writer and editor Frederik Pohl had taken over the editorship of *Galaxy* and its companion magazine *If* from Horace Gold in June of 1961, and he was the one who brought me back into science fiction. So a word about Fred Pohl is necessary here:

As I write this in the summer of 2002, he and I have maintained a close and warm friendship for more than forty years. It has been, as many friendships and a good many marriages tend to be, often a turbulent relationship, in which each of us has done things displeasing to the other, and sharp words have been exchanged, after which we go right back to being friends. We have disagreed over politics, over story themes, over matters of professional responsibility, and any number of other things, including the nature and purpose of science fiction itself. In the beginning, when I was a brash and seemingly incorrigible young writer and Fred (who had made many of the same early mistakes I was then making) felt obliged to show me the error of my ways, he was something of a Dutch uncle to me. Later on, when I entered into the maturity of my career and Fred himself tumbled into difficult personal circumstances, it was I who lectured him, once or twice quite angrily. These days, now that I'm a senior citizen and Fred is an even more senior one, there's no lecturing at all between us, only the occasional half-hearted tossing of a barbed quip. (Usually over political matters, since we're farther apart than ever there.)

In the late 1950s Fred had been vexed with me for my willingness to churn out all that lucrative junk, and he believed (rightly, as time would prove) that a top-rank sf writer was hidden behind the pyramid of literary garbage that I had cheerfully been producing over the past few years. So he made me an offer shrewdly calculated to appeal to my risk-abhorring nature. He agreed to buy any

Robert Silverberg with John W. Campbell Jr., editor of ASTOUNDING SCIENCE FICTION/ ANALOG magazine from 1938 to his death in 1971.

I started reading ASTOUNDING when I was 13, in 1948. I found most of the stories and all of the articles quite baffling. But I caught the drift quickly and in 1949 and 1950 I bought dozens of back issues, until I had them all.— RS

Baycon banquet, 1968, Berkeley, California. Harlan Ellison helping RS, as toastmaster, present the Hugos. Philip Jose Farmer, to RS's right, is guest of honor.

story I cared to send him — a guaranteed sale — provided I undertook to write it with all my heart, no quick-buck hackwork. If he wanted revisions, I would pledge to do one rewrite for him, after which he would be bound to buy the story without asking anything more of me. If I turned in a story he didn't like, he would buy it anyway, but that would be the end of the deal. I was, of course, to say nothing about these terms to any of my fellow writers, and I kept the secret until long after Fred had left the magazine.

It was an irresistible arrangement, as he damned well knew. I would get three cents a word — the top rate at the time — without the slightest risk, and without any necessity whatever to slant my work to meet the imagined prejudices of a dictatorial editor. All I had to do was write what I believed to be good science fiction, and Fred would buy it. I had never had an arrangement like that with a first-class sf magazine before, and I lost no time in writing "To See the Invisible Man," the first of what would be a great many stories for Fred Pohl's *Galaxy*.

That story, written in June of 1962, marks the beginning of my real career as a science fiction writer, I think. The 1953-58 stories are respectable professional work, some better than others but all of them at least minimally acceptable but most of them could have been written by just about anyone. They were designed to slip unobtrusively into the magazines of their time, efficiently providing me with regular paychecks. By freeing me from the need to calculate my way around the risk of rejection, Fred Pohl allowed — indeed, required — me to reach as deep into my literary resources as I was capable of doing. I would reach deeper and deeper, in the years ahead, until I had moved so far away from my youthful career as a hack writer that latecomers would find it hard to believe that I had been emotionally capable of writing all that junk, let alone willing to do it. In "To See the Invisible Man" the distinctive Silverberg fictional voice is on display for just about the first time.

(The voice of another and greater writer can be heard in the background, though. I found the idea for my story in the opening paragraph of Jorge Luis Borges' "The Babylon Lottery," where he says, "Like all men in Babylon I have been a proconsul; like all, a slave. . . . During one lunar year, I have been declared invisible; I shrieked and was not heard, I stole my bread and was not decapitated." Borges chose to do no more with the theme of statutory Invisibility in that story — it was, for him, nothing more than an embellishment in a story about something else entirely. So I fell upon the notion and developed it to explore its practical implications, thus doing the job Borges had left undone.)

Oddly, the story didn't appear in *Galaxy* despite my arrangement with Fred. Soon after taking over the editorial post, he created a new magazine, *Worlds of Tomorrow*, and shifted some stories out of the *Galaxy* inventory to fill its first issue, dated April, 1963. "To See the Invisible Man" was among them. To those readers who quite rightly thought of me as a heartless manufacturer of mass-produced fiction, the story was something of a revelation — and there would be more such surprises to come.

Many years later, by the way, it was adapted for television's *Twilight Zone* program, with a superb screenplay by Steve Barnes.

2004

FLIES (1965)

So I was writing sf again, slowly at first, then with greater frequency as I began to savor the advantages of my deal with Fred Pohl. Now that I had had a taste of what tackling complex science fictional themes or modes of narrative without fear of rejection was like, I grew more and more enthusiastic about writing stories for him. Next I did a story called "The Pain Peddlers," and then one called "Neighbor," and in February 1964, a fourth, "The Sixth Palace." But those four did not represent a return to my old bang-em-out prolificity of the 1950s. Each was carefully planned and closely revised. They showed the new pride I was taking in my work.

Fred was pleased with them too. He encouraged me to keep going. By the summer of 1964 he and I were discussing my doing a series of five novellas for him — the "Blue Fire" stories, which became the novel *To Open the Sky*. I had told him at the outset that my contributions to his magazine would probably be few and far between, because I was more interested in writing nonfiction — I had launched a new career as a successful writer of popular books on archaeological subjects — and at the beginning that was true: but, bit by bit, he had lured me back into science fiction. (Or I had lured myself.) I did the first of the "Blue Fire" stories in November 1964, the second in December, the third in March, 1965. For someone who planned to dabble in sf on a purely part-time basis, I was suddenly getting very active again after six or seven years away from the center of the scene.

I was beginning to edit anthologies, too. A book called *Earthmen and Strangers* was the first, and for my sins I chose to reprint a story by Harlan Ellison in it. Ellison was willing to grant me permission to use his story, but not without a lot of heavy muttering and grumbling about the terms of the contract, to which I replied on October 2, 1965:

"Dear Harlan: You'll be glad to know that in the course of a long and wearying dream last night I watched you win two Hugos at last year's Worldcon. (He

had never won an award at this point in his career.) You acted pretty smug about it, too. I'm not sure which categories you led, but one of them was probably Unfounded Bitching. Permit me a brief and fatherly lecture in response to your letter of permission on the anthology...."

Whereupon I dealt with his complaints at some length, and then, almost gratuitously, threw in a postscript:

"Why don't *you* do an anthology? *Harlan Ellison Picks Offbeat Classics of SF,* or something...."

From the placement of the italicized word in that sentence, I suppose I must already have suggested to Harlan that he edit an anthology of controversial sf. He was running a paperback line then called Regency Books, published out of Chicago — but for some reason he had brushed the idea aside. Now, though, it kindled something in him. He was back to me right away, by telephone this time, to tell me that he would do a science fiction anthology, all right, but for a major publishing house instead of little Regency, and instead of putting together a mere compilation of existing material he would solicit previously unpublished stories, the kind of sf that no magazine of that era would dare to publish. Truly dangerous stories, Harlan said — a book of dangerous visions. "In fact, that's what I'll call it," he told me, in mounting excitement. "*Dangerous Visions.* I want you to write a story for it, too."

And so I unwittingly touched off a publishing revolution.

By the eighteenth of October Harlan had sold the book to Doubleday and was soliciting stories far and wide. Requests for material — material of the boldest, most uncompromising kind — went out to the likes of Theodore Sturgeon, Frederik Pohl, Poul Anderson, Philip K. Dick, Philip Jose Farmer, Fritz Leiber, J. G. Ballard, Norman Spinrad, Brian Aldiss, Lester del Rey, Larry Niven, R. A. Lafferty, John Brunner, Roger Zelazny, and Samuel R. Delany. Dick, Pohl, Sturgeon, Anderson, del Rey, Farmer, Brunner, Aldiss, and Leiber were well-established authors, but the work of Ballard, Zelazny, Delany, Niven, and Spinrad, believe it or not, was only just beginning to be known in the United States in

1965. Harlan's eye for innovative talent had always been formidably keen.

As the accidental instigator of the whole thing — and the quickest man with an sf story since Henry Kuttner in his prime — I sat down right away and wrote the very first dangerous vision, "Flies," in November of 1965, just as soon as Harlan told me the deal was set. It was about as dangerous as I could manage: a demonstration of the random viciousness of the universe and a little blasphemy on the side. (I would return to both these themes again and again in the years ahead: my novel *Thorns* of 1966 was essentially a recasting of the underlying material of "Flies" at greater length.) Back at once came Harlan's check for $88.

Which was the first of many, for *Dangerous Visions* would turn out to be the most significant sf anthology of the decade, and was destined to go through edition after edition. It is still in print, more than thirty-five years later. All of the extraordinary writers whose names I rattled off above came through with brilliant stories, along with fifteen or twenty others, some well known at the time but forgotten now, some obscure then and still obscure, but all of them fiercely determined to live up to Harlan's demand for the kind of stories that other sf editors would consider too hot to handle.

Dangerous Visions appeared in 1967. "An event," said the *New York Times*, "a jubilee of fresh ideas . . . what we mean when we say an important book." Its success led to the publication of an immense companion volume in 1972, *Again, Dangerous Visions* — 760 pages of stories by writers who hadn't contributed to the first book (Ursula K. Le Guin, Gene Wolfe, Kurt Vonnegut, Gregory Benford, James Tiptree, Jr., . . .) And ultimately Harlan began to assemble the mammoth third book in the series, *The Last Dangerous Visions*, though the project became stalled and its publication now will be an event in some alternate universe.

I knew not what I was setting in motion with my casual postscript of October 2, 1965, suggesting that Harlan edit an anthology. Certainly I had no idea that I was nudging him toward one of the great enterprises of his career. Nor did I suspect that my own 4,400-word contribution to the book would open a new and darker phase of my own career — in which, ultimately, almost everything I wrote would become a dangerous vision of sorts.

2004

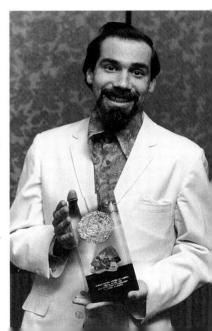

RS holding Nebula Award for "Passengers," 1969. Photo by Jay Kay Klein.

PASSENGERS (1967)

1966 — the year of "Hawksbill Station," *The Time Hoppers*, *Thorns*, and my big El Dorado book, *The Golden Dream* — was a watershed year for me. I had found my own voice as a writer and had attained a degree of skill surprising even to me; publishers were crowding around me, eager for my science fiction and for my nonfiction work as well; the days of grinding out hack assignments for magazines like *Trapped* or *True Men Adventures* were receding into history. And as the major works of 1966 began to find their way into print the following year, critics who had dismissed me as a cynical opportunist were taking a second look at what I was doing. I felt a heady sense of new beginnings, of having entered into a mature and fulfilling phase of my career. (I also managed to damage my health in the joyous overwork of it all, coming down with a bout of hyperthyroidism and spending most of the summer of 1966 as an invalid, frail and exhausted — a new experience for me. But by autumn I was back to normal and ready to tackle a full schedule, as the writing of a novel like *Thorns* in just ten working days in September of 1966 demonstrated. If that seems improbable to you, please accept my assurance that it seems pretty improbable to me, too. But the ledger entries are incontrovertibly there: ten working days.)

Suddenly, now, I found I had won the respect of my peers in the science fiction world for something other than my ability to turn out salable work in high volume. Though barely into my thirties, I was elected president of the newly founded Science Fiction Writers of America early in 1967. I made my first appearance on the awards ballots since winning the Hugo as Most Promising New Author in 1956: *Thorns* was a Nebula nominee in 1967, and so was the novella version of "Hawksbill Station." (I finished second both times.) Both stories would be on the Hugo ballot as well, the following year, the Hugos following a somewhat different chronological schedule in those days. (More second-place finishes would be the result.)

And in January, 1967, I offered a story to the most difficult, cantankerous, . demanding editor of the era — Damon Knight, famous for his well-aimed and ferocious attacks on all that was slovenly in science fiction. He had started an anthology of original fiction called *Orbit*. Selling a story to Damon struck me as a challenge that had to be surmounted; and so I sent him "Passengers," and on January 16 he sent it back, saying, "I can't fault this one technically, & it is surely dark & nasty enough to suit anybody, but I have a nagging feeling that there's something missing, and I'm not sure I can put my finger on it." But he offered some suggestions for revisions anyway, and I decided to try another draft, telling him on January 26, "You and your *Orbit* are a great tribulation to me. I suppose I could take "Passengers" and ship it off to Fred Pohl and collect my $120 and start all over trying to sell one to you, but I don't want to do that, because I believe this story represents just about the best I have in me, and if I can't get you to take it it's futile to go on submitting others."

The rewrite, Knight said, was close — not quite there. So I rewrote it again. And again. The hook was in me, and all I could do was wriggle. On March 22 he wrote to me again to say, "God help us both, I am going to ask you to revise this one more time. The love story now has every necessary element, but it seems

Silverberg c. 1970s.

to me it's an empty jug. Now I want you to put the love into it. I say this with a feeling of helplessness, because I don't know how to tell you to do it."

And then he proceeded to tell me, not how to do it, but why I should do it; and I did it and he bought the story, and published it in *Orbit Four* in 1968. And the following year it won me my first Nebula, for Best Short Story of the Year. (It was nominated for the Hugo, too.) Since then it has become a standard anthology piece, has been purchased by a Hollywood studio, has in general become one of my best-known stories. The five drafts of it that I did between January and March of 1967 were an almighty nuisance but I have never regretted doing them.

2004

GOING DOWN SMOOTH (1968)

"Going Down Smooth" is a story of serious intent founded on a pair of backstage jokes.

The first involves the process, now I think obsolete, of commissioning science fiction writers to construct stories around a previously painted cover illustration. Why this should ever have become standard practice in the magazine business puzzles me; the usual explanation had to do with the deadlines and such, but it still seems to me more efficient to have had artists illustrate scenes from stories, rather than vice versa. How-be-it, many magazines worked that way and some remarkable science fiction stories did emerge, the writer's ingenuity often being taxed to the extreme to make narrative sense out of the picture with which he was presented. I think particularly of James Blish's masterful "Common Time" as the archetypical written-around-a-cover story; but I did dozens of them myself, including some of my best short pieces.

"Going Down Smooth" was probably among the last such stories I did. I was then writing fiction regularly for *Galaxy* — Frederik Pohl had dragooned me out of the first of my retirements from sf writing about 1963 with an exceptionally generous offer, and by easy stages I had moved from the periphery of *Galaxy*'s life to quite a central position as one of the most prolific contributors. This reached something of a frenzied pitch a little later, under Pohl's successor Ejler Jakobsson, when *Galaxy* serialized four of my novels in virtually consecutive issue over a year and a half — *Downward to the Earth, Tower of Glass, The World Inside*, and *A Time of Changes*. I don't think any science fiction magazine had given so much space to a single writer since Heinlein's heyday at *Astounding* thirty years earlier.

Anyway, Fred Pohl asked me to do a cover story for *Galaxy* sometime late in 1967, and his assistant, Judy-Lynn Benjamin (later Judy-Lynn Del Rey, the powerful and influential science fiction editor at Ballantine's Del Rey Books), sent me a photostat of a cover "rough" by a gifted young artist named Vaughn Bodé. It was a typically perplexing write-a-story-around-*this*-one sort of thing, showing an oceangoing vessel with a cluster of colossal periscopes rising from the water behind it. Bodé had deviated from the usual cover-rough format in one respect, though, *Galaxy*'s traditional cover format for decades made use of a white panel down the left side of the page in which the names of stories were printed. Bodé had not only drawn that panel into his painting, but had gone to the prankish extent of making up a bunch of bizarre story titles. I went right along with the joke, picking out the least implausible of his titles and using it for my story. (I think I lost my photostat of the rough in the fire that swept my home in February 1968; otherwise I'd list the other titles here. I've forgotten them, but they were fine crazy ones.) That was backstage joke number one.

The other one was a prank at Fred Pohl's expense. Though he was in most respects a superbly intelligent editor, Pohl had decided, circa 1966 or 1967, that the basic readership of his magazine consisted of fourteen-year old boys, whose parents might forbid them to buy it if they were to glance inside and discover anything pornographic, as pornography was understood in those quaintly innocent days. So Pohl forbade his authors any sort of erotic content and deleted from their manuscripts even the mildest of what used to be called "unprintable" Anglo-Saxonism. I took issue with this policy to some degree, although later on I came, alas, to realize that Pohl was probably right, and that the readership of the sf magazines back then did consist largely of fourteen-year-old boys of all ages. Anyway, in the grand old manner of science fiction pros rebelling tepidly against editorial censorship, fighting repression with slyness, I built my entire story around the earthiest of procreative obscenities — but, since my protagonist was a computer, I flanged together a binary-equivalent alphabet and disguised the forbidden word in chaste numerals. To me, and doubtless to Fred Pohl, there is not a whole lot of karmic distinction between saying "fuck you" and saying "1000110 you" — the baleful energy, as I see it, lies in the underlying sentiment, not in the verbal or pseudoverbal packet that carries it. But not so with parents of Fred's fourteen-year-old audience, I guess, because the story was published, no subscriptions were canceled, and we all lived happily ever after.

During the later Jakobsson editorial regime at *Galaxy* I actually did get the dread word into the magazine, by the way. It was a passage in "The World Inside" in which a twenty-fourth-century historian, musing on the twentieth century's obsession with "forbidden" language, repeats such words as "fuck" and "cunt" in bewilderment, trying to comprehend why entire books would have been suppressed for containing them. They are mere noises to him, and the concepts they represent seem utterly harmless. Ironically, these explorations of the innately innocuous nature of sexual slang touched off so many irate letters from the readership that the publisher became aware of the situation and asked Jakobsson to reinstate the old magazine taboos. The first victim of this was Robert A. Heinlein, whose novel *I Will Fear No Evil* was being serialized in *Galaxy*. Never in his career had Heinlein used language that would offend the most prudish, but in the climatic paragraph of this novel he allowed himself a lyrical affirmation of the power of love, and this is how it came out in *Galaxy*:

"Thank you, Roberto, for letting me welcome you into my body. It is good to touch — to f—, to be f—ed. It's not good — to be — too much alone...."

And so the immortal souls of the readers were protected by the vigilant publisher. And so everybody got f—ed again. Nowadays the fourteen-year-olds are too busy f—ing one another to read *Galaxy* at all, and nobody worries much about the terrible issues of obscenity that caused us such anguish in the far-off ancient days of 1967.

1980

NIGHTWINGS (1968)

The messy, chaotic, and ultimately well-nigh apocalyptic year of 1968 — the year of the Tet offensive and other dismal military events in Vietnam, the year Robert F. Kennedy and Martin Luther King, Jr. were assassinated, the year when student protesters turned universities all over the world into armed camps, when Soviet troops marched into Prague to snuff out Czech liberty, when the Democratic Party's national convention produced open warfare in the streets of Chicago — gave me a private foretaste of the turmoil it was destined to bring when, on a bitterly cold February night, I awakened at half past three in the morning to discover that my house was on fire.

By dawn I knew the worst. The roof was gone; the attic, where I kept a reference library, had been gutted; my third-floor office was partially destroyed; the lower floors of the house had suffered such extensive water damage that the entire structure would have to be rebuilt from within. And so, amidst the general lunacy and nightmarish frenzy of that strange year, I would for nine months find myself living in exile from that splendid house in one of New York City's loveliest neighborhoods — nine months of exhaustion, depression, improvised quarters, cartons and packing crates, limited access to the reference materials I needed in my work, to my own files and notes, to everything that was part of an inordinately active literary career. While the rest of the world was exuberantly taking leave of its sanity, that year of 1968, I was struggling to hang on to mine.

The cost of rebuilding the house was immense (and kept climbing from week to week as the roaring war-driven inflation of the Vietnam years took hold.) The insurance money would, as it always does, fall short of the actual expense; and the first payment was delayed by the usual bureaucratic snafus for three full months. Though the impact of the fire on every aspect of my life had left me drained of energy, I had no choice but to get back to work as soon as I

NIGHTWINGS *1970 hardcover edition with Jack Gaughan jacket artwork.*

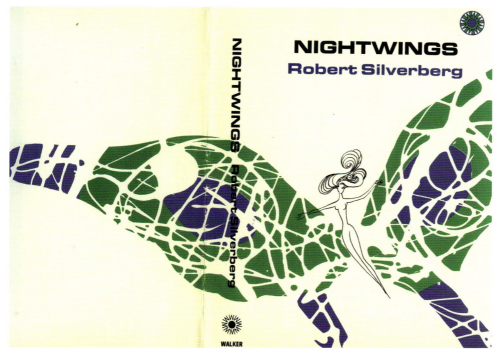

could replace my typewriter and find a flat surface on which to place it.

The first thing I wrote after the fire — I began it about ten days later, and completed it, groggy as I was, in something like five days — was a 19,000 word novella called "Nightwings."

I had no idea that I was beginning a novel, then. I was too weary to think about anything so long term. A quick story for one of the top-level science fiction magazines would bring me about $500 — something like $5,000 in modern purchasing power-and that would get me through the basic living expenses of the first few weeks. The story came to me, as so many of mine do, with the title first — "Nightwings." I asked myself. "What could that possibly refer to?" — and then a group of images, a winged girl, a sky full of invading alien ships, a blinded prince. Within moments a story had come together in my mind, by a process I have never dared to try to understand. I knew that I would set it in the very far future and try for a certain romantic, incantatory tone. Even the first sentence arrived in that early wonderful rush: "Roum is a city built on seven hills."

I sat down and wrote it as fast as I could. And sent it to Frederik Pohl of *Galaxy* early in March 1968, and Fred, who had had a house fire of his own and knew precisely what I was going through, sent me a check by return mail. What he didn't manage to tell me was just how much he liked the story. As he explained in some chagrin a couple of months later, "I just discovered that I dictated a letter to you on 'Nightwings' when I got it, and it was never typed up. This is a serious oversight, because what I said in the letter was that I thought it was a great story and admired you enormously for having written it."

That was a good thing to hear, because Fred and I had had some pretty heated correspondence in the interim about the two sequels to the original story that I had written for him by then, and I welcomed this pacifying gesture. But at the time I wrote the original one I had no time to worry about whether it was a great story, or even a good one, or whether Fred Pohl really and truly loved it. What mattered was the check for $513 that the story produced, which would pay several weeks' rent at my current temporary quarters.

I went on quickly to write a story called "Ishmael in Love" for *Fantasy & Science Fiction*, one of the other top sf magazines of the time, and then a short book on the wonders of ancient Chinese science for young readers. At the pace I worked back then, I got both of these projects out of the way before the end of March. By that time it had occurred to me that the "Nightwings" novella was, in fact, the opening section of a three-part novel that would carry my protagonist deeper and deeper into the strange world I had created until he, and the entire conquered Earth, attained rebirth and redemption. And so on March 18 I told Fred Pohl — who tended to like series stories anyway — that I was going to write two sequels of about the same length as the first story. "Go ahead," he told me. Which is how, eventually, the novel-length book called *Nightwings*, of which the novella of the same title is the opening sequence, came into being.

The world outside was a pretty wild place while I was writing those stories. Police stormed five student-occupied buildings at my alma mater, Columbia University, to end a sit-in by war protesters; all of France was paralyzed by a general strike; the U. S. Supreme Court upheld a new law making it illegal to burn draft cards; and Robert F. Kennedy was assassinated while campaigning for the Presidency in Los Angeles. Against this background of personal stress and mount-

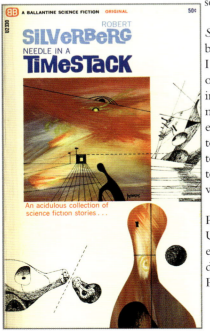

Ballantine PB edition of NEEDLE IN A TIMESTACK, *1966. Cover art by Richard Powers.*

ing global madness I wrote the second and third of my three stories about the far-future civilization of Earth's Third Cycle.

"Nightwings," the first of the three, was published in July, in the edition of *Galaxy* dated September 1968. It won immediate reader acclaim, and when I showed up at that year's World Science Fiction Convention in Berkeley, California (where the People's Park riots were going on practically next door, and whiffs of tear gas drifted through the convention hotel), I heard much in its praise. Story number two, called "Perris Way," appeared in the issue after next, dated November 1968. The final story, "To Jorslem," followed in the February 1969 issue.

In the spring of 1969 "Nightwings" was one of five stories to make the final Nebula Award ballot in the Best Novella category, but finished second to Anne McCaffrey's "Dragonrider." Then, a few months later, running against the same group of stories, it won me that year's Best Novella Hugo award my first Hugo award, for a specific piece of fiction. (An earlier one, in 1956, was for being the best new writer of the year.) As for the novel that I made out of the three magazine stories by dint of slight revisions and the addition of a small amount of new connective tissue, it was published in September, 1969, has been translated into many languages and mentioned in various lists of great science fiction novels, and remains in print to this day.

2004

SUNDANCE (1968)

This was another product of the dark year of 1968 — written for Edward L. Ferman, the publisher and now also the editor of *Fantasy & Science Fiction*, in late September, a couple of months after I finished the "Nightwings" sequence. I was still living in rented quarters — in exile, that was exactly how I thought of it — but I had begun to adapt by that time to the changed circumstances that the fire had brought, and I was working at something like the old pace. Since I was writing too many stories for Pohl to handle all at once, I began offering every other one to Ferman. I was working at a new level of complexity, too — sure of myself and my technique, willing now to push the boundaries of the short-story form in any direction that seemed worth exploring. I had always been interested, from the beginning of my career, in technical experimentation, when and as the restrictions imposed on me by my pulp-magazine editors allowed any. But now I was in my thirties and approaching the height of my powers as a writer. So I did "Sundance" by way of producing a masterpiece in the old sense of the word — that is, a piece of work which is intended to demonstrate to a craftsman's peers that he has ended his apprenticeship and has fully mastered the intricacies of his trade.

Apparently I told Ed Ferman something about the story's nature while I was working on it, and he must have reacted with some degree of apprehensiveness, because the letter I sent him on October 22, 1968, accompanying the submitted manuscript, says, "I quite understand your hesitation to commit yourself in advance to a story when you've been warned it's experimental; but it's not all that experimental.... I felt that the only way I could properly convey the turmoil in the protagonist's mind, the gradual dissolution of his hold on reality, was through the constant changing of persons and tenses; but as I read it through I think everything remains clear despite the frequent derailments of the reader." And I

THORNS was written in two breathless weeks in September 1966.— RS

THORNS, Ballantine paperback, 1967; cover art by Robert R. Foster.

THOSE WHO WATCH, Signet paperback.

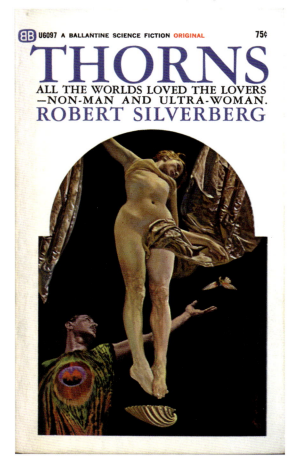

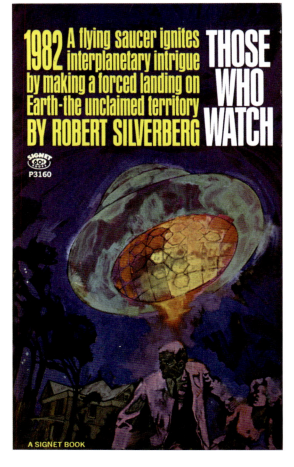

added, "I don't mean to say that I intend to disappear over the deep end of experimentalism. I don't regard myself as a member of any 'school' of sf, and don't value obscurity for its own sake. Each story is a technical challenge unique unto itself, and I have to go where the spirit moves me. Sometimes it moves me to a relatively conventional strong-narrative item . . . and sometimes to a relatively avant garde item like this present 'Sundance;' I'm just after the best way of telling my story, in each case."

Ferman responded on Nov 19 with: "You should do more of this sort of thing. 'Sundance' is by far the best of the three I've seen recently. It not only works; it works beautifully. The ending — with the trapdoor image and that last line — is perfectly consistent, and just fine." He had only one suggestion: that I simplify the story's structure a little, perhaps by eliminating the occasional use of second-person narrative. But I wasn't about to do that. I replied with an explanation of why the story kept switching about between first person narrative, second person, third person present tense, and third person past tense. Each mode had its particular narrative significance in conveying the various reality-levels of the story, I told him: the first-person material was the protagonist's interior monologue, progressively more incoherent and untrustworthy; the second-person passages provided objective description of his actions, showing his breakdown from the outside, but not so far outside as third person would be — and so forth. Ferman was convinced, and ran the story as is.

And it became something of a classic almost immediately after Ed ran it in his June 1969 issue. Though it was certainly a kind of circus stunt, it was a stunt that worked, and it attracted widespread attention, including a place on the ballot for the Nebula award the following year. (But I had "Passengers" on the same ballot, and had no wish to compete with myself. Shrewdly if somewhat cynically, I calculated that the more accessible "Passengers" had a better chance of winning the award, and had "Sundance" removed from the ballot. And that was how I came to win a Nebula with my second-best story of 1969.) "Sundance" has since been reprinted dozens of times, both in science fiction anthologies and in textbooks of literature.

2004

THE WORLD INSIDE
was put together out of five or six shorter pieces, most of which first saw print in the lamented mag **GALAXY.**
— RS

GOOD NEWS FROM THE VATICAN (1971)

Ever since I read Baron Corvo's remarkable novel *Hadrian the Seventh* in 1955 I have amused myself with the fantasy of being elected Pope — an ambition complicated to some degree by the fact that I am not in holy orders, nor a Roman Catholic, nor, indeed, any kind of Christian at all. As my friends know, I duly submit an application whenever a vacancy occurs at the Vatican, but as of this date the Church has not yet seen fit to make use of my services.

All the same, I keep close watch over events in the Holy City as I bide my time, and in the pursuit of this not entirely serious career plan I've learned a good deal about the rituals and tensions surrounding the elections of a pontiff. This led me, one chilly but lighthearted day in February 1971, to produce this sly, playful story of the accession of the first robot to the Holy See. (The robot is, in fact, meant to be my own successor, though the point is made only through an

(top)
RS with Roger Zelazny,
1967.

(opposite)
Cover art by Jack Gaughan
for "Nightwings" in
GALAXY *Magazine.*

SIGNET·451·Y6113·$1.25

EDITED BY

ROBERT SILVERBERG
NEW DIMENSIONS

FEATURING: IV
R. A. LAFFERTY   DAVID R. BUNCH
TERRY CARR   GARDNER R. DOZOIS
BARRY N. MALZBERG   LAURENCE M. JANIFER
RICHARD A. LUPOFF   FELIX C. GOTSCHALK
    ROGER ELWOOD

oblique private reference in the final paragraph.)

At that time a year and a half had passed since the completion of rebuilding work on my New York house, and it was even more handsome than it had been before the fire. I assumed I would live there for the rest of my life. But some sort of uneasiness was stirring in my soul even then, for the winter of 1970-71 was unusually snowy in New York, and as the white drifts piled up outside the door I began to tell people that I yearned for some warmer climate. On the February day when Terry Carr called to ask me to write a story for *Universe*, his new anthology of previously unpublished short stories, I was, as a matter of fact, writing *The Book of Skulls*, a novel set in the torrid Arizona desert.

Carr, then at the peak of his distinguished career as a science fiction editor for Ace Books, told me that he was approaching the deadline for delivery of the first volume of *Universe* and was badly in need of work by authors with recognizable names. He had been asking me for a story for weeks, but I was busy with my novel, and I put him off; but now he appealed bluntly to me to help him out. Since Terry was a persuasive man and a close friend besides, I agreed to do a quick short story for him. What to write about? Well, I thought, casting about quickly, suppose they elect a robot as Pope? That ought to be worth 3,000 words or so of amiable foolery, right? My own pretense of interest in attaining the Papacy and my knowledge of the mechanics of Papal elections would help me make the story reasonably convincing. A couple of hours' work and Terry and his new anthology would be off my conscience.

So I sat down and wrote "Good News from the Vatican" just about as fast as I could type it out. Terry was amused by its cool, detached, tongue-in-cheek mode of irony (which I was beginning to employ more and more, as I entered my third decade as a writer) and published it in the first issue of *Universe* with a brief introduction noting that although my stories were usually quite serious in tone, this one was a bit on the silly side, although nevertheless quite thoughtful and ingenious, et cetera, et cetera.

A couple of unexpected ironies proceeded from this enterprise. The little story I had written so quickly that snowy February day caught everybody's attention, was nominated for a Nebula award, and won the trophy for me the second of, ultimately, five Nebulas — the following spring. (I won my third the same night, for the novel *A Time of Changes*.) I collected my awards not in New York but at a ceremony held in California, for, much to my astonishment, the inner uneasiness of February had culminated by late summer in a series of explosive personal upheavals that had caused me to sell my New York house and move westward, a few months after Terry Carr himself had done the very same thing.

And also — rather sadly, actually — a decade and a half after I had helped Terry get *Universe* started by hastily writing an award-winning story for his first issue, I found myself taking his place as its editor, when his publisher decided to continue the anthology as a memorial to him following his untimely death in 1987.

2004

CAPRICORN GAMES (1972)

Jesus was a Capricorn; so was Richard M. Nixon; and so am I. I am not much of a believer in the astrological sciences — the whole theory that the stars govern our lives makes no sense whatever to me — but I do accept, however inconsistent with the previous statement it may be, the conventional notion of the sort of people those born under the sign of Capricorn tend to be. (Stubborn, dedicated, talented, self-centered, always planning things out ahead of time. I think of Capricorns as being excellent chess players, though I'm a terrible one myself.) I look upon Capricorns as somewhat manipulative, which is not necessarily a negative attribute: "manipulative" is a term that can be applied to jugglers, novelists, surgeons, musicians, and others who are quick with their hands in a literal rather than metaphorical sense, But some of the Capricorn energy does flow into the work of organizing other human beings into patterns that serve the needs of the Capricorn, I feel. Certainly that's the sort of Capricorn that Nikki is in this story, which dates from October, 1972. I was a Californian by the time I wrote it, and you know how Californians are about things like astrology.

I was also at the beginning of a serious slowdown in my productivity, after a decade and a half's output of short stories and novels at a fantastic and almost unreal pace. After the heavy exertions of 1971, a year in which I wrote the novels *The Book of Skulls* and *Dying Inside* and nine or ten lesser items while in the midst of moving myself from New York to California, I wrote no novels at all in 1972, only short stories and novelets, (I did manage to produce fifteen of them during the year, a pretty hefty rate of production by the standards of normal writers, and far more than I've done in any year since, but nothing at all compared with what I was routinely doing in 1956 or 1957.) The early 1970s were the heyday of hardcover anthologies of original science fiction, a peculiar publishing phenomenon that had, so far as I could tell, no economic justification whatever for its existence. A go-getter named Roger Elwood was editing eight or ten such books a year, and much of my 1972 output was written for him — "Capricorn Games" for a collection

25th Year of Publication

THE MAGAZINE OF

Fantasy AND

special SILVERBERG issue

Science Fiction

APRIL   75c • UK 30p.

Born With The Dead
a new novella by
Robert Silverberg

called *The Far Side of Time,* published by the now-forgotten house of Dodd, Mead.

This story has always been a particular favorite of mine, and not just because its January-born author often sees himself as sitting at the keyboard playing games with his characters, playing games with his readers' minds. Nikki's birthdate happens to be — by sheer one-out-of-365 coincidence — the same as that of a young woman who was living in Houston, Texas, in 1981, when I — also by sheer coincidence — was in town to speak at the local university. She came upon the story somehow, was startled and amused to find that she shared a birthdate with its protagonist and that the author of the story was making a public appearance locally, and went to meet him. It turned out that we had a lot to say to each other. Her name was Karen Haber and — to make a long story short — we play our Capricorn games under the same roof these days.

2004

BORN WITH THE DEAD (1973)

The slowdown in my productivity continued in 1973. Life was pretty crazy for most of us that year — the United States was suffering the gigantic hangover of the post-Vietnam years, and even for the most prosaic suburban people it was a time of weird clothing, weird hairstyles, massive drug consumption, and outlandish sexual revelry. Here in California we were churning through some sort of societal revolution every six weeks or so. My first marriage was falling apart, besides. And I was simply worn out after years and years of super-prolific writing. All that work had left me fairly independent financially, however, and although I was not yet 40 I was beginning to think of abandoning my career and spending the rest of my life traveling, reading, and caring for my new Californian garden of exotic semitropical plants.

As a result I wrote practically nothing in 1973 — my output for the entire year was a piddling 81,000 words, which would have been two weeks' work ten years before. Though whatever work I did manage to produce was of a high level of quality, every word was an effort and it was only the pressure of other people's deadlines that got me to do anything at all.

Nevertheless, in the middle of that deadly year I embarked on a long story that surely ranks near the top of my entire vast array of work. Weary as I was, reluctant to work as I was, I found myself unable to keep this one from coming into being — thanks to a little timely encouragement from Ed Ferman of *Fantasy & Science Fiction.*

For most of its half-century-plus of existence the magazine that is formally known as *The Magazine of Fantasy & Science Fiction,* but more usually *F&SF,* has been a bastion of civilized and cultivated material. That was true under its founding editors, Anthony Boucher and J. Francis McComas, and under such succeeding editors as Robert P. Mills and Avram Davidson. By the 1970s, editorial control had passed into the hands of Ed Ferman, who also happened to be the publisher of the magazine, and who functioned in admirable fashion in both capacities for many years thereafter. My fiction had been appearing on and off in *F&SF* since the days of the Boucher-McComas administration; but it was Ed Ferman

(above)
Photo by Bill Rotsler c. 1971, used as source image for Ed Emshwiller painting to April, 1974 **MAGAZINE of FANTASY & SF** *tribute issue shown on opposite page.*

who turned me into a steady contributor. He published a flock of my short stories in the magazines in the 1960s, of which the best known was the much-anthologized "Sundance," and then, as I began to turn away from shorter fiction in favor of novellas and novels, Ferman let me know that he would be interested in publishing some of my longer work also.

In December 1972, just after the publication of my novel *Dying Inside*, I got a note from Ed saying that he had just received a review copy of that book. "I simply wanted to tell you what a fine and moving and painful experience it was to read it," he wrote, going on to compare the novel favorably to recent works by Bernard Malamud and Chaim Potok. And he added in a postscript, "The editor in me has just popped up, and I can't help asking what I have to do to see your next novel. If it's anything near the quality of *Dying Inside*, I'll go higher than our top rate."

I already knew that I wasn't going to write another novel just then, not with all the turbulence going on in my life, and perhaps would never write one ever again. Therefore I felt uneasy about committing myself to any very lengthy work. And I was already working on a longish short story called "Trips" for an anthology Ferman was editing in collaboration with Barry Malzberg. But despite everything, I did have another long story in mind to write after that, one that would probably run to novella length, and I could not keep myself from telling Ferman it was his if he wanted it. He replied at once that he did.

The story was "Born With the Dead."

It had the feel of a major story from the moment I conceived it. I had played with the idea of the resuscitation of the dead in fiction since my 1957 novel *Recalled To Life*, and now, I felt, I was ready to return to it with a kind of culminating statement on the subject. A few days after I began work on it I let Ferman know that it was going to be a big one. To which he replied on April 16, 1973 that I should make it as big as it needed to be, because he proposed to make the story the centerpiece of a special Robert Silverberg issue of the magazine.

That had real impact on me. Over the years *F&SF* had done a handful of special issues honoring its favorite contributors — Theodore Sturgeon, Ray Bradbury, Fritz Leiber, Poul Anderson, James Blish, and one or two others. Each special issue featured a portrait of the writer on the cover, a major new story by him, several critical essays, and a bibliography. All of the writers chosen had been favorites of mine since my days as an avid adolescent reader; and now, suddenly, in my mid-thirties and at what plainly was the peak of my career, I found myself chosen to join their company. It gave me a nice shiver down the spine.

But of course I had to write a story worthy of that company — and this at a time when my private life was in chaos and the world about me, there in the apocalyptic days of the late Nixon era, was pretty chaotic too. So every day's work was an ordeal. Sometimes I managed no more than a couple of paragraphs. At best I averaged about a page a day. Writing it required me to do battle with all kinds of internal demons, for the story springs from areas within me that I found it taxing to explore: I had to confront my own attitudes toward death, love, marriage, responsibility, and the like in every paragraph. I was, in addition, growing ever more uneasy about my relationship to the science fiction readership, and found myself wondering constantly whether one more Silverbergian exploration of the dark side of existence might not be asking too much. And I was mentally exhausted besides.

The weeks dragged by; I entered the second month of the project with more than half the story still to tell. (By way of comparison: *Dying Inside*, also a difficult thing to write and three times as long, took me just nine weeks.) And now it was the middle of May; I had begun the story in late March. But somehow, finally, I regained my stride in early June, and the closing scenes, grim as their content was, were much easier to write than those that had gone before. One night in early June I was at the movies — Marlon Brando's *Last Tango in Paris*, it was — when the closing paragraphs of the story began to form in my mind. I turned to my wife and asked her for the notebook she always carried, and began to scribble sentences in the dark during the final minutes of the film. The movie ended; the lights came on; the theater emptied; and there I sat, still writing. "Are you a movie critic?" an usher asked me. I shook my head and went on writing.

So the thing was done, and I knew that I had hooked me a big fish. The next day I typed out what I had written in the theater, and set about preparing a final draft for Ed Ferman, and on June 16, 1973 I sent it to him with a note that said, "Here It Is. I feel exhausted, drained, relieved, pleased, proud, etc. I hope the thing is worthy of all the sweat that went into it. What I'm going to do tomorrow is don my backpack and head for the Sierra for a week in the back country at 10,000 feet, a kind of rite of purification after all these months of crazy intense typing."

"I could not be more pleased with "Born With the Dead," Ferman replied four days later. (E-mail was mere science fiction in those days.) "It seems to me that it brings to a peak the kind of thing you've been doing with *Book of Skulls* and *Dying Inside*." (I had not noticed until that moment the string of death-images running through the titles of those three practically consecutive works of mine.) "I don't think there is a wrong move in this story, and it comes together beautifully in the ending, which I found perfect and quite moving."

RS c. 1970s.

The story appeared in the April 1974 *F&SF*, which was indeed the special Robert Silverberg issue, with an Ed Emshwiller portrait of me on the cover in my best long-haired 1970s psychedelic mode, and essays about me within by Barry Malzberg and Tom Clareson, along with a Silverberg bibliography in very small type (so it didn't fill half the issue). "Born With the Dead" went on to win the Nebula award in 1975 and the Locus award as well. In the Hugo voting, though, it finished second, an event which I seemed to confirm what I had already come to believe, that my current output was far removed from the needs and interests of the science fiction mass audience. But, Hugo or no, the story has, since then, been generally acclaimed as a classic. It has been reprinted in innumerable anthologies, translated into ten foreign languages, and optioned for motion picture production. I have rarely had so much difficulty writing a story as I had with this one; but the anguish and trauma that it cost me now lie three full decades behind me, and the story is still here, to my great delight as its creator and, I hope, to yours as reader. 2004

SCHWARTZ BETWEEN THE GALAXIES (1973)

In the two years since finishing *Dying Inside* in the fall of 1971, I wrote nothing but short stories and the novella "Born with the Dead." Despite the struggle that those stories, and "Born with the Dead" in particular had been, I allowed myself to take on commitments to write two more novels, which would eventually become *The Stochastic Man* and *Shadrach in the Furnace*. I also let two friends talk me into writing short stories for publications they were editing. But, even as I locked myself into these four projects, I felt an increasing certainty that I was going to give up writing science fiction once those jobs were done.

My own personal fatigue was only one factor in that decision. Another was my sense of having been on the losing side in a literary revolution. Among the many revolutions that went on in the era known as the Sixties (which actually ran from about 1967 to 1972) there was one in science fiction. A host of gifted new writers, both in England and the United States, brought all manner of advanced literary techniques to bear on the traditional matter of sf, producing stories that were more deeply indebted to Joyce, Kafka, Faulkner, Mann, and even e. e. cummings than they were to Heinlein, Asimov, and Clarke. This period of stylistic and structural innovation, which reached its highest pitch of activity between 1966 and 1969, was a heady, exciting time for science fiction writers, especially newer ones such as Thomas Disch, Samuel R. Delany, R. A. Lafferty, and Barry Malzberg, although some relatively well-established people like John Brunner, Harlan Ellison, and, yes, Robert Silverberg, joined in the fun. My stories grew more and more experimental in mode — you can see it beginning to happen in "Sundance" and "Good News from the Vatican" — and most of them were published, now, in anthologies of original stories rather than in the conventional sf magazines.

What was fun for the writers, though, turned out to be not so much fun for the majority of the readers, who quite reasonably complained that if they wanted to read Joyce and Kafka, they'd go and read Joyce and Kafka. They didn't want their sf to be Joycified and Kafkaized. So they stayed away from the new fiction in droves, and by 1972 the revolution was pretty much over. We were heading into the era of *Star Wars*, the trilogy craze, and the return of literarily conservative, action-based science fiction to the center of the stage.

One of the most powerful figures in the commercialization of science fiction at that time was the diminutive Judy-Lynn del Rey, a charming and ferociously determined woman whose private reading tastes inclined toward *Ulysses* but who knew, perhaps better than anyone else ever had, what the majority of sf readers wanted to buy. As a kind of side enterprise during her dynamic remaking of the field, she started a paperback anthology series called *Stellar*, and despite my recent identification with the experimental side of science fiction, asked me, in May 1973, to do a story for it.

Her stated policy was to bring back the good old kind of sf storytelling, as exemplified in the magazines of the 1950s, a golden age for readers like me. "I don't want mood pieces without plots," she warned. "I don't want vignettes; I don't want character sketches; and I don't want obvious extrapolations of current fads and newspaper stories. These yarns should have beginnings, middles, and ends. I want the writers to solve the problems they postulate...."

Since most of what I had been writing recently embodied most of the characteristics she thus decried, there was a certain incompatibility between Judy-Lynn's strongly voiced requirements and her equally strong insistence on having a Silverberg story for her first issue. And yet I had no real problem with her stated policy. My own tastes in sf had been formed largely in the early 1950s, when such writers as C. M. Kornbluth, Alfred Bester, James Blish, Theodore Sturgeon, and Fritz Leiber had been at the top of their form. I had always felt more comfortable with their kind of fiction than with the wilder stuff of fifteen years later; I thought myself rather a reactionary writer alongside people like Disch, Lafferty, Malzberg, or J. G. Ballard. And I thought "Schwartz Between the Galaxies," which I wrote in October 1973, was a reasonably conservative story, too — definitely a story of the 1970s but not particularly experimental in form or tone.

Judy-Lynn bought it — it would have been discourteous not to, after urging me so strenuously to write something for her — but she obviously felt let down, even betrayed. Here she was putting together her theme-setting first issue, and here I was still trying to write literature. To her surprise and chagrin, though, the story was extremely popular — one of the five contenders for the Hugo award the following year — and was fairly widely anthologized afterward. So I won the skirmish; but Judy-Lynn, bless her, won the war. Our little literary revolution ended in total rout, with the space sagas and fantasy trilogies that she published sweeping the more highbrow kind of science fiction into oblivion, and many of the literary-minded writers left science fiction, never to return.

I was among those who left, although, as you will note, I did come back: after a while. But it seemed certain to me as 1974 began that my days as a I science fiction writer were over forever. For one thing, the work had become terribly hard: my work-sheets indicate that "Schwartz Between the Galaxies" took me close to three weeks to write. In happier days I could have written a whole novel, and a good one, in that time. Then, too, despite that Hugo nomination, I felt that the readers were turning away from my work. I was still getting on the awards ballots as frequently as ever, but I wasn't winning anything. That seemed symptomatic. The readers no longer understood me, and I felt I understood them all too well.

So in late 1973 I wrote one more short story — "In the House of Double Minds" — because I had promised it to an editor, and then I swore a mighty oath that I would never write short sf again. In the spring of 1974 I wrote the first of my two promised novels, *The Stochastic Man*. About six months later I launched into the second one, *Shadrach in the Furnace*, and finished it in the spring of 1975 after a horrendous battle to get the words down on paper.

That was it. I had spent two decades as a science fiction writer, and had emerged out of my early hackwork to win a considerable reputation among connoisseurs, and now it was all over. I would never write again, I told myself. (And told anyone else who would listen, too.)

And I didn't. For a while, anyway.

2004

THE FAR SIDE OF THE BELL-SHAPED CURVE (1980)

After lying fallow for more than four years, my mind suddenly presented me with a novel that I could not refuse to write. And so I came out of my permanent and irrevocable retirement to produce *Lord Valentine's Castle*, which I completed in the spring of 1979.

Even after finishing that long and complicated novel, I had no desire to go back to short-story writing. Short-story writing is hard on the nerves: you have no room to make any real mistakes, by which I mean that every word has to count, every line of dialogue has to serve three or four simultaneous purposes, every scene has to sweep the story inexorably along toward the culminating moment of insight that is the classic short-story payoff. In a novel you can go off course for whole chapters at a time and no one will mind; you may even find yourself being praised for the wonderful breadth of your concept. But a short story with so much as half an irrelevant page is a sad, lame thing, and even the casual and uncritical reader is aware that something is wrong with it.

Having been through the tensions of short-story creation so many times over a twenty-year period, I resolved to excuse myself from further struggle with the form. In a collection of my stories published in 1978 I said, "I suppose I might someday write another short story, but it has been almost five years since the last and I see no sign that the impulse is coming over me."

I felt only relief, no regret, at giving up short stories. The short form was a challenge I felt no further need to meet. You needed a stunning idea, for one thing — the ideal science fiction short story, I think, should amaze and delight — and you had to develop it with cunning and craft, working at the edge of your nervous system every moment, polishing and repolishing to hide all those extraneous knees and elbows. Doing a good short story meant a week or two of tough work, bringing an immediate cash reward of about $250, and then maybe $100

RS with Samuel R. Delany,

Judging by the longish hair and goofy shirt, dating from 1971. — RS

Photo by Jay Kay Klein.

every year or two thereafter if you had written something that merited reprint-ing in anthologies. Though money isn't the most important factor in a writer's life (if it were, we'd all be writing the most debased junk possible), it is a consid-eration, especially when a good short story takes fifty or a hundred working hours, as mine were tending to take by 1973. At $2.50 an hour short stories hard-ly seemed worth the effort.

But then came a magazine called *Omni*.

It was printed on slick, shiny paper and its publishers understood a great deal about the techniques of promotion, and it started its life with a circulation about six times as great as any science fiction magazine had ever managed to achieve. After some comings and goings in the editorial chair, the job of fiction editor went to my old friend Ben Bova, who began to hint broadly that it would be a nice idea if I wrote a short story for him. He mentioned a sum of money. It was approximately as much as I had been paid for each of my novels prior to the year 1968. Though cash return, as I've just said, is not the most important factor in a writer's life, the amount of money Ben mentioned was at least capable of caus-ing me to rethink my antipathy to short-story writing.

By the time I was through rethinking, however, Bova had moved upstairs to become *Omni's* executive editor. The new fiction editor was another old friend of mine, the veteran science fiction writer Robert Sheckley, who also thought I ought to be writing stories for *Omni*. All through 1979 he and Bova sang their siren song to me, and in the first month of the new year I gave in. I phoned Sheckley and somewhat timidly told him I was willing to risk my nervous sys-tem on one more short story after all. "He's going to do it," I heard Sheckley call across the office to Bova. It was as though they had just talked Laurence Olivier into doing one more Hamlet. So much fuss over one short story!

But for me it was a big thing indeed: at that moment short-story writing seemed to me more difficult than writing novels, more difficult than learning Sanskrit, more difficult than winning the Olympic broad-jump. I had promised to write a story, though; and I sat down to try. Though in an earlier phase of my career I had thought nothing of turning out three or four short stories a week, it took me about five working days to get the opening page of this one written satisfactorily, and I assure you that that week was no fun at all. But then, magical-ly, the barriers dissolved, the words began to flow, and in a couple of days the rest of the story emerged. "Our Lady of the Sauropods," I called it, and when *Omni* published it in the September 1980 issue, the cover announced, "Robert Silverberg Returns!" I imagined the puzzled readers of *Omni*, who surely were unaware that it was seven years since I had deigned to write short stories, turn-ing to each other and saying, "Why, wherever has he been?"

Having done it once, I realized I could do it again. Bob Sheckley was ask-ing for more; and in the summer of 1980 an idea for a fairly complex time-trav-el story wandered into my head. Since time travel is one of my favorite science fiction themes, I set about immediately sketching it out.

It turned out to be the most ambitious story I had done in ten years or so, involving not only a very tricky plot but also a lot of historical and geographical research. (Sarajevo, where the story opens, would be all over the front pages of the newspapers a decade later, but this was 1980, remember, and the only thing anyone knew about the place then was that it was where the Austrian archduke

Franz Ferdinand was assassinated in 1914, touching off the First World War.)

So I worked hard and long, with much revising along the way (a big deal, in those pre-computer days), and on August 16, 1980, I mailed it to Sheckley with a note that said, "Somehow I finished the story despite such distractions as the death of my cat and a visit from my mother and a lot of other headaches, some of which I'll tell you about as we sit sobbing into our drinks at the Boston convention and some of which I hope to have forgotten by then."

Though I was now writing regularly again — this was my fourth short story in eight months — I had not yet returned to full creative confidence, and, though I thought "Bell-Shaped Curve" was a fine story, I wasn't completely sure that Sheckley would agree. When we met two weeks later in Boston for that year's World Science Fiction Convention, though, he told me at once that he was going to publish it. But he hoped I'd take a second look at it and clean up some logical flaws.

"Sure," I said. "Just give me a list of them."

But Bob Sheckley, sweet man that he is, was not that sort of editor. He didn't have any list of the story's logical flaws — he simply felt sure there must be some. I was on my own. So after the Boston trip I went back to the story, giving it a very rigorous reading indeed, and, sure enough, there were places where the time-travel logic didn't make sense. That came as no surprise to me, because time-travel logic never does make sense, but I did see some ways of concealing, if not removing, the illogicalities. I revised the story and sent it back to him in late September, telling him this in my accompanying letter:

"I have reworked 'Bell-Shaped Curve' to handle most of the obvious problems, without pretending that I have made time travel into anything as plausible as the internal combustion engine. Aside from a bunch of tiny cosmetic changes, the main revision has been to eliminate the discussion between Reichenbach and Ilsabet about being wary of duplication; they now speak in much more general terms of paradox problems. But in fact they don't understand any more about time travel than I do about what's under the hood of my car....

"And remember that a story that may contain logical flaws is a story that will give the readers something to exercise their wits about. That will be pleasing to them. If they can come away from the issue feeling mentally superior to Robert Silverberg and the entire editorial staff of *Omni*, haven't they thereby had their two dollars' worth of gratification?"

Omni published the story in 1981. It's been reprinted in a lot of anthologies since then. And you all know what eventually happened to Sarajevo.

2004

NEEDLE IN A TIMESTACK (1982)

I was back in the swing of things, now, after getting my "retirement" out of my system, and although I still had no plans for undertaking any novels, short stories were emanating from me all through 1981 with a swiftness that I had not experienced in a decade and a half. I had begun to do the cycle of tales that would be collected in the book called *Majipoor Chronicles*; I sold more stories to *Omni*, and to other such high-paying magazines as *Playboy* and *Penthouse*.

The *Playboy* relationship was particularly stimulating. *Playboy's* fiction editor, Alice K. Turner, was bright, irreverent, funny, and as knowledgeable about the craft of the short story as any editor I've ever known. Over the course of nearly two decades she bought perhaps fifteen stories from me, and just about every one involved a battle royal down to the last semicolon — a series of good-humored author/editor confrontations from which both of us drew tremendous pleasure. (Most of the time I ultimately came to see the wisdom and logic of her objections to a story. Her big secret was that she knew when to let me win in cases where I didn't.)

Alice accepted a story from me ("Gianni") in February of 1981 and another ("The Conglomeroid Cocktail Party") in October of that year. Since she could publish only one story a month and every writer in America was sending her material, that should have been enough out of me for a while. But I was on a roll, writing with an ease and freedom I had not known since the prolific days of 1967, and when another *Playboy*-quality story idea came to me in January 1982, I sent it to her unhesitatingly.

I had heard Bill Rotsler, a friend of mine, say to a young man who was bothering him at a science fiction convention, "Go away, kid, or I'll change your future." Upon hearing that I said, "No, tell him that you'll change his PAST," and suddenly I realized that I had handed myself a very nice story idea. I wrote it in Januar, 1982 — its intricate time-travel plot unfolded for me with marvelous clarity as I worked — and Alice Turner bought it immediately for *Playboy's* July 1983 issue.

A few years ago a major American movie company bought it also. They gave me quite a lot of money, which was very pleasant, but so far they haven't done anything about actually making the movie. I hope they do, sooner or later. It's one science fiction movie I'd actually like to see.

I played a nasty trick on bibliographers with this one, incidentally. In 1966 Ballantine Books published a short-story collection of mine called *Needle in a Timestack* — a delicious title dreamed up by Betty Ballantine, my editor there (and one of the two owners of the company.) In the fullness of time the book went out of print, and when I sold it to a British publisher in 1979 I dropped all but four of the original group of stories and replaced them with others, to avoid duplicating a different British collection of my stories. So there were two books of mine with the same name, one American, one British, made up of substantially different groups of stories!

Neither book, of course, contained the story called "Needle in a Timestack," because as of 1979 I hadn't written it yet. Three years later, though, when I wrote the story, "Needle in a Timestack" seemed a perfectly fitting title for it, and I reached for it unhesitatingly, only too aware of the havoc I was creating for scholars of my work.

The final twist came a few years later, when the British *Needle in a Timestack*, almost entirely different in contents from the original American one, was published in the United States. I suppose it might have seemed logical to add the *Playboy* story to the group, thus uniting story title and book title for the first time, but I didn't, because I had already collected it in a different book, 1984's *The Conglomeroid Cocktail Party*.

NEW WORLDS SCIENCE FICTION, *May 1960, (UK) with "Ozymandias" by RS.*

2004

RS holding Nebula Award for "Sailing To Byzantium," 1986. Photo by Jay Kay Klein.

SAILING TO BYZANTIUM (1984)

It was the spring of 1984. I was back on track as a writer after the self-inflicted derailment of a decade earlier. I had just completed my historical fantasy novel *Gilgamesh the King*, set in ancient Sumer, and antiquity was very much on my mind when Shawna McCarthy, who had just begun her brief and brilliant career as editor of *Isaac Asimov's Science Fiction Magazine*, came to the San Francisco area, where I live, on holiday. I ran into her at a party and she asked me if I'd write a story for her. "I'd like to, yes." And, since the novella is my favorite form, I added, "a long one."

"How long?" "Long," I told her. "A novella."

"Good," she said. We did a little haggling over the price, and that was that. She went back to New York and I got going on "Sailing to Byzantium" and by late summer it was done.

It wasn't originally going to be called "Sailing to Byzantium." The used manila envelope on which I had jotted the kernel of the idea out of which "Sailing to Byzantium" grew — I always jot down my story ideas on the backs of old envelopes — bears the title, "The Hundred-Gated City." That's a reference to ancient Thebes, in Egypt, and this was my original note:

"Ancient Egypt has been recreated at the end of time, along with various other highlights of history — a sort of Disneyland. A twentieth century man, through error, has been regenerated in Thebes, though he belongs in the replica of Los Angeles. The misplaced Egyptian has been sent to Troy, or maybe Knossos, and a Cretan has been displaced into a Brasilia-equivalent of the twenty-ninth century. They move about, attempting to return to their proper places."

It's a nice idea, but it's not quite the story I ultimately wrote, perhaps because I decided that it might turn out to be nothing more than an updating of Murray Leinster's classic novella "Sidewise in Time," a story that was first published before I was born but which is still well remembered in certain quarters. I *did* use the "Hundred-Gated" tag in an entirely different story many years later — "Thebes of the Hundred Gates." (I'm thrifty with titles as well as old envelopes.) But what emerged in the summer of 1984 is a story, which quickly acquired the title it now bears as I came to understand the direction my original idea had begun to take.

From the earliest pages I knew I was on to something special, and "Sailing to Byzantium" remains one of my favorite stories, out of all the millions and millions of words of science fiction I've published in the past fifty years. Shawna had one or two small editorial suggestions for clarifying the ending, which I accepted gladly, and a friend, Shay Barsabe, who read the story in manuscript, pointed out one subtle logical blunder in the plot that I hastily corrected; but otherwise the story came forth virtually in its final form as I wrote it.

It was published first as an elegant limited-edition book, now very hard to find, by the house of Underwood-Miller, and soon afterward it appeared in *Asimov's* for February 1985. It met with immediate acclaim, and that year it was chosen with wonderful editorial unanimity for all three of the best-science fiction-of-the-year anthologies, those edited by Donald A. Wollheim, Terry Carr, and Gardner Dozois. "A possible classic," is what Wollheim called it, praise that gave me great delight, because the crusty, sardonic Wollheim had been reading science fiction almost since the stuff was invented, and he was not one to throw such words around lightly. "Sailing to Byzantium" won me a Nebula award in 1986, and was nominated for a Hugo, but finished in second place, losing by four votes out of 800. Since then the story has been reprinted many times and translated into a dozen languages or more. Whenever I have one of those bleak four-in-the-morning moments when I ask myself whether I actually did ever accomplish anything worthwhile as a science fiction writer, "Sailng to Byzantium" is one of the first pieces of evidence I offer myself to prove that I did.

2004

ENTER A SOLDIER.
LATER: ENTER ANOTHER (1987)

A curious phenomenon of American science fiction publishing in the late 1980s, one which will probably not be dealt with in a kindly way by future historians of the field, was the" shared world" anthology. I use the past tense for it because the notion of assembling a group of writers to produce stories set in a common background defined by someone else has largely gone out of fashion today. But for a time in 1987 and thereabouts it began to seem as though everything in science fiction was becoming part of some shared world project.

I will concede that some excellent fiction came out of the various shared world enterprises, as well as a mountain of junk. The idea itself was far from new in the 1980s; it goes back at least to 1952 and *The Petrified Planet*, a book in which the scientist John D. Clark devised specifications for an unusual planet and the writers Fletcher Pratt, H. Beam Piper, and Judith Merril produced superb novellas set on that world. Several similar books followed in the next few years.

In the late 1960s I revived the idea with a book called *Three for Tomorrow* — fiction by James Blish, Roger Zelazny, and myself, based on a theme proposed by Arthur C. Clarke — and I did three or four others later on. In 1975 came Harlan Ellison's *Medea*, an elaborate and brilliantly conceived colossus of a book that made use of the talents of Frank Herbert, Theodore Sturgeon, Frederik Pohl, and a whole galaxy of other writers of that stature. But the real deluge of shared-world projects began a few years afterward, in the wake of the vast commercial

RS at Brian Aldiss' home in the U.K., taken after the Brighton Worldcon in 1987.

success of Robert Asprin's fantasy series, *Thieves' World*. Suddenly, every publisher in the business wanted to duplicate the *Thieves' World* bonanza, and from all sides appeared platoons of hastily conceived imitators.

I dabbled in a couple of these books myself — a story that I wrote for one of them won a Hugo, in fact — but my enthusiasm for the shared-world whirl cooled quickly once I perceived how shapeless and incoherent most of the books were. The writers tended not to pay much attention to the specifications, and simply went off in their own directions; the editors, generally, were too lazy or too cynical or simply too incompetent to do anything about it; and the books became formless jumbles of incompatible work.

Before I became fully aware of that, though, I let myself be seduced into editing one shared-world series myself. The initiator of this was Jim Baen, the publisher of Baen Books, whose idea centered around pitting computer-generated simulacra of historical figures against each other in intellectual conflict. That appealed to me considerably, and I agreed to work out the concept in detail and serve as the series' general editor.

I produced an elaborate prospectus outlining the historical background of the near-future world in which these simulacra would hold forth; I rounded up a group of capable writers; and to ensure that the book would unfold with consistency to my underlying vision, I wrote the first story myself in October of 1987, a 15,000-word opus for which I chose Socrates and Francisco Pizarro as my protagonists.

The whole thing was, I have to admit, a matter of commerce rather than art: just a job of work, to fill somebody's current publishing need. But a writer's intention and the ultimate result of his work don't bear any necessary relationship. In this case I was surprised and delighted to find the story taking on unanticipated life as I wrote, and what might have been a routine job of word-spinning turned out, unexpectedly, to be rather more than that when I was done with it.

Gardner Dozois published it in *Isaac Asimov's Science Fiction Magazine*, and then I used it as the lead story in the shared-world anthology, Time Gate. Dozois picked it for his 1989 *Year's Best Science Fiction Collection*, and in 1990 it was a finalist on both the Nebula and Hugo ballots — one of my most widely liked stories in a long time. The Nebula eluded me, but at the World Science Fiction Convention in Holland in August 1990, "Enter a Soldier" brought me a Hugo award, my fourth, as the year's best novelet.

Even so, I decided soon after to avoid further involvement in the shared world milieu, and have done no work of that sort in many years. Perhaps it was always unrealistic to think that any team of gifted, independent-minded writers could produce what is in essence a successful collaborative novel that has been designed by someone else. But my brief sojourn as editor of *Time Gate* did, at least, produce a story that I now see was one of the major achievements of my career.

2004

(opposite)
INFINITE JESTS, *edited by RS; published by Chilton; 1974.*

DEATH DO US PART (1994)

Though most of the 1980s and 1990s my writing rhythm involved beginning a novel when the California rainy season starts in November, finishing it about March, and following it with several short stories before the coming of summer called a halt to all work during the dry, sunny months that commence here in April. If the novel ran long, short-story production got shorter shrift: some years none got written at all.

My book for 1993-94 was the relatively short novel *The Mountains of Majipoor*, which I finished so early in the rainy season that there was time to do several shorter pieces afterward, before shutting the fiction factory down for its traditional summer recess. So I wrote this one in February 1994, tacking a couple of new twists on the old notion of the quasi-immortal who falls in love with someone of normal lifespan, and thereby once again coming to grips with some virtually obsessive themes of my fiction.

Ellen Datlow bought it for *Omni*, but it never saw print there, because *Omni*, once so successful, had run into hard times and was beginning a Cheshire-Cat routine of vanishing into the mysterious online world of the Internet. The idea was to distribute both a conventional print version of *Omni* and an online version, but the printed magazine gradually disappeared, leaving only the electronic edition. Though I have, like almost everyone else, become a daily user of the Internet, I still have not come to feel comfortable about reading fiction on a computer, and I tend to believe that anything published on the Internet might just as well have been published on Mars, at least so far as I'm concerned. The online version of *Omni* did indeed make the story available to its cyberspace following, finally, in December of 1996, and technically that's its first publication. But to my outmoded way of thinking "Death Do Us Part" made its publishing debut in the August, 1997 issue of *Asimov's Science Fiction*, an actual paper-and ink operation. As a concession to the realities of the twenty-first century, I've given the *Omni* use of the story priority in the copyright acknowledgments at the back of books reprinting it, though.

2004

THREE: AUTOBIOGRAPHY

SOUNDING BRASS, TINKLING CYMBAL

> *…and even Silverberg, who some-*
> *times, with all his skill and knowl-*
> *edge and sophistication, does tend to*
> *the androidal. …."*

— John Clute in *New Worlds 5*

Though I speak with the tongues of men and of angels, and have not charity, I am becomes as sounding brass, or a tinkling cymbal.

And though I have the gift of prophecy, and understand all mysteries, and all knowledge; and though I have all faith, so that I could remove mountains, and have not charity, I am nothing.

— I Corinthians, 13: 1-3

At last to speak of one's self. An odd temptation, which mostly I have resisted, in the past, maintaining that I'm not yet ready to undertake a summing up, or that I'm in the midst of some intricate new transition still not fully understood, or that I'm bored with myself and talking about myself. Yet I have granted all sorts of interviews, and spoken quite explicitly, all the while protesting my love of privacy; the one thing I've never attempted is explicit written autobiography. I manage to hold all poses at once, modest and exhibitionistic, esthete and man of commerce, puritan and libertine: probably the truth is that I have no consistent positions at all. We'll see.

Autobiography. Apparently one should not name the names of those one has been to bed with, or give explicit figures on the amount of money one has earned, those being the two data most eagerly sought by readers; all the rest is legitimate to reveal. Very well. The essential starting point, for me, is the confession (and boast) that I am a man who is living his own adolescent fantasies. When I was sixteen or so I yearned to win fame as a writer of science fiction, to become wealthy enough to indulge in whatever amusements I chose, to know the love of fair women, to travel widely, to live free from the pressures and perils of ordinary life. All these things have come to me, and more; I have fewer complaints to make about the hand destiny has dealt me than anyone I know. Here at what I assume is my midpoint I feel a certain inner security, a self-satisfaction, which I suppose borders occasionally on smugness. (But not on complacency. The past is unchangeable and the present delightful, yet the future still must be regarded warily. I live in California, a land where the earth might literally open beneath my feet this afternoon; and I've already once had, in my pre-California incarnation, the experience of awakening before dawn to find my world in flames.)

Because my life has been so generally satisfactory, and because I'm a literary enough man to know the dangers of *hubris*, I sometimes affect a kind of self-deprecatory shyness, a who-*me?* kind of attitude, whenever I am singled out for special attention. This pose gets more and more difficult to maintain as the years go on and the accomplishments and money and awards pile up; by now certain objective measures of achievement exist, for me, and there's an element of hypocrisy in trying to deny them purely for the sake of trying to avoid the fate that chops down

(opposite)
Silverberg 1970s portrait
by Jay Kay Klein.

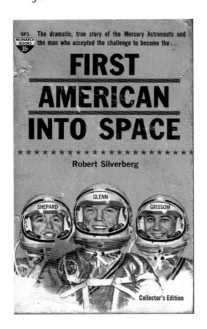

FIRST AMERICAN INTO SPACE *(Monarch Books paperback, 1961).*

the boastful. Ten years ago, or even five, I probably would have refused the opportunity to contribute to this book, claiming that I was unworthy (and privately fearing that others would say so if I did not). To hell with that now.

I am the youngest of the six contributors here [Alfred Bester, Harry Harrison, Damon Knight, Frederick Pohl, and Brian Aldiss]: the youngest by nearly a decade, I suspect, since as I write this I'm still more than a year short of my fortieth birthday, and my companions, I know, all cluster around the half-century mark. A familiar feeling, that one. I was always the youngest in any group, owlishly precocious, a nastily bright little boy who was reading at three, writing little stories at six, spouting learned stuff about European dynasties and the sexual habits of plants at seven or eight, publishing illegible magazines at thirteen, and selling novels at eighteen. I was too unruly and too clever to remain in the same class at school with my contemporaries, so I grew up two years younger than all my friends, thinking of myself as small and weak and incomplete. Eventually, by surviving, I caught up with everyone. I am the oldest in my immediate circle of friends, with a beard alas now tinged with grey, and I am as tall as most and taller than many, and within the tiny world of science fiction I have become something of an elder statesman, and the wounds I received by being fourteen years old in a universe of sixteen-year-olds are so well sheathed in scar-tissue now that I might as well consider them healed. And yet it still is strange to be included as an equal in this particular group of writers, since three of them — Alfred Bester, Damon Knight, Frederik Pohl — were among my own literary idols when I was indulging in those adolescent fantasies of a writer's career twenty-odd years ago. A fourth, Harry Harrison, had not yet begun writing seriously then himself, but he was the editor who first paid me for writing anything, in 1953; and only Brian Aldiss, the originator of this collection of autobiographical essays, played no part in shaping me in my teens, for I had never heard his name until I myself was an established writer. Yet I make no apologies for being here among my elders. Here we all are: professional writers, diligent craftsmen, successful creators — artists, if you will. And good friends as well.

I am an only child, born halfway through the Great Depression. (There would have been a sibling, I think, when I was about seven, but it miscarried; I often wonder what pattern my life would have taken had I not grown up alone, pampered, self-indulgent.) My ancestors were Jews from Eastern Europe, and my grandparents, three of whom survived well into my adulthood, were reared in Poland or Russia in villages beyond my easy comprehension. My father was born in London in the first year of the 20th Century, and came to the United States a few years thereafter. My mother was born in Brooklyn, New York, and so was I.

I have no very fond recollections of my childhood. I was puny, sickly, plagued with allergies and freckles, and (I thought) quite ugly. I was too clever by at least half, which made for troubles with my playmates. My parents were remote figures; my father was a certified public accountant, spending his days and many of his evenings adding up endless columns of red figures on long yellow sheets, and my mother taught school, so that I was raised mainly by Lottie, our mulatto housekeeper, and by my loving and amiable maternal grandmother. It was a painful time, lonely and embittering; I did make friends but, growing up in isolation and learning none of the social graces, I usually managed to alienate them quickly, striking at them with my sharp tongue if not my feeble fists. On the other hand, there were compensations: intelligence is prized in Jewish households, and my parents saw to it that mine was permitted to develop freely. I was taken to museums, given all the books I wanted, and allowed money for my hobbies. I took refuge from loneliness in these things; I collected stamps and coins, harpooned hapless butterflies and grasshoppers, raided the neighbors' gardens for specimens of leaves and flowers, stayed up late secretly reading, hammered out crude stories on an ancient typewriter, all with my father's strong encouragement, and it mattered less and less that I was a troubled misfit in the classroom if I could come home to my large private room in the afternoon and, quickly zipping through the too-easy homework, get down to the serious business of the current obsessional hobby.

Children who find the world about them distasteful turn readily to the distant and the alien. The lure of the exotic seized me early. These were the years of World War II and real travel was impossible, but in 1944 a friend of my father's gave me a subscription to the *National Geographic Magazine*, and I was off to Zanzibar and Surinam and Jamaica in my imagination decades before I ever reached those places in actuality. (Typically, I began buying old *National Geographics* with lunatic persistence, and didn't rest until I had them all, from the 1880s on. I still have them.) Then, an hour's journey from home on the subway, there was the American Museum of Natural History, with its mummies and arrowheads, its mastodons and glyptodons, above all its brontosaurs and tyrannosaurs; Sunday after Sunday my father and I made the pilgrimage, and I reveled in the wonders of prehistory, soberly lecturing him on the relative chronological positions of Neanderthal and Peking and Piltdown Man. (Yes, Piltdown, this was 1944, remember.) From dinosaurs and other such fantastic fossils to science fiction was but a short journey: the romantic, exotic distant past is closely tied to the romantic, exotic distant future in my imagination.

So there was Jules Verne when I was nine — I must have taken that voyage with Captain Nemo a hundred times — and H. G. Wells when I was ten, most notably *The Time Machine* (which promised to show me all the incredible eons I would never live to know) but also *The Island of Dr. Moreau* and *War of the Worlds*, the myriad short stories, and even an obscure satire called *Mr. Blettsworthy on Rumpole Island*, to which I often returned because Mr. Blettsworthy encountered living ground-sloths. There was Twain's *Connecticut Yankee in King Arthur's Court*, which also I read repeatedly. (How early my fascination with time travel emerged!) I dabbled in comic books, too, and I have gaudy memories of Buck Rogers and *Planet Comics*. But somehow I missed Edgar Rice Burroughs altogether; and it was not until early 1948, when I was already a veteran of scores of hardbound science fiction books, that I even knew such things as science fiction magazines existed.

The magazines mostly repelled me by their covers and their titles. I did buy *Weird Tales* — my first one had an Edmond Hamilton novelet about the Norse gods, which delighted me since I had gone through whole libraries of Norse mythology in early boyhood. I bought *Amazing Stories*, then the sleaziest representative of the genre, because it happened to publish an uncharacteristically respectable-looking issue about then. I bought John Campbell's dignified little *Astounding Science Fiction*, but found the stories opaque and unrewarding to my thirteen-year-old mind. Because I was rather a snob, I would not even open magazines with names like *Thrilling Wonder Stories* and *Famous Fantastic Mysteries* and *Startling Stories*, especially since their covers were bright with paintings of hideous monsters and scantily clad damsels. (Sex was very frightening to me just then, and I had sworn never to have anything to do with women.) More than a year passed before I approached those magazines in what was by then an unquenchable thirst for science fiction, and discovered they were publishing some of the best material of the day.

Then there were the books: the wondrous Healy-McComas *Adventures in Time and Space*, the big Groff Conklin titles, Wollheim's *Pocket Book of Science Fiction*, and the other pioneering anthologies. My father was more than a little baffled by my increasing obsession with all this trash, when previously I occupied myself with decent books on botany and geology and astronomy, but he saw to it that I bought whatever I wanted. One collection in particular had enormous impact on me: Wollheim's *Portable Novels of Science*, published in 1945 and discovered by me three years later. It contained Wells' *First Men in the Moon*, which amused me; Taine's *Before the Dawn*, which fed my always passionate interest in dinosaurs; Lovecraft's *Shadow Out of Time*, which gave me that peep into unattainable futures that originally led me to science fiction; and above all Stapledon's *Odd John*, which spoke personally to me as I suppose it must to any child who is too bright for his own good. I was up almost till dawn reading that book, and those novels marked me.

I was at that time still talking of some sort of career in the sciences, perhaps in botany, perhaps in paleontology, perhaps astronomy. But some flaws in my intelligence were making themselves apparent, to me and to my teachers if not to my parents: I had a superb memory and a quick wit, but I lacked depth, originality, and consistency; my mind was like a hummingbird, darting erratically over surfaces. I wanted to encompass too much, and mastered nothing, and though I always got high marks in any subject that caught my interest, I noticed, by the time I was thirteen, that some of my classmates were better than I at grasping fundamental principles and drawing new conclusions from them. I doubt that I would have been of much value as a scientist. But already I was writing, and writing with precocious skill — for school newspapers and magazines, for my own abominably mimeographed magazine, and, without success, for professional science fiction magazines. Off went stories, double-spaced, and bearing accurate word-counts (612; 1814; 2,705). They were dreadful, naturally, and they came back, usually with printed rejection slips but sometimes — when the editors realized they were dealing with a bright child of thirteen or fourteen and not with a demented adult — with gentle letters suggesting ways I might improve my style or my sense of plot. And I spoke openly of a career in writing, perhaps earning my living as a journalist while writing science fiction as a sideline.

Why science fiction? Because it was science fiction that I preferred to read, though I had been through Cervantes and Shakespeare and that crowd too. And because writing science fiction allowed me to give free play to those fantasies of space and time and dinosaurs and supermen that were so gratifying to me. And because I had stumbled into the world of science fiction fandom, a world much more comfortable than the real world of bullies and athletes and sex, and I knew that my name on the contents page of *Astounding* or *Startling* would win me much prestige in fandom, prestige that I could hardly hope to gain among my classmates.

So, then, the stories went forth, awkward imitations on a miniature scale of my favorite moments out of Lovecraft or Stapledon or Taine or Wells, and the stories came back, and I read textbooks on the narrative art and learned a good deal, and began also to read the stories in the science fiction magazines with a close analytical eye, measuring the ratio of dialogue to exposition, the length of paragraphs, and other technical matters that, I suppose, few fifteen-year-olds study as carefully as I did. Nothing got published, or even came close, but I was growing in skill.

I was growing in other ways, too. When I was about fourteen I went off, for the first time, to summer camp, where I lived among boys (and girls) of my own age and no longer had to contend with being the youngest and puniest in my peer-group. I had always been known as "Robert," but at camp I was speedily dubbed "Bob," and it seemed to me that I was taking on a new identify. *Robert* was the spindly misfit, that maladjusted, isolated little boy; *Bob* was a healthy, outgoing, normal young man. To this day I wince when some stranger presumes on my public persona and addresses me as Robert — it sends me rocketing backward in time to the horrors of being ten again. Although I sign my stories *Robert* for reasons of formality, my friends know me as *Bob*, and my parents managed the transition fairly gracefully at my request (although my father sometimes slips, a quarter of a century after the change), and when I occasionally encounter some childhood friend I let him know, rapidly, the name I prefer and the reason I prefer it.

This new Bob was able to cope. He grew to a reasonable height, halting just a bit short of six feet; he became a passable athlete; he discovered how to sustain friendships and how to manage conversations. For a few years I led a split life, introverted and lonely and secretive at home, open and lighthearted and confident during the summers; and by the time I was about seventeen, some integration of the two lives had begun. I had finished high school (where I had become editor of the high-school newspaper and was respected for my skill as a writer) and, by way of surrendering some of my precocity, had declined to go immediately into college. Instead I spent a few months reading and writing, and a few months working in a furniture warehouse on the Brooklyn waterfront, among rough, tough illiterates who found my cultivated manner a charming novelty rather than a threatening intrusion, and then I went off to the summer camp, not as a camper but as an employee. In the autumn I entered Columbia University with old slates wiped clean: I was no longer morbidly too young. I was free of the local playmates who could never forget the maladjustments of my childhood, I was able to begin in the *Bob* persona, without hauling the burden of my past problems.

I lived away from home, in a little apartment of my own. I manifested previously unknown skills for drinking and carousing. I discovered that women were not really very frightening after all. I plunged myself into new worlds of the mind: into Aquinas and Plato, into Bartok and Schoenberg, into Kafka, Joyce,

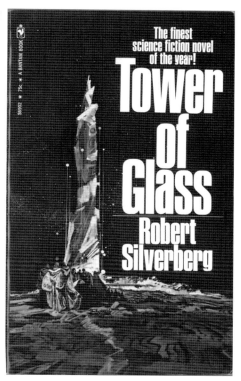

TOWER OF GLASS
Bantam Books, Inc., NY;
1971 paperback edition.

Mann, Faulkner, Sartre. I continued to read science fiction, but dispassionately, with the eye of one who was soon to be a professional; I was less interested in visions of ultimate tomorrows and more in seeing how Messrs Bester, Pohl, Knight, Sheckley, Dick etc. , carried off their tricks. One of my stories was published — for a fee of $5, I think — by an amateur magazine called *Different*, operated by a poetess named Lilith Lorraine. Harry Harrison asked me to do an article about fandom for a science fiction magazine he was editing, and I turned in a competent journalistic job and was paid $30. That was in September 1953. I sent a short story called "Gorgon Planet" off to a magazine called *Nebula*, published in Scotland by Peter Hamilton, and in January 1954 he notified me that he would use it, and sent me his check for $12. 60.

That same month I sold a novel to a major American publisher. The earlier sales could be brushed aside as inconsequential — two weak short stories accepted by obscure magazines, and one specimen of mere journalism — but the novel was something else. I was not yet nineteen years old, and I was a professional writer. I had crossed the threshold.

That novel! Its genesis went back almost three years. When I was editor of my high-school newspaper in 1951 a book appeared for review, a science fiction novel for boys, published by the Thomas Y. Crowell Company, an old-line New York firm. Steeped as I was in Wells and Heinlein and Stapledon and such, I reviewed this clumsy, naïve book scornfully, demolishing it so effectively that in the summer of 1953 the publishing company invited me to examine and criticize, prior to publication, the latest manuscript by that author. I read it and demolished it too, with such thoroughness that the book was never published. This time the Crowell editor asked me to the office and said, in effect, "If you know so much about science fiction, why don't you try a novel for us yourself?" I accepted the challenge.

I had attempted a novel once before, at the age of thirteen. It began as two short stories, but I subsequently combined them, elaborated, padded most shamefully, and ended up with an inch-thick manuscript that must have been one of the least coherent hodgepodges ever committed to paper. The outline of the book I suggested to Crowell in September 1953 was better, but not much. It concerned the trip of four young space cadets to Alpha Centauri on a sort of training cruise. No plot, not much action. The cadets are chosen, leave for space, stop at Mars and Pluto, reach Alpha Centauri, become vaguely entangled in a revolution going on there, become disentangled and go home. Some novel.

Every weekend that autumn I wrote two or three chapters, working swiftly despite the pressures of college. When eight chapters were done I submitted them and received an encouraging note urging me to complete the book. It was done by mid-November: nineteen chapters, 145 pages of typescript. I sent it in, heard nothing for two months, and on a Sunday in January 1954, received a stunning telephone call from the Crowell editor: they were sending me a contract for my novel. Of course, some changes would be required before it could be published.

In March I was sent a severe four-page letter of analysis. Anticlimax after anticlimax, they said; first part of book fine, last half terrible. Though immensely discouraged, I set to work rewriting, trying to build complications and a resolution into my rudimentary story. On June 5 this revision came back to me: I had

(opposite)
I have always kept a ledger, entering each sale as it was made and noting down the amount I was paid, the number of words, the date and place of publication. (Some pages of that ledger were damaged in my 1968 fire and are too faint now for me to read.) Until some time in the 1970s I also assigned a number to each individual item, not numbering any reprint of that item. "Warm Man" got number 175. The numbering ran up into the 1,100s and then I wondered why I was bothering to do it and stopped. I still keep the ledger, though.

Here's a ledger page from 1956. I was still in college when I was writing and selling all this stuff — my final semester, January-June 1956. The pay seems low (my earnings for Feb. 1956 were $460.80 after commissions, and April was $779), but the 1956 dollar was worth at least ten times as much as today's, maybe more, and $4,600 a month, let alone $7,790, is still pretty good going for a college senior's part-time job, I think.— RS

Date Accep.	Date Paid	Title	Publisher	Words	Pay	Comm.	Net	Cum. Wordage	Published	
1/56	1/56	Man of Many Bodies	Ziff-Davis	6000	60.00	6.00	54.00	2122200	Fantastic Dec 56	✓
1/56	1/56	False Prophet	ASF	16000	240.00	24.00	216.00	2282200	ASF 12/56	✓
1/56	10/56	Walkdown	Lowndes	3000	30.00	3.00	27.00	2312200	Western Action 4/56	✓
1/56	8/56	O Captain My Captain	Z-D	3500	35.00	3.50	31.50	2347000	Fan 8/56	✓
1/56	9/56	Soccer to the Ocean Travelers	Larry Shaw	13500	67.50	6.75	60.75	2482000	SFA 12/56	✓
1/56	11/56	The Guest Rites	Larry Shaw	3300	45.00	4.50	40.50	2515000	Infinity 2/57	✓
1/56	1/56	A World of His Own	Z-D	6000	60.00	6.00	54.00	2575000	Amz 12/56	✓
1/56	8/56	Bat-Shy	Lowndes	6000	45.00	4.50	40.50	2635000	10-Story Sports 7/56	✓
1/56	1/56	Run of Luck	Z-D	3000	30.00	3.00	27.00	2665000	Amz 7/56	✓
1/56		9		60300	612.50	61.25	551.25			✓
2/56	2/56	Guardian of the Crystal Gate	Z-D	11500	115.00	11.50	103.50	2780000	Fan 8/56	✓
2/56	7/56	The Lonely One	Lowndes	6500	51.00	5.10	45.90	2845000	SFS 7/56	✓
2/56	2/56	Stay Out of My Grave	Z-D	5000	50.00	5.00	45.00	2895000	Amz 7/56	✓
2/56	8/56	The Final Challenge	Infinity	6000	60.00	6.00	54.00	2955000	Inf 8/56	✓
2/56	2/56	Choke Chain	Z-D	8000	80.00	8.00	72.00	3035000	Fan 12/56	✓
2/56	2/56	A Mind for Business	ASF	5200	156.00	15.60	140.40	3087000	ASF 9/56	✓
2/56		6		42200	512.00	51.20	460.80			✓
3/56	4/56	The Macauley Circuit	Fant. Univ.	4000	40.00	4.00	36.00	3127000	FU 8/56	✓
3/56	3/56	Revolt of the Synthetics	Z-D	5000	50.00	45.00	45.00	3177000	Fan 8/56	✓
3/56	3/56	Look Homeward Spaceman	Z-D	5000	50.00	5.00	45.00	3227000	Amz 8/56	✓
3/56	4/56	Clifford Odets	Exposed	2100	125.00	12.50	112.50	3248000	Exposed #9 9/56	✓
3/56	4/56	Bitter Homecoming	Z-D	7700	77.00	7.70	69.30	3325000	Amz 12/57	✓
3/56	4/56	The Rivals	Z-D	4300	43.00	4.30	38.70	3368000	Amz 4/56	✓
3/56	4/56	Yachting	Z-D	1500	15.00	—	15.00	3383000		✓
3/56		7		34600	400.00	36.50	363.50			✓
4/56	7/56	Songs of Summer	Lowndes	6200	48.00	4.80	43.20	3445000	SF Stories 9/56	✓
4/56	4/56	The Psychiatry Boom	Exposed	2100	125.00	12.50	117.50	3466000	Exposed #8 9/58	✓
4/56	4/56	Vault of the Ages	Z-D	3000	30.00	3.00	27.50	3496000	Amz 8/56	✓
4/56	10/56	Stretch Drive	Lowndes	12000	70.00	7.00	63.00	3616000	10-Story Sports 10/56	✓
4/56	4/56	Middle-Aged Rookie	Z-D	7500	75.00	7.50	67.50	3691000	Fantastic 5/59	✓
4/56	4/56	Sourdough	ASF	4500	135.00	13.50	121.50	3736000	ASF 11/56	✓
4/56	4/56	The Hunted Heroes	Z-D	5000	35.00	5.00	30.00	3786000	Amz 9/56	✓
4/56	4/56	Deus Ex Machina	Lowndes	12000	60.00	6.00	54.00	3906000	SFQ 11/56	✓
4/56	4/56	Royalties	Crowell	—	16.70	—	16.70			✓
4/56	4/56	Sound Decision	ASF	15500	271.25	27.12	244.13	4061000	ASF 10/56	✓
4/56		9		68800	865.95	86.42	779.53			✓

Jim Warren, Forry Ackerman, and RS at the 1963 Discon in Washington, D.C. Photo by Jay Kay Klein.

allowed my main protagonist to achieve his goal by default rather than by positive action, and the publishers wouldn't let me get away with that. I promised to spend the summer considering ways to restructure the book; meanwhile Crowell would consult an outside reader for suggestions and evaluations.

The summer passed. I did no writing, though I began vaguely to hatch a completely new plot turning on my hero's climactic conversion to the revolutionary party. At the end of October the long-awaited reader's report on the manuscript landed in the mailbox of my campus apartment. It made the job I had done on that unpublished book the year before look like praise. What was wrong, I learned, was that I really didn't know how to write. I had no idea of characterization or plotting, my technique was faulty, virtually everything except my typing was badly done. If possible, the reader said, I should enroll in a writing course at New York University.

A year earlier, I might have been crushed; but by the autumn of 1954 I had sold a couple of competent if uninspired short stories, I had written five or six more that seemed quite publishable to me (ultimately, I sold them all), and I felt that I had a fairly firm technical grasp on the art of fiction, however faulty the execution of my novel might be at the moment. Instead of abandoning the project, I spent three hours considering what I could do to save it, and in the afternoon I telephoned my editor to tell her that I proposed a total rewrite based on the conversion-to-revolution theme. By this time she must have come to doubt her original faith in my promise and talent, but she told me to go ahead.

I knew this was my last chance. The first step was to throw out the first nine chapters, which had survived intact through all the earlier drafts. They were good, solid chapters — it was the end of the story that was weak, not the beginning — but they had little relevance to my new theme. I compressed them into two pages and got my characters off to the Alpha Centauri system as fast as I could. In six weekends of desperate work the new novel, wholly transformed, was done. And on January 2, 1955 — one year almost to the hour since I had been notified that a contract would be offered me — I received a telegram: CONGRATULATIONS ON A WONDERFUL REVISION JOB ALL SET TO GO.

Revolt on Alpha C was published in August 1955, to generally indifferent reviews. ("inept and unreal......a series of old-hat adventures," said *The New York Times*.) Perhaps that was too harsh a verdict: the book is short, innocent, a little foolish, but not contemptible. It remained in print, in its Crowell edition, for seventeen years, earning modest but steady royalties until the printing was exhausted. A paperback edition published in 1959 still seems to enjoy a healthy life, having been through seven or eight printings so far, and in 1972 the book was reissued on two microfiche cards as part of the Xerox Micromedia Classroom Libraries series. This strange persistence of a very young author's very unimportant first novel does not delude me into thinking I must have created a classic unrecognized in its own day, nor do I believe it has much to do with my latter-day prominence in science fiction. That *Revolt on Alpha C* remains in print after nearly twenty years is no more than an odd accident of publishing, but one that I find charming as well as profitable. My father never ceases to ask if the book still brings in royalties, and he is as wonderstruck as I that it does.

I was launched. On the strength of having sold a novel and a few short stories, I was able to get an agent, Scott Meredith, and he has represented me now for two decades. (There are writers and publishers who will tell you that drawing and quartering is too gentle a fate for him, and there are other writers who have been with him longer than I, with every intention of continuing the relationship until time's end. I think every agent evokes a similarly wide spectrum of responses.) I sent my agent all the unsold short stories in my file, and, assuming that manuscripts bearing his sponsorship would sell far more readily than ones coming in unsolicited from an unknown writer, I awaited a flow of publishers' checks. The flow was a bit sluggish, though. Two trifling stories sold to minor magazines in June 1954 and February 1955 for a total of $40.50; in May 1955 came $49.50 for a rather more elaborate piece. But several quite ambitious stories, which I thought worthy of the leading magazines of the time, failed to sell at all, from which I began to draw a sinister conclusion: that if I intended to earn a livelihood writing fiction, it would be wiser to use my rapidly developing technical skills to turn out mass-produced formularized stories at high speed, rather than to lavish passion and energy on more individual works that would be difficult to sell.

In the summer of 1955, just as that somber insight was crystallizing in me, Randall Garrett appeared in New York and rented a room in the hotel near Columbia University where I was living. Garrett was about eight years older than I, and had had some two dozen stories published, including several in *Astounding*, the premiere magazine of the era. Alone in a strange city, down on his luck, he struck up a curious friendship with me. We were markedly different in personal habits and rhythms, in philosophy, in background; but somehow these differences were a source of vitality rather than disharmony in the collaborative partnership that swiftly evolved. We complemented one another. Garrett was an established professional writer, but his discipline had collapsed and he was writing very little; I was unknown but ambitious, and could force an entire short story out of myself at a single sitting. Garrett had had a scientific education; mine was literary. Garrett was an efficient storyteller, but his prose was mechanical; I had trouble constructing internally consistent plots, but I wrote smoothly and with some grace. Garrett's stories rarely delved into character; I was already concerned, as much as I could be at the age of twenty, with emotional and psychological depth. We began to work together.

Until then, I had submitted all my stories by mail or else through my agent. Garrett took me to editorial offices. I met John Campbell of *Astounding*, Bob Lowndes of the esteemed but impoverished *Science Fiction Stories*, Howard

Philip K. Dick with RS. Photo taken at the 1968 Worldcon by David A. Kyle.

A fascinating, crazy guy, straight out of one of his own books.—RS

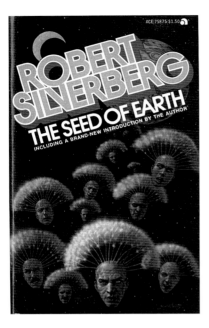

THE SEED OF EARTH
*Ace paperbeck edition,
1977. Cover art by Don
Ivan Punchatz.*

Browne of *Amazing*, Larry Shaw of the newly founded *Infinity*. Editors, Garrett said, bought more readily from writers they had met than from strangers who had only postal contact with them, and lo! it was so. I sold five stories in August 1955, three in September, three in October, six in November, nine in December. Many of these were collaborations with Garrett, but quite a few were stories I did on my own, capitalizing on contacts I had made with his help. Suddenly I was something more than a beginner, here in my final year of college: I was actually earning a living, and quite a good living, by writing. I think the partnership with Garrett accelerated the progress of my career by several years.

Unfortunately there were negative aspects. Once I had assumed, naively, that if I merely wrote the best stories that were in me, editors would recognize their merits and seek my work. Now I was coming to see that there was a quicker road to success — to live in New York, to visit editors regularly, learn of their issue-by-issue needs and manufacture fiction to fit them. I developed a deadly facility; if an editor needed a 7,500-word story of alien conquest in three days to balance an issue about to go to press, he need only phone me and I would produce it. Occasionally I took my time and tried to write the sort of science fiction I respected as a reader, but usually I had trouble selling such stories to the better markets, which reinforced my growing cynicism. By the summer of 1956 — by which time I had graduated from college and had married — I was the complete writing machine, turning out stories in all lengths at whatever quality the editor desired, from slam-bang adventure to cerebral pseudo-philosophy. No longer willing to agonize over the gulf between my literary ambitions and my actual swiftness, selling fifteen stories in June of 1956, twenty the following month, fourteen (including a three-part serial, done with Garrett, for *Astounding*) the month after that.

This hectic productivity was crowned at the World Science Fiction Convention in September 1956, when I was voted a special Hugo as the most promising new writer of the year. The basis for the award could only have been my ubiquity, since most of what I had published was carefully-carpentered but mediocre, and much was wholly opportunistic trash. It is interesting to note that the writers I defeated for the trophy were Harlan Ellison, who at the time had had only one or two dismal stories published, and Frank Herbert, whose impressive *Under Pressure* had appeared in *Astounding* the year before. A week after the convention I went with my bride, Barbara, to the first Milford Science Fiction Writers' Workshop, an awesome assembly of titans — Theodore Sturgeon, Fritz Leiber, Cyril Kornbluth, Lester del Rey, Damon Knight, Frederik Pohl, James Blish, William Tenn, and a dozen more of equal stature. Ellison and I were the only neophytes present. Harlan had not yet begun to show a shadow of his future abilities, and he made an easy whipping-boy for the patriarchs, but I was a different matter: self-contained, confident, quite sure of what I was doing and why.

Del Rey and a few others tried to shake my cynicism and persuade me to aim higher than sure-thing potboilers, but it was clear that potboilers were what I wanted to write, and no one could argue with my success at hammering out penny-a-word dreadfuls. I was only a boy, yet already my annual income was beyond that of anyone in the field except Asimov, Heinlein, Clarke, and Bradbury, those long-enshrined demigods. What I dared not say was that I had opted to write mechanical junk because I had no faith, any longer, in my ability to write anything better. It had been my experience that whenever I assayed the kind of fiction that Sturgeon or Leiber or Kornbluth wrote, I had trouble getting it published. My craftsmanship was improving steadily, in the narrow sense of craft as knowing how to construct a story and make it move; possibly some fatal defect of the soul, some missing quality, marred my serious work, so that it was idle of me, I thought, to try to compete with the Sturgeons and Leibers. I will leave art to the artists, I said quietly, and earn a decent living doing what I do best.

By the end of 1956 I had more than a million published words behind me. I lived in a large, handsome apartment in what was then a desirable neighborhood on Manhattan's Upper West Side. I was learning about fine wines and exotic foods and planning a trip to Europe. The collaboration with Garrett had long since ended, but the impetus he had given me was sufficient and reliable. (A few, notably Horace Gold of *Galaxy*, swore at me for ruining a potentially important talent, but Horace bought my artfully aimed *Galaxy*-type potboilers all the same.) My fellow writers viewed me with alarm, seeing me as some sort of berserk robot that would fill every page of every magazine with its output; they deplored my utter lack of literary ambition, yet accepted me as one of their number, and I formed strong friendships within the close-knit science fiction fraternity. And I wrote, and I sold, and I prospered, and with rare exceptions abandoned any pretense at literary achievement. I wanted to win economic security — to get enough money into the bank so that I would be insulated against the financial storms that had buffeted most of the writers I knew, some of the greatest in the field among them. Lester del Rey pointed out to me that simply on the money-making level I was going about things the wrong way. The stuff I was writing earned me a cent or two a word and then dropped into oblivion, while stories written with more care, with greater intensity of purpose, were reprinted again and again, earning their authors fees far beyond the original sale. I knew that this was so, but I preferred to take the immediate dollar rather than the hypothetical future anthology glory.

So it went through 1957 and 1958. I grew a beard and acquired other, less superficial, stigmata of sophistication. I journeyed to London and Paris, to Arizona and California, treating myself at last to the travels I had not had in boyhood. I learned the lore of the investment world and made some cautious and quite successful forays into the stock market, seeking always the financial independence that I believed would free me from the karmic wheel of high-volume hackman-ship.

Not everything I wrote was touched by corruption. I still loved science fiction for its soaring visionary expansiveness, for its mind-liberating power, and however dollar-oriented I became I still yearned to make some valuable contribution to the field, and felt guilty that the stuff I was churning out was the sort of thing I had openly scorned in my fan-magazine critical essays seven or eight years before. I recall in particular a Sunday afternoon party at Harlan Ellison's Manhattan apartment in 1957 where I talked shop with Cyril Kornbluth, Algis Budrys, James Blish, and one or two other sf writers of their level, and went home in an abyss of self-contempt because these men, my friends, were trying always to publish only their best while I was content to do my worst. Whenever I felt the sting, I put aside hackwork and tried to write honest fiction.

Scattered through my vast output of the late 1950's, then, are a good many

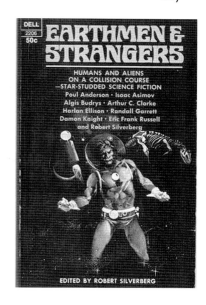

EARTHMAN & STRANGERS, *Dell 1966 paperback edtion, cover art: Jeff Jones. RS' first book as editor.*

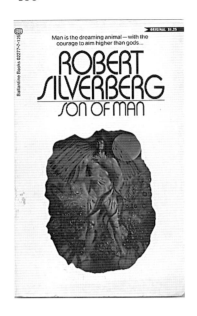

Ballantine Books 02277-7-125

Man is the dreaming animal—with the
courage to aim higher than gods...

ROBERT
SILVERBERG
SON OF MAN

ORIGINAL $1.25

SON OF MAN
*I wrote it in three weeks,
maybe less. Big chunks of it
came right out of my dreams
of the night before. I began
to think I might go on
writing it forever, since the
plot is open-ended and
essentially infinite, but then
came a day when I realized
I had reached the end of my
story, a very curious realization, and I stopped. I've
rarely enjoyed writing a
book so much. I wish I
could do something like it
again, but it's the sort of
book that can be done only
once.— RS*

*Ballantine paperback, 1971;
cover art by Gene Szafran.*

quite respectable stories, not masterpieces — I was still very young, and much more callow than most people suspected — but decently done jobs. Occasionally even now they find their way into anthologies. They were my comfort in those guilt-ridden days, those stories and the novels. In longer lengths I was not so commercially-minded, and I genuinely hoped to achieve in books what was beyond me in the magazines. There were few publishers of science fiction novels then, however: the market consisted, essentially, of three houses, Doubleday, Ballantine, and Ace. With the leading writers of the day keeping the first two well supplied with books, I found no niche for myself, and turned of necessity to Donald Wollheim's Ace Books. This small company published scores of novels a year in a rather squalid format, and was constantly searching for new writers to meet its hunger for copy. The shrewd and experienced Wollheim worked mira-cles on a tiny budget and produced an extraordinarily broad list, ranging from juvenile action stories to superb novels by Philip K. Dick, A. E. van Vogt, Clifford D. Simak, Isaac Asimov, and other luminaries. Wollheim saw potential in me, per-haps as a mass-producer of action fiction and perhaps as something more than that, and encouraged me to offer him novels. He purchased the first, *The Thirteenth Immortal*, late in 1956, and I wrote nine more for him, I think, in the next seven years.

My Ace novels would be fruitful material for somebody's thesis. The first was melodramatic, overblown, a little absurd, yet sincerely conceived; its faults are those of its author's youth, not his cynical approach toward his trade. The second, *Master of Life and Death* (1957), was something of a tour de force, a maze of plot and subplot handled, I think, with some dexterity. *Invaders from Earth* (1958), the third, attempts a sophisticated depiction of psychological and political realities. I liked those two well enough to allow them to be reprinted a decade later. *Stepsons of Terra* (1958) was an intricate time-paradox novel with a certain van Vogtian intensity. On the evidence of these four books alone I would seem an earnest and ambitious young writer striving constantly to improve. But the rest of the novels I wrote for Wollheim were slapdash adventure stories, aiming no higher than the least of his line; I had learned there was little money and less prestige in doing books for Ace, and without those rewards I was content to do the minimum acceptable job. (A few of my later Ace books were better than that, but they were aimed at better markets and went to Wollheim only after others had rejected them.) I know that Wollheim was disappointed in the trend my work for him had taken, but I was too far gone in materialism to care.

During the high-volume years I wrote a good deal that was not science fic-tion — crime stories, a few westerns, profiles of movie stars, and other odds and ends. Some of this work came to me on assignment from my agent, and some I sought because my rate of productivity was now so high that the science fiction field could not absorb all the wordage I was capable of turning out. I had the conviction, though — shared by a surprisingly large number of science fiction writers — that to write sf was the One True Task, and any other kind of writing was mere hackwork done to pay the bills. This was a legitimate enough attitude when held by people like James Blish or William Tenn, who in their early days were forced to write sports fiction and other trivia because the sf market was so tiny; but it was a bit odd for me to feel that way when virtually everything I wrote, sf or not, was pounded out in the same cold-blooded, high-velocity manner. Still, I did feel that way, and whatever my private feelings about the quality of most of my science fiction at that time, I still saw it as a higher endeavor than my westerns and crime stories.

Then, late in 1958, the science fiction world collapsed. Most of the magazines for which I was writing regularly went out of business as a result of upheavals in distribution patterns, and those that survived became far more discriminating about what they would publish. My kind of mass production became obsolete. To sustain what had become a comfortable standard of living I found it necessary to leave the cozy, incestuous science fiction family and look for work in the general New York publishing scene.

The transition was quick and relatively painless. I was facile, I was confident, and my friends had friends. I hired out to any editor who would undertake to pay on time; and, though I continued to write some science fiction in 1959 and 1960, my records for those years show all sorts of strange pseudonymous stories and articles: "Cures for Sleepless Nights," "Horror Rides the Freeway," "I Was a Tangier Smuggler," "Hot Rod Challenge," "Buried Billions Lie in Wait," and so many others that it strains my own credulity. I recall writing one whole piece before lunch and one after lunch, day in, day out: my annual output climbed well above a million words in 1959 and went even higher in 1960 and 1961.

These were years of wandering in the wilderness. I was earning more money

Two separate Ace Double paperback editions. **NEXT STOP THE STARS** *and* **INVADERS FROM EARTH.**

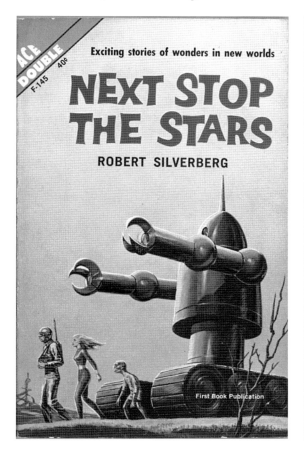

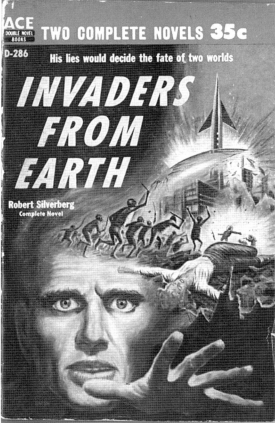

than I had in science fiction, and I had no problems of guilt, for in pouring out this grotesque miscellany I did not need to flagellate myself with the knowledge that I was traducing a literature I loved. On the other hand, I had no particular identity as a writer. In the past, when people asked me what I did, I had answered that I wrote science fiction; now, working anonymously in twenty different sub-literate markets, I had no ready reply, so I went on saying I was a science fiction writer. In truth I did have the occasional story in *Galaxy* or *Astounding*, and an Ace book now and then, to make the claim legitimate. I was mainly a manufac-turer of utilitarian prose, though, churned out by the yard. It was stupefyingly boring, and, as the money piled up, I invested it shrewdly and talked of retiring by the time I was thirty, living on my dividend income, and spending my days traveling, reading, and studying. Already I was doing a good bit of that. In the winters my wife and I fell into the habit of going to the West Indies, where we became skindivers and explored coral reefs. In the summers we made other jour-neys — Canada in 1959, Italy in 1960, the American Northwest in 1961. I was working only four or five hours a day, five days a week, when at home, which left me ample leisure for my private interests — contemporary literature and music, art, ancient history. There was an almost total split between my conscience-less commercialized working-hours self and the civilized and fastidious man who

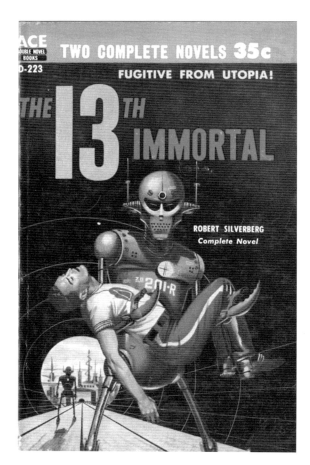

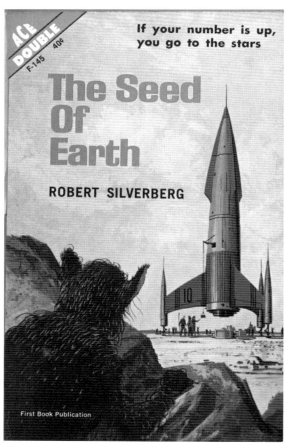

replaced him in early afternoon. I was still only about twenty-five years old.

Unexpectedly, the seeds of a new writing career began to sprout. One of my few science fiction pieces of 1959 was a little novel for children, *Lost Race of Mars*, published by the notable house of Holt, Rinehart and Winston. (My earlier connection with Crowell had fallen apart in 1956, after their rejection of my proposed successor to *Revolt on Alpha C*, and this was my first contact with a major publishing house since then.) *Lost Race of Mars* was short and simple, but it was an appealing book; *The New York Times* chose it as one of the hundred best children's books of the year, and the publisher expressed eagerness to do more of my work. (*Lost Race* is still in print and selling well, both in hardcover and a paperback edition.) I had visited Pompeii while in Italy in 1960, and now I saw a way of capitalizing on my interest, strong since childhood, in antiquity and its remains: I suggested a book for young readers on the excavation of Pompeii.

The people at Holt, Rinehart and Winston considered the idea for quite a while but ultimately declined it. Henry Morrison, who then was handling my affairs at the Scott Meredith agency and who since has become an important agent in his own right, told me he thought the project would fare better if I wrote not about one ancient site but several — say, Chichén Itzá and Angkor and Babylon as well as Pompeii — and he even offered me a title for the expanded book, *Lost Cities and Vanished Civilizations*. When I agreed he sold the book, on the basis of a brief outline, to a Philadelphia house of which I knew nothing, Chilton Books.

With my agent's help I began to emerge from that wilderness of anonymous potboilerei. I began to work in book-length nonfiction, and displayed gifts for quick, comprehensive research and orderly uncluttered exposition. For a minor paperback company called Monarch, now defunct, I did books on the American space program, the Rockefeller family, and the life of Sir Winston Churchill; and for Chilton, in the summer of 1961, I wrote my lost-cities book. None of this was art, but it was far from despicable work. I used secondary sources and wrote with journalistic speed, but what I produced was clear, generally accurate, an honest kind of popularized history. Chilton liked *Lost Cities* and hastened to accept my next proposal, for a book on underwater archaeology. Early in 1962 a suggestion for a young readers' book on great battles found favor at the old-line house of G. P. Putnam's Sons. In April of that year *Lost Cities and Vanished Civilizations* was published and — to my amazement, for I thought of it as no more than a competent rehash of other writers' books — was chosen as one of the year's five best books for young people by an annual awards committee in the field of juvenile publishing, and was selected by the Junior Literary Guild, an important book club. Once again I found myself launched.

Many of New York's leading hardcover publishing houses were willing, on the strength of the success of *Lost Cities*, to give me contracts for nonfiction juvenile books on whatever subject happened to interest me. As rapidly as I dared I severed my connections with my sleazy magazine outlets and ascended into this new, astoundingly respectable and rewarding career. Chilton took another general archaeology book, *Empires in the Dust*. Holt, Rinehart and Winston accepted a biography of the great Assyriologist, Austen Henry Layard. The New York Graphic Society commissioned a book on American Indians, and Putnam one on the history of medicine.

(opposite)
I wrote 13th IMMORTAL in 1956. Not exactly my finest novel, but readers may find some interest in seeing how I wrote three months after getting my college degree.— RS

I met Ed Emshwiller either at the 1956 World SF Convention in New York or at the first Milford Writer's Conference that immediately followed it. Not certain about the convention, because there were so many people there, but we definitely spent time together at Milford, and he and his wife Carol drove my wife (Barbara, then) and me back to New York City after the conference, since we didn't have a car at that time. (He got a ticket for speeding during the drive, somewhere in rural New Jersey, and was much unpleased by it. It's also possible that I encountered him earlier that year at some editorial office — Lowndes's, or Campbell's — but it was surely some time in 1956. I do remember a genial, seemingly easy-going man, a ready smile, no affectations, somebody one could (and I did) take an immediate liking to. I was a New Yorker and I was accustomed to the darker New York style, and Ed's affability was a pleasant novelty. Later, as I got to know him and learned something about his real artistic ambitions, I realized that he was far more complex within than one might think at first meeting.

One day Emsh and I were both in John Campbell's office when Kelly Freas came in to discuss illustrations for a Jack Vance story called "The Miracle Workers," and he did a quick sketch of the two of us that wound up as an interior illustration for that story when it appeared in **ASTOUNDING** *around 1958. — RS*

The rhythm of my life changed dramatically. I still wrote in the mornings and early afternoons — wrote at almost the same incredible velocity as when I had been doing tales of Tangier smugglers — but now I spent the after-hours taking notes in libraries and museums, and I began to assemble a vast private reference library at home. Although my early nonfiction books had been hasty compilations out of other popularizations, I swiftly became more conscientious, as though to live up to the high opinion others had formed of those early books; I went to primary sources whenever possible, I visited actual sites, I did intensive research in many ways. The results were visible. Within a year or two I was considered one of the most skilled popularizers of the sciences in the United States, with publishers eagerly standing in line as my changing interests took me from books on Antarctica and ancient Egypt to investigations of scientific hoaxes and living fossils. For the first time since I had become a professional writer, nearly a decade earlier, I won my own respect.

I maintained a tenuous link with science fiction, largely social, since then as now my closest friends were science fiction writers. I attended parties and conventions, and kept up with what was being published. But of actual science fiction writing I was doing very little. There seemed no commercial reason to get back into sf, even though it had recovered considerably from its 1958 swoon; I had more work than I could handle in the lucrative juvenile nonfiction hardcover field. Only the old shame remained to tweak me: I had served science fiction badly in my 1955-8 days, and I wanted to atone. When Frederik Pohl became editor of *Galaxy* he suggested that I do short stories for him and offered me absolute creative freedom: I could write what I pleased and, within reason, he undertook to buy it. In such an arrangement I could blame neither editorial shortsightedness nor constricting editorial policies for the quality of what I wrote: I was my own master. In the summer of 1962 I offered Pohl a short story, "To See the Invisible Man," inspired by Borges, which was out of an entirely different artistic universe from anything I had written in my first go-around in science fiction — a mature, complex story. He published it and, over the next couple of years, half a dozen more of similar ambitious nature, and, bit by bit, I found myself drawn back into science fiction, this time not as a producer of commodities but as a serious, dedicated artist who turned away from more profitable work to indulge in sf out of love.

During those years — 1962 to 1965 — when I dabbled in science fiction for sheer diversion only, science fiction was undergoing radical changes. The old pulp-magazine rigidities were dissolving. New writers were everywhere: Brian Aldiss, J. G. Ballard, Roger Zelazny, Samuel R. Delany, R. A. Lafferty, Michael Moorcock, and a dozen more. In the bad old days one had to be an established writer of mighty stature, a Bester or a Blish or a Sturgeon, to "get away" with any sort of literary adventurousness; most editors rightly thought that their readers were hostile to unusual modes of narrative, and nearly everyone wrote in an interchangeable manner, unquestioningly adopting universal conventions of style and construction. Suddenly the *way* of telling stories was released from convention. The familiar old robots and starships were being put through strange and fascinating new paces. Pulp-magazine requirements for neat plots and "upbeat" positive resolutions were abandoned. I had been only too willing, in 1957 and thereabouts, to conform to the prevailing modes, for it seemed quixotic to try to do otherwise. Now an army of younger, or at any rate newer, writers had boldly overthrown the traditional rules, and, a trifle belatedly, I joined the revolution.

Even after I returned to science fiction, the nonfiction books remained my chief preoccupations. For one thing, to go back to the mass production of sf would be to defeat the purpose of returning; for another, I was so overwhelmed with nonfiction contracts stretching two and three years into the future, that there was no question of a full-time resumption of sf. The nonfiction was becoming ever more ambitious and the books took longer; in the summer of 1965 I spent months working on one title alone, which I had never done before. (It was a book on the Great Wall of China — no mere cut-and-paste job, but an elaborate and unique synthesis of all available knowledge about the Wall.) Then, too, science fiction had become more permissive but there was still not much money to be had in writing it, and I was continuing to pursue my goal of economic independence, which mandated my centering my career in other fields.

One gigantic item of overhead had entered my life. Early in 1962 I had purchased an imposing house — a mansion, in fact — in a lovely, almost rural enclave near the northwest corner of New York City. I had always lived in apartments; now I joined the landed classes, and had my own lawn and garden, my own giant oak trees, my own wild raccoons wandering about at night (in New York!). There was room for all my books and all I was likely to acquire for many years to come. The third floor of the house, a separate four-room suite, became my working area, and we filled the rest of the place with books and paintings and *objets d'art*. It was a magnificent house, beautiful and stately, and not at all costly in terms of my income at the time. What *was* costly was the upkeep, taxes and cleaning and heat and all, running to many thousands of dollars a year; though I still intended to retire from full-time high-volume writing as soon as possible, I recognized that by buying the house I had postponed that retirement by at least five years.

The nonfiction books grew ever more demanding as — driven by vanity, I suppose, or by intellectual pride, or merely by the feeling that it was time for my

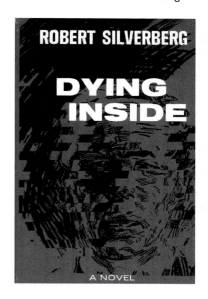

ROBERT SILVERBERG

DYING INSIDE

A NOVEL

There's a lot of autobiographical data in **DYING INSIDE** *(David Selig is the same age I am, went to the same school, etc.) but there's a lot that's fictional (I'm not telepathic, don't have a sister, didn't live his lonely isolated life). In any case I don't consider ghosting term papers, which I also never did, to be professional writing in the sense that I practice it. (The term papers in the novel, though, were my own from my college days!) — RS* reach to begin exceeding my grasp — I tackled bigger and bigger projects. Though I still was doing books for readers in their teens, a biography of Kublai Khan and one of Socrates, a book on bridges and one on coral reefs, I was aiming primarily for older readers in much of what I did, and endeavoring now to deal with subjects that had had no serious examinations in recent times. The Great Wall book was the first of these; and early in 1966 I embarked on a far more arduous task, a book called *The Golden Dream*, a study of the obsessive quest for the mythical land of El Dorado. Working an impossible, brutal schedule, pouring out thousands of words a week, I knew more than a little about the psychology of obsession, and the book, 120,000 words long, was surely the finest thing I had ever done. It was published in an appropriately handsome edition by the Bobbs-Merrill Company, was treated with respect by reviewers, and, I grieve to report, dropped into oblivion as fast as any of my hackwork. The book earned me no income beyond the small initial advance in the United States, was never published at all in Great Britain, and achieved only one translation, in France. I was disappointed but not discouraged; it would have been agreeable to grow rich on the book, but this was secondary to the joy and challenge of having written it. I was learning to love my work for its own sake, regardless of its fate in the marketplace. Growing up, that is.

About the time of the *The Golden Dream* I inaugurated still another aspect of my career by asking the publisher of some of my nonfiction juveniles to let me edit a science fiction anthology. Here at last I could put to some practical use all those years of collecting and reading sf; I had built a superb science fiction library, with literally every magazine ever published and most of the books. The anthology, *Earthmen and Strangers*, was released in the autumn of 1966. I found editing so much to my taste that I sought other anthology contracts and ultimately was devoting as much time to editing as to my own writing.

In that same period — 1965-66 — I built close associations with the two major science fiction houses of the era, Ballantine and Doubleday. When I first became a professional writer these houses were the exclusive preserves of the Clarkes and Heinleins and Sturgeons and Asimovs and Bradburys, and seemed unattainable to the likes of me; now, still having not much of a reputation in science fiction but solidly established outside the field and confident of my skills, I found no difficulty convincing Betty Ballantine of Ballantine and Larry Ashmead of Doubleday to publish my sf. (Even though I considered myself a very part-time science fiction writer in those days, I was still prolific enough to require two regular publishers.) To Ballantine I gave *To Open the Sky*, a pseudo-novel constructed from five novelettes I had written for Fred Pohl's *Galaxy*. To Doubleday I offered *The Time Hoppers*, an expansion of one of those ambitious short stories of my youth that I had had so much trouble placing in 1954. They were both good, middle-of-the-road science fiction, not exactly of Hugo quality but several notches above anything I had published in the field before.

Ballantine also agreed to do a collection of my short stories; and, in January 1966, I proposed a new novel, a book called *Thorns*, telling Mrs. Ballantine, "Much of the texture of the story will rely on background details that can't be sketched in advance. I hope you can gather enough of my intentions from the outline to go ahead with it. What I have in mind is a psychological sf novel, somewhat adventurous in style and approach and characterization, and I think I can

All I remember of **THE SILENT INVADERS** *is its last sentence, which I thought was pretty good at the time and still like. The book itself was written in about seven minutes around 1961 to pay the rent.*
— RS

bring it off. It's worth trying, at any rate." She agreed to the gamble.

I spent the next few months writing the El Dorado book, and in June I fell into a mysterious illness. All energy went from me and I lost close to twenty pounds — though I was slender to begin with — in a few weeks. I had not been ill since finishing with the standard childhood maladies, indeed was not even prone to minor upsets, and this was a startling event to me. The symptoms answered well to leukemia and other dire things, but turned out to be only a metabolic change, a sudden hyperactivity of the thyroid gland. Such thyroid outbreaks, I learned, are often caused by the stress of prolonged overwork, and I think the forced marches of El Dorado had much to do with this one. I took it as a warning: I was past thirty and it was time to think realistically about slowing down. Though I had enough book contracts to keep me busy for two or three years, I resolved to reduce my output and gradually to make drastic reductions in the time I devoted to work.

Though greatly weakened, I wrote steadily — but at a slower pace — through the infernally hot summer of 1966, while at the same time planning *Thorns* and doing preliminary research for another major nonfiction work, a study of the prehistoric Mound Builder cultures of the central United States. I was still gaunt and haggard when I attended the annual science fiction conven-

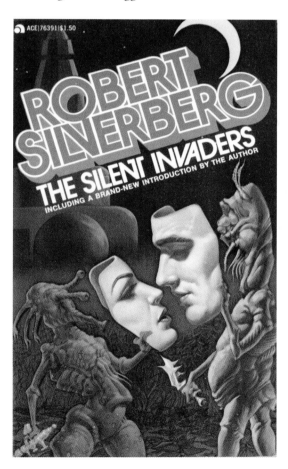

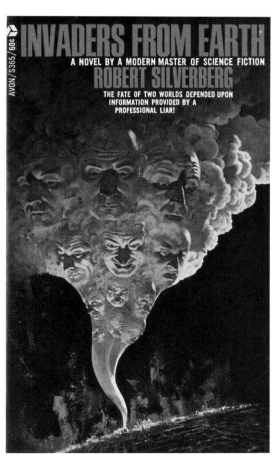

tion in Cleveland at the beginning of September, but the drug therapy for my thyroid condition was beginning to take hold, and immediately after the convention I felt strong enough to begin *Thorns*. The title describes the book: prickly, rough in texture, a sharp book. I worked quickly, often managing twenty pages or more a day, yet making no concessions to the conventions of standard science fiction. The prose was often oblique and elliptical (and sometimes shamefully opaque in a way I'd love to fix retroactively); the action was fragmented in the telling, the characters were angular, troubled souls. Midway in the job I journeyed out to Pennsylvania to attend a party at Damon Knight's Milford Workshop. I knew nearly all the writers there, and they knew me. They all knew how prosperous I was, and some were aware that I had achieved worthwhile things with my non-fiction, but they couldn't have had much respect for me as a writer of science fiction. They might admire my professionalism, my productivity, my craftsmanship — but to them I was still that fellow who had written all that zap-zap space-opera in the 1950s. Their gentle and not-so-gentle comments hardly troubled me, though, for I knew I was no longer that mass-producer of garbage, and sooner or later they would all know it too. While at Milford I glanced at an Italian science fiction magazine and found a harsh review of one of my early Ace novels, recently published in Italy. Badly done and wordy, the critic said — *malcondotto e prolisse*. Perhaps it was. The next day, when I went home to finish *Thorns*, Malcondotto and Prolisse joined the cast of characters.

I regained my health by the end of the year and eventually made a full and permanent recovery. I withdrew, bit by bit, from my lunatic work schedule: having written better than a million and a half words for publication in 1965, I barely exceeded a million in 1966, and have never been anywhere near that insane level of productivity since. Though I still wrote daily except when traveling, I worked less feverishly, content to quit early if I had had a good morning at the typewriter, and I began alternating science fiction and nonfiction books to provide myself with periodic changes of rhythm. I looked forward to 1967 with some eagerness — and with much curiosity, too, for that was the year in which my first really major science fiction, *Thorns* and *The Time Hoppers* and a novella called "Hawksbill Station," would finally be published. Would they be taken as signs of reform and atonement for past literary sins, or would they be ignored as the work of a writer who by his own admission had never been much worth reading?

I began the year by writing a short story, "Passengers," for Damon Knight's new *Orbit* anthology series. He asked for revisions, minor but crucial, five times, and though I grumbled I saw the wisdom of his complaints and did the rewriting. I wrote a novel for Doubleday, *To Live Again*, which surpassed anything I had done in complexity of plot and development of social situation. I expanded "Hawksbill Station" into a novel. I did my vast Mound Builder book, bigger even than El Dorado, a book that was as much a study of the myth-making process as it was an exploration of American Indian culture. (When it appeared in 1968, as *Mound Builders of Ancient America: The Archaeology of a Myth*, many reviewers, even those in the archaeological journals, assumed I was myself an archaeologist, and I received flattering if embarrassing invitations to lecture, to teach, and to write reviews. The book was greeted enthusiastically by professional archaeologists and has become a standard reference item, to be found in most libraries. Having said so many uncomplimentary things about my own writing in these pages, I think

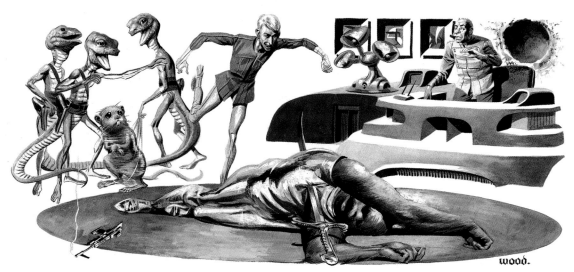

wood.

I've earned the right to be a bit boastful about this one.) There were three other big projects in this year of supposedly reduced output: the novels *The Masks of Time* and *The Man in the Maze* and another Goliath of a nonfiction work, *The Longest Voyage*, an account of the first six circumnavigations of the world.

I was, in truth, riding an incredible wave of creative energy. Perhaps it was an overcompensation for my period of fatigue and illness in 1966, perhaps just the sense of liberation and excitement that came from knowing I was at last writing only what I wanted to write, as well as I could do it. In any event I look back in wonder and awe at a year that produced *To Live Again, Masks of Time, Man in the Maze*, two 150,000-word works of history, several short stories, and — I have as much trouble believing this as you — no less than seven non-fiction books for young readers, each in the 60,000-word range. No wonder my peers regarded me as some sort of robot: I have no idea myself how I managed it all, working five hours a day, five days a week, with time off for holidays in Israel and the West Indies and a week at Montreal's Expo 67.

Thorns was published in August of 1967. All of Ballantine's science fiction titles were then automatically being distributed free to the members of the two-year-old Science Fiction Writers of America, and so all my colleagues had copies in hand at the time of that year's sf convention. Many of them had read it, and — as I hoped — it shook their image of my work. At least a dozen of my friends told me, with the frankness of true friendship, that the book had amazed them: not that they thought me incapable of writing it, but rather that I would be willing to take the trouble. If seemed such a radical break from my formularized science fiction of the 1950's that they thought of it as the work of some entirely new Robert Silverberg. I was pleased, of course, but also a little pained at these open admissions that I had been judged all these years by the basest of what I had written between 1955 and 1958. *Thorns* was not all that much of a breakthrough for me; it represented only a plausible outgrowth of what I had begun to attempt in 1962's short story, "To See the Invisible Man," and in the work that followed it over a period of four years.

Even before the publication of *Thorns* I found my position in the American

"Birds of a Feather"
GALAXY, *Nov. 1958,*
art by Wally Wood.

science fiction world undergoing transformations. In the summer of 1967 I had become President of the Science Fiction Writers of America, succeeding Damon Knight, founder of the organization. The job was not an award for literary merit but rather a tribute to the experience I had had in building a career and dealing with publishers. Certainly I was well qualified for the job, and I felt no hesitation about accepting it, especially since the organization would have collapsed if I had declined — no one else was willing to take it on. Doubtless if I had run against some writer whose work was more highly regarded than mine, James Blish or Poul Anderson or Philip José Farmer, I would have been defeated; but willy-nilly I ran unopposed, gladly letting myself in for a year of drudgery on behalf of my fellow writers. At least *Thorns* soon showed the rank-and-file of the membership that their new president would not disgrace the organization.

Thorns did not universally give delight. Those who found pleasure in my old straightforward action stories were appalled by this dark, disturbing book. One of my dearest friends, an old-line writer conservative in his tastes, explicitly accused me of a calculated sellout to the "new wave" of science fiction — of writing a deliberately harsh and freaky book to curry favor with the influential leaders of the revolution within science fiction. That charge was particularly painful to me. Having blithely sold out so many times as a young man to any editor with the right price in his hand, I was hurt to find myself blamed for selling out again, this time to the opposite camp, when I finally wrote something that grew from my own creative needs instead of the market's demands. Such criticisms were rare, though. *Thorns* was nominated both for the Hugo and for the Science Fiction Writers' Nebula trophy — the first time anything of mine reached the final ballot in either contest.

They won no awards, nor did "Hawksbill Station," which was also up for a Nebula; but the critics were re-evaluating my place in science fiction, invariably invoking my seamy early work before getting around to saying how much better a writer I was nowadays. 1968 promised to be a rewarding year. It was less than six weeks old, though, when I awakened at half past three one frigid winter morning to the glare of an unaccustomed light in the house. Burglars have broken in, I thought, groping toward wakefulness — but no, there were no burglars. The glare I saw was fire.

So out into the miserable night we went and watched the house burn. Papers stored in the attic, I think, had ignited. My wife and I carried our four cats and a flock of kittens to the dubious safety of the basement, and I seized the manuscript of my current book and a few ancient artifacts and cached them in the garage; then the firemen refused to let us return to the building, and we took refuge in the house across the way. By dawn it was over. The roof was gone; the attic had been gutted; my third-floor office was a wreck; and the lower floors of the house, though unburned, were awash in water rapidly turning to ice. A priest from a nearby Catholic college appeared and, unbidden, took several Volkswagenloads of our houseplants to safety in his cabin, lest they freeze in the unprotected house. Then he returned and offered consolation, for I was in a bad way. No Catholic I, but I had felt the hand of some supernatural being pressing against me that night, punishing me for real and imagined sins, leveling me for overweening pride as though I had tried to be Agamemnon.

Friends rallied round. Barbara performed prodigies, arranging to have our belongings taken to storage (surprisingly, most of our books and virtually all the works of art had survived, though the structure itself was a ruin) and negotiating with contractors; I was not much good for anything for days — stupefied, Godhaunted, broken. We moved to a small, inadequate rented house about a mile away as the immense job of reconstruction began. I bought a new typewriter, reassembled some reference books, and, after a few dreadful weeks, began once more to work in strange surroundings.

In nine months the house was ready to be occupied again, and by the spring of 1969 the last of the rebuilding was done and the place was more beautiful than ever — an exact replica of its former self, except where we had decided on improvements. But I was never the same again. Until the night of the fire I had never, except perhaps at the onset of my illness in 1966, been touched by the real anguish of life. I had not known divorce or the death of loved ones or poverty or unemployment, I had never experienced the challenges and terrors of parenthood, had never been mugged or assaulted or molested, had not been in military service (let alone actual warfare), had never been seriously ill. The only emotional scars I bore were those of a moderately unhappy childhood, hardly an unusual experience. But now I had literally passed through the flames. The fire and certain more personal upheavals some months earlier had marked an end to my apparent immunity to life's pain, and drained from me, evidently forever, much of the bizarre energy that had allowed me to write a dozen or more books of high quality in a single year. Until 1967, I had cockily written everything in one draft, rolling white paper into the machine and typing merrily away, turning out twenty or thirty pages of final copy every day and making only minor corrections by hand afterwards. When I resumed work after the fire I tried to go on that way, but I found the going slow, found myself fumbling for words and losing the thread of narrative, found it necessary in mid-page to halt and start over, pausing often to regain my strength. It has been slower and slower ever since, and I have only rarely, and not for a long time now, felt that dynamic sense of clear vision that enabled me to write even the most taxing of my books in wild, joyous spurts. I wasted thousands of sheets of paper over the next three years before I came to see, at last, that I had become as other mortals and would have to do two or three or even ten drafts of every page before I could hope to type final copy.

I hated the place where we settled after the fire — it was cramped, dirty, confused, ugly — but the rebuilding job called for thousands of dollars beyond the insurance settlement, and I had to go on writing regardless of externals. With most of my reference library intact but in storage for the duration, I was forced back into virtual full-time science fiction, the nonfiction temporarily impossible for me. One of the first things I wrote, in the early days of the aftermath, was a curiously lyrical novella, "Nightwings," to which I added a pair of sequels some months later to constitute a novel. Later in the year came a novel for young readers, *Across a Billion Years*, almost unknown among my recent books — a rich, unusual book that never found an audience. There was a short story, "Sundance," a display of technical virtuosity, my favorite among all my myriad shorter pieces. And, in my despair and fatigue, I managed somehow to write a bawdy comic novel of time travel, *Up the Line*. The fire had shattered me emotionally and for a time physically, but it had pushed me, I realized, into a deeper, more profound expression of feelings. I had been through a monstrous tempering of my artistic skills.

In September of 1968 I went to California for the science fiction convention — my third visit to that state, and I was struck once again by its beauty and strangeness. I was toastmaster at the convention's awards banquet, a last-minute replacement for the late Anthony Boucher, and for five hours toiled to keep a vast and restless audience amused — a fascinating, almost psychedelic experience. November saw me back in my restored house, working on the biggest of all my nonfiction books, an immense exploration of the Zionist movement in the United States. The publishers invested a huge sum of money in it, and planned to promote it to best-seller status, but, as usual, nothing came of it but good reviews: I was destined never to win wide attention for my long nonfiction works.

My science fiction, though, was gathering acclaim. *Masks of Time* failed by only a few votes to win a Nebula, as did the novella "Nightwings." But "Nightwings" did take a Hugo at the St. Louis convention in 1969. In the spring of that year, I wrote a novel, *Downward To the Earth*, which was in part inspired by a journey to Africa (and in which were embedded certain homages to Joseph Conrad) and in part by my own growing sense of cosmic consciousness: I had never been a religious man, had never belonged to any organized church, but something had been set ticking in me by the fire, a sense of connections and compensating forces, and *Downward to the Earth* reflected it. *Galaxy* purchased it for serialization and New American Library for book publication. In the autumn — slowly, with much difficulty — I wrote *Tower of Glass*, for Charles Scribner's Sons, the publishers of Hemingway and Wolfe and Fitzgerald, now experimenting with science fiction. *Galaxy* bought that one too. And at the end of the year I wrote my strangest, most individual book, *Son of Man*, a dream-fantasy of the far future, with overtones of Stapledon and Lindsay's *Voyage to Arcturus* and a dollop of psychedelia that was altogether my own contribution. It was becoming extremely hard for me to get words on paper, despite this long list of 1969's accomplishments, and, with the expenses of the fire behind me, I was again talking of retirement. Not total retirement — writing was a struggle, but *having written* was a delight — but at least a sabbatical of some months, once I had dealt with the contractual obligations I had taken on for the sake of rebuilding my home.

The paradox of this stage of my career manifested itself ever more forcefully in 1970: I felt continual growth of my art, my power, my vision, and simultaneously it became constantly more difficult to work. I tired more easily, I let myself be distracted by trifles, and when I did write I was over-finicky, polishing

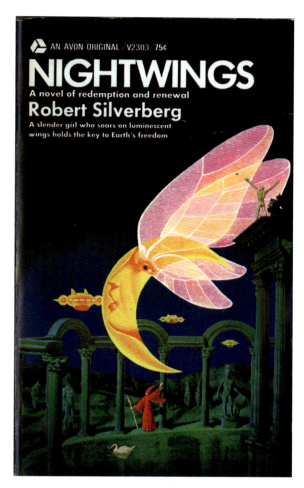

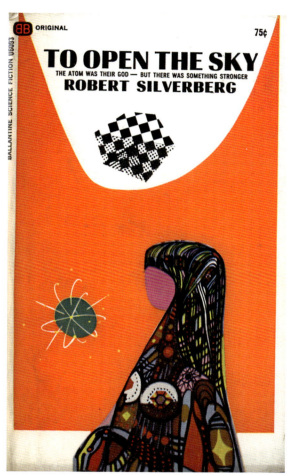

and polishing so that on a good day I was lucky to get nine or ten pages written. Still an immense output, but not what I had grown accustomed to pulling from myself in the vanished days of indefatigable productivity. Nevertheless it was an active year. I did *The World Inside*, a novel composed of loosely related short stories set within a single great residential tower; I think it and *Tower of Glass* (another story of a giant erection!) are closer to pure science fiction, the exhaustive investigation of an extrapolative idea, than anything else I have written. I did *A Time of Changes*, more emotional than most of my work and heavily pro-psychedelic. I did *The Second Trip*, a rough and brutal novel of double identity, and I wrote the last of my major nonfiction books, *The Realm of Prester John*, which I regard as a genuine contribution to scholarship. (Doubleday published it and no one bought it.)

By now it was clear that the science fiction world had forgiven me for the literary sins of my youth. My short story "Passengers" won a Nebula early in 1970. *Up the Line* and one of the "Nightwings" series were on the ballot also, though they failed to win. In the summer I was American Guest of Honor at the World Science Fiction Convention in Heidelberg, a little to my surprise, for

NIGHTWING, *Avon paperback 1969 edition, with Don Ivan Punchatz cover art.*

TO OPEN THE SKY, *Ballantine Book, 1967, with Richard Powers cover art.*

THOSE WHO WATCH.
Cover art by Tim White.

though I was beginning to think I would someday be chosen for this greatest of honors in science fiction, I had assumed it was at least ten years in the future. I was a triple Hugo nominee that year too, but came away, alas, with a bunch of second and third-place finishes. Another quite improbably boyhood fantasy was eerily fulfilled for me in 1970. When I was about sixteen and *Galaxy* was the newest and most controversial of science fiction magazines, I diverted myself one day with an amiable daydream in which I was the author of three consecutive serials in that magazine — an awesome trick, since the authors of *Galaxy*'s first five novels were Simak, Asimov, Kornbluth and Merrill, Heinlein, and Bester. But there I was in 1970 with *Downward to the Earth, Tower of Glass*, and most of *The World Inside* running back-to-back, and *Time of Changes* following them in 1971. I remembered my old daydream and felt a little disbelieving shiver.

My new working habits were entrenching themselves: revise, revise, revise. Projects that might have taken me two weeks in 1965 took three months in 1970. I refused to sign new contracts, knowing that I no longer had much control over the length of time it took me to finish anything, and I could not therefore guarantee to meet delivery dates. Nonfiction in particular I was phasing out; I had had a good run in that career for a decade, but the burden of research now was more than I cared to carry, and the failure of my big books to have much commercial success had eventually had a depressing effect. Now that I was in my full stride in science fiction, working at the top of my form and enjoying public favor, I wanted to devote as much of my dwindling literary energies to that field as I could.

Strangely, it was becoming impossible for me to take the stuff of science fiction seriously any more — all those starships and androids and galactic empires. I had come to believe that the chances that mankind would reach and colonize the planets of other stars were very slight indeed, and the stories set on such worlds now seemed idle fantasy to me, not serious projection. So too with many of the other great themes of science fiction: one by one they became unreal, though they continued to have powerful metaphorical and symbolic value for me. I discovered that much of what I was writing in 1971 was either barely sf at all (*The Book of Skulls*) or was a kind of parody of science fiction ("Good News from the Vatican," "Caliban," and other short stories) or borrowed a genuine science fiction theme for use in an otherwise "straight" mainstream novel (*Dying Inside*). This realization inspired flickers of new guilt in me. I no longer had to apologize, certainly not, for shortcomings of literary quality; but was this new Silverberg really serving the needs of the hardcore science fiction audience? Was he providing the kind of sincerely felt fiction about the future that the readers still seemed to prefer, or was he doing fancy dancing for his own amusement and that of a jaded elite?

The pattern of awards in the field reinforced these doubts. I was getting nominated by twos and threes every year now for the Hugo and the Nebula; indeed, I have by now amassed more final-ballot nominations than any other writer. In 1972 the Science Fiction Writers of America favored me with two Nebulas, an unusual event, for my novel *A Time of Changes* and my short story "Good News from the Vatican" — but the writers have relatively sophisticated tastes, and I have fared far less well with the Hugos, awarded by a broader cross-section of the sf readership. Though nominated every year, my books and stories have finished well behind more conservative, "safer" works. This causes me no serious anguish or resentment, for I have hardly been neglected in the passing around of honors in the sf world, but it does lead me to brood a bit in idle hours. Not that it affects what I write: I am bound on my own course and will stay to it. I wish only that I could be my own man and still give pleasure to the mass of science fiction readers.

In 1971 I at last achieved the partial retirement of which I had been dreaming for so many years. The press of contracts abated, and in late spring I simply stopped writing, not to resume until autumn. I had never, not since early college days, gone more than four weeks away from my typewriter; now I was away from it five whole months, and felt no withdrawal symptoms at all. I read, swam, loafed; now and then I would work on anthology editing for an hour or so in the morning, for such editing was becoming increasingly important to me, but essentially I was idle all summer. A more complete break with the old Silverberg could not have been imagined. To underscore the transformation, I had spent some weeks just before the holiday revising an early novel of mine, *Recalled to Life*, for a new edition. When I wrote it, in 1957, I had exaggeratedly high regard for it, seeing it as a possible Hugo nominee and hoping it would gain me a place with Ballantine or Doubleday or some other major publishing house. Looking at this

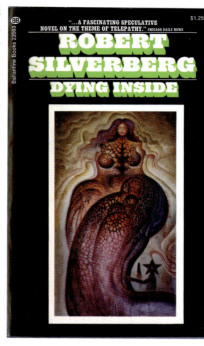

DYING INSIDE *(1973) Ballantine paperback.*

DOWNWARD TO THE EARTH *(1971) Signet paperback. Cover by Gene Szafran.*

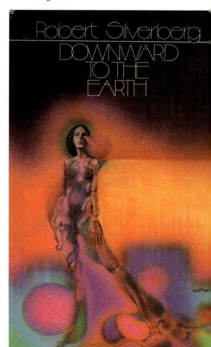

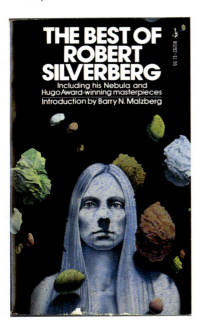

(apposite)
Art by Tim White for
THORNS (NEL), 1978.

(below)
Danish edition (1960)
ALIENS FROM SPACE
by RS writing as "David
Osborne," cover art by
Richard Powers.

masterpiece of my youth fourteen years later, I was appalled at its crudity, and repaired it as best I could before letting it be reissued. That experience gave me a good yardstick to measure my own growth.

Further transformations of my life, unexpected ones, lay in wait for me. My wife and I were native New Yorkers, and, however extensively we traveled, we always returned to New York, the home base, after a few weeks. We loved the city's vitality, its complexity, the variety of experience it offered, and we had money enough to insulate ourselves from its inconveniences and perils. Our rebuilt house was more than a dwelling to us, it was a system of life, an exoskeleton, and we assumed we would live in it the rest of our lives. But New York's deterioration and decline was driving away our friends. Two by two they trooped away, some to distant suburbs, many to California; and by the autumn of 1971 we found ourselves isolated and lonely in a city of eight million. New York now was dangerous, dirty, ever more expensive; taxes were rising alarmingly and the amenities we prized, the restaurants and galleries and theaters, were beginning to go out of business. We were held fast by pride and pleasure in our house — but did we want to find ourselves marooned in our magnificent fortress while everything dissolved about us? Timidly we began talking about joining the exodus. It still seemed unthinkable; we toyed with the notion of moving to California the way loyal Catholics might toy with the idea of conversion to Buddhism, enjoying the novelty and daring of such an outlandish idea, but never taking it seriously. In October 1971 we flew to San Francisco for a reunion with many of our transplanted Eastern friends; we said we were considering moving, and they urged us to come. It was impossible to give up our house, we said. We went back to California in November, though, still hesitating but now willing to look, however tentatively, at areas where we might find a comparable place to live. And just after the turn of the year we discovered ourselves, to our amazement, boarding a plane for a sudden weekend trip west to see a house that a friend had located for us.

That house turned out not to work — it was too big even for us, and too decayed — but before the weekend was over we had found another, strange and beautiful, an architectural landmark in a park-like setting, and we placed a bid on it and after some haggling the bid was accepted, and, as if in a dream, we put our cherished New York place up for sale and made arrangements to move West. It all happened so swiftly, in retrospect — less than six months from the moment the temptation first struck to the day we arrived, with tons of books and furniture, in golden California, in the new El Dorado.

California, then. A new life at the midpoint. For reasons of climate, my 1971 scheme of working autumn and winter and taking a holiday in spring and summer did not seem desirable, though I still wanted to work only half the time. I hit on a plan of working mornings, normally a cloudy time of day here, and giving myself the afternoons free, with frequent total interruptions of work for short holidays away from home. This has worked well for me. My output continues to decline: 1971 saw me write about a quarter of a million words, 1972 only some 115,000, or about what I would have done in an average month a decade earlier. Since *Dying Inside* in 1971 I have written no novels, though doubtless that datum will be obsolete before this essay is published: my major work in California has been a novella, "Born with the Dead," but a novel soon will be upon me, I think. Mainly I have written short stories, ostensibly science fiction, though the

definition has required some stretching; they are strange and playful pieces, qualities evident in the titles of the two story collections I have made of them: *Unfamiliar Territory* and *Capricorn Games*.

Though one good quiver of the San Andreas Fault could destroy all I have built in a moment, I am at present in a comfortable situation, invulnerable to the demands of the marketplace, able to write what I choose and have it published by people I respect. The work comes slowly, partly because I revise so much, partly because the temptations of lovely California are forever calling me from my desk, partly because the old pressures — to prove myself artistically, to make myself secure financially — no longer operate on me. I keep close to nature, regularly visiting the mountains and deserts nearby and, when at home, laboring in my well-stocked and ever-expanding garden; I read a good deal, I edit anthologies of original material that bring me into contact with younger writers, I maintain many friendships both within and outside the science fiction cosmos, and, as the mood takes me, I pursue such old interests — music, archaeology, the cinema, whatever — as still attract me. Though I may eventually write more nonfiction, if only for the sake of learning more about the natural environment here by studying it systematically in preparation for a book, I expect that such writing as I do henceforth will be almost exclusively science fiction, or what passes for science fiction in my consciousness these days, I still respond to it as I did as a child for its capacity to open the gates of the universe, to show me the roots of time. I have little admiration for most of the science fiction I read today, and even less for the bulk of what I wrote myself before 1965, but I do go on reading it however short it falls of my ideal vision of it, and I do go on writing it in my fashion, pursuing an ideal vision there too and always falling short, but coming closer, coming closer now and then, close enough to lead me to continue.

1974

(opposite top)
NEW DIMENSIONS 3.

(below)
…for LORD VALEN-
TINE'S CASTLE I
very deliberately used
the schema from Joseph
Cambell's **HERO WITH**
A THOUSAND FACES.
— RS

LORD VALENTINE'S
CASTLE, *Harper & Row,*
Publishers, NY; 1980. Dust
jacket art by Ron Walotsky.

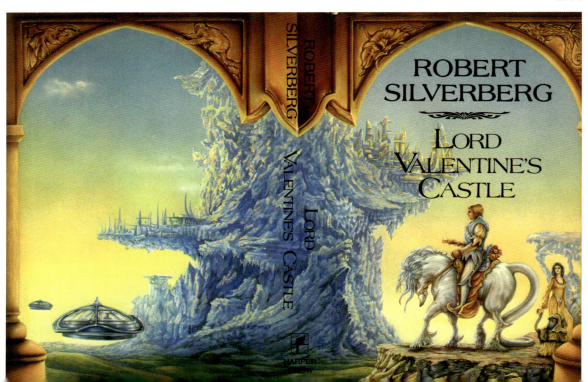

ROBERT
SILVERBERG

LORD
VALENTINE'S
CASTLE

Postscript to "Sounding Brass, Tinkling Cymbal", October 1975:

"To continue," I said — I wrote the piece you have just read in the summer of 1973 — and continue I did, for a while: two short stories that autumn, and a novel, *The Stochastic Man*, during the winter of 1973-74. But late in 1974 I began to discover depressing things about the state of my career: books were going out of print, my publishers were in no hurry to reissue them, readers seemed baffled and even hostile, critics seemed to be paying no attention. Suddenly I was neither commercially viable nor acclaimed as an artist; Mammon alone might have kept me going, and so might a steady diet of praise, but the simultaneous disappearance of both robbed me of any desire to go on with science fiction. I didn't need to do it for a living; I wasn't getting much creative joy out of it; the public response was not encouraging. Worst of all, the strain of these perplexities was affecting my health: a whole assortment of psychosomatic troubles began plaguing me. I began a long and ambitious novel, *Shadrach in the Furnace*, in the autumn of 1974, and, before I was fifty pages into it, I decided that it would be my last. Science fiction was damaging me, that was clear. Editors who I believed were friends told me, quite sincerely, that there was no room in commercial publishing for such books as *Dying Inside* or *Son of Man*. To produce, at a rate of a page or two a day, books that angered the science fiction community (because they were too much like literature) — and were ignored by the readers of mainstream literature (because they were science fiction), was too frustrating, too depressing. Although my work was in demand in Europe, suddenly commanding not only critical attention but also royalties greater than I had known in the United States, it seemed folly to go on. My motivation was undermined. It seemed simplest and best to give it up.

And so I have. I have no science fiction books under contract now and have refused all offers; I have written no short stories for two years; *Shadrach* will appear in 1976 and that will be the end, at least for a long while. I intend to continue editing *New Dimensions* and the reprint anthologies, and, by so doing, to help writers more courageous or more durable than I; I'll continue also to accept speaking engagements and to make convention appearances, so that I can put forth my views on what science fiction ought to be. But I have no desire to jump back into the crucible myself. When I think of how my career in science fiction ended, I feel sad, bitter, and confused; I still find it hard to accept the idea that I ceased to be of value to the general science fiction audience just as I reached my creative peak, but that's what seems to have happened. (As witness the 1975 Hugo results.) So I am out of it, and well out of it, puzzled but slowly healing, sadder but wiser. Evidently modern American commercial science fiction is no place for a serious writer. I have learned my lesson; the seriousness has been burned out of me by it; I am off to Hollywood for a period of rest and rehabilitation as a screenwriter. I feel no sense of unfinished business in science fiction, for I did, after all, manage to write *Tower of Glass, Downward to the Earth, Son of Man, Dying Inside, The Book of Skulls, To Live Again, Hawksbill Station, Nightwings*, and *A Time of Changes*, books which helped in some measure to shape current American sf. If you think it's cowardly of me to throw in the towel, consider those nine titles for a moment — and then consider that not one of them is in print in the United States as I write this epilogue today.

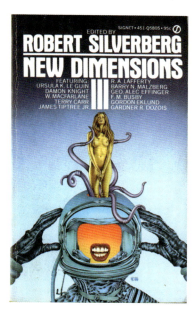

In the early days of my career I wrote just one draft, white paper/ carbon/ yellow paper, and made whatever minor corrections were necessary by hand after I'd finished the story. By 1968 or so I had lost the ability to compose final draft copy in a single go, or else had become too picky to let myself do it, and so I began doing a complete draft on yellow paper, reading it and correcting by hand, and retyping all the way through in final draft. Took twice as long but the product was at least twice as good, and rethinking each sentence as I retyped it was exceedingly useful. As the books grew longer (the LVC manuscript ran 600 pages), this became an interminable process, and I was grateful for the coming of the word processor, which enabled me to do a continuous first/ second/ third draft without the need to retype sections that needed no reworking.— RS

MY *STAR TREK* TREATMENT

I briefly unretired last September (1976) to do the screenplay for the *Star Trek* movie. It seemed like a whole lot of fun to write a movie, and there would of course have been a ton on money in it too, so what the hell, what the hell, I went down to Hollywood and talked to Paramount, and fabricated a story idea for them, and sold them a treatment. A treatment is what we prose writers sometimes call an "outline." My *Star Trek* treatment ran about 10,000 words, and I received for it a sum larger than any book publisher has ever advanced me for a novel. But I never wrote the screenplay. That's Hollywood, as the man said.

In the course of the project, though, I watched ten or twelve *Star Trek* episodes, never having paid much attention to the show when it was alive, and a little to my surprise I found myself quite charmed by the whole thing, even fascinated. A lot of people who ought to know better thought I was slumming when I took the *Star Trek* job — obviously a writer like Silverberg, who turns out that arty high-falutin' fiction and who is in no need of money for its own sake, has no business working on anything as trashy as *Star Trek*, they said — but in fact I was rather looking forward to the job, because I perceived, after my period of research, just how well done the show had been, what a genuine sf accomplishment it was. (At least in the first two years.) So no, I didn't clamber aboard the *Enterprise* to make a quick buck, nor did I ever have a patronizing attitude toward the assignment, and I think that if Paramount had let me make the movie I wanted to write, the result would have been something extraordinary. On the other hand, they probably would have hobbled the script mercilessly after it left my hands, and I'd have nothing to show for my efforts except a big blotch on my escutcheon and seventy-odd paltry thousand dollars.

Anyway, I'm not going to write the *Star Trek* movie, and I'm not currently fishing for Hollywood work of any other kind, although I've been fished for by Hollywood on a couple of other thus far abortive projects; I'm available but not actively so. I have no immediate plans for writing fiction, either. The mood of bitterness and anger with which I terminated my career has largely dissipated, but in retirement I've found plenty of other creative ways to amuse myself, and the thought of interrupting them just to write more stories seems altogether bizarre to me. One reason I quit, of course, is that my books were going out of print; now it seems that they're mostly going to come back in print, and there is also a vast and very gratifying Silverberg boom going on in five or six foreign countries; but, paradoxical as it may seem, the more reprints and foreign sales that turn up, the less likely I am to do

This is the original idea for **LORD VALENTINE'S CASTLE,** *which arrived in my head on a summer afternoon (I think) as I was lolling around by the pool; I grabbed the envelope that the monthly announcement from the SF Book Club had arrived in and scribbled this hastily on the back.— RS*

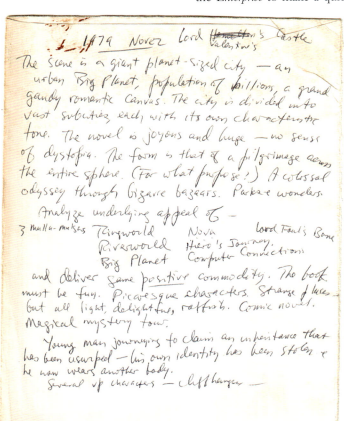

new writing. I think if my work had vanished from view everywhere forever, I might ultimately have been driven to write something else if only to see my name in print again — for it is, you know, the unceasing lust for ego that is the only motivation for writing anything. But here I am signing contracts for Urdu and Swahili editions of *Dying Inside,* for Antarctic rights to *The Thirteenth Immortal*, for a Polish edition with introductions by Ivar Jorgenson. My cup runneth over.

1978

THE MAKING OF MAJIPOOR (1979)

It began with my scribbling some hasty notes on the back of an envelope, one spring day in 1978: 1979 NOVEL

"The scene is a giant planet-sized city — an urban Big Planet, population of billions, a grand gaudy romantic canvas. The city is divided into vast subcities, each with its own characteristic tone. The novel is joyous and huge — no sense of dystopia. The form is that of a pilgrimage across the entire sphere. (For what purpose?) A colossal odyssey through bizarre bazaars. Parks & wonders ….

Deliver a *positive commodity*. The book must be fun. Picaresque characters. Strange places — but all light, delightful, raffish. Comic novel. Magic mystery tour."

I paused, a little startled by all this. I hadn't written any fiction for nearly five years, nor had any desire to — I had "retired" forever from writing, bored with it, burned out, blocked, whatever. Did I really mean to write a new novel after all? Apparently I did; for after a moment I added, at the bottom of the envelope:

"Young man journeying to claim an inheritance that has been usurped — his own identity has been stolen & he now wears another body."

And then, finally, at the top next to "1979 NOVEL," the words "Lord Hamilton's Castle." After which I crossed out "Hamilton," substituted "Valentine," and I was off and running. What I had in mind that day, and, I think, ultimately achieved, was successful light entertainment. What would be required of me, before I was through, was to draw on a whole host of intellectual resources in the fields of history, mythology, psychology, literature, geography, geology, botany, and more.

The phrase "urban Big Planet" in my back-of-the-envelope sketch needs some explaining. *Big Planet* is a novel by Jack Vance, first published in 1952, that takes place on an enormous world somewhat like India in climate, divided into hundreds or thousands of independent principalities. Because the crust of Big Planet is devoid of the heavier elements, Vance's planet has "no metal, no machinery, no electricity, no long distance communication," and therefore — despite its immense size, with a circumference seven or eight times that of Earth — Big Planet is a low-density world with a gravitational pull about the same as ours, making possible human settlement.

Vance's novel is a lovely colorful romp, which I read several times with great pleasure back in the 1950s. But, because of the constraint of publishing limitations then, it's only about 50,000 words long, and merely nibbles at the infinite complexity of the planet on which it is set. Had he wished, Vance could have placed another dozen novels there without exhausting the territory. But, since he never wrote them, the notion came to me of creating a Big Planet of my own

Dust jacket author's photo from 1983.

and exploring its topographic possibilities with greater thoroughness than he had cared to apply.

The notation, "an *urban Big Planet,*" indicates my desire to distinguish my world from Vance's, which is predominantly a tropical jungle wilderness. I imagined a single huge city spreading thousands of miles in all directions — the very opposite of Vance's concept. But very quickly I saw the impossibility of that. If I wanted a population of many billions, I would need extensive agricultural zones to support them; and if I wanted (as I very much did) to create a host of fascinating plants and animals, I would have to have a variety of wild places.

So the back-to-back urban development made no sense, and in the end I fell back on a model that was even more like a giant India than Vance's planet: a place of teeming cities surrounded by vast farming districts, and yet, nevertheless, huge wilderness areas ranging from parched desert to jungle to snow-capped mountains, all of it surrounded by an ocean so enormous that no expedition had ever succeeded in crossing it. What I had in mind, in other words, was a planet so big that it could encompass a host of varying environments — stupendous jungles, seemingly interminable swamps, torrid plateaus, great rolling savannas, rivers seven thousand miles long, cities of thirty billion people — without any sense of crowding whatever.

To populate such a world with human beings, which was my intention, I would need to adopt the Vancean low-density planetary model, with its concomitant shortage of useful metals. Which told me at once that I would have to veer somewhat from a strictly science-fictional mode of thinking, because without metals there could be very little in the way of machinery — no aircraft and no telecommunications system, for example — and how, then, could I justify the existence of those cities with thirty billion people in them, with no rapid transit, no telephones, no elevators, indeed no high-rise structures? How could there be any sort of coherent central government, let alone the hierarchical and quasi-feudal monarchy that would justify a title like *Lord Valentine's Castle*?

I began to see that I would have to operate on that blurry borderline where science fiction shades into fantasy: a dollop of telepathy here and there for communication, a certain amount of vagueness about technology (an ancient civilization that has long ago used up its sparse metals and forgotten how its own mechanisms work), and some kind of ground-effect vehicles ("floaters") that didn't require internal-combustion engines or electricity to drive them. The lack of air transport, I figured, would work in my favor, adding to the sense of planetary immensity that was one of my primary goals: it would take just about forever to get from anywhere to anywhere there.

Suddenly I had a name for my planet: MAJIPOOR, "maji" to provide a subliminal hint of the magic that makes the whole place work, and the Hindi-sounding suffix "-poor" to remind me that my geographic model was the subcontinent of India blown up to superplanetary size.

While the planet itself was taking shape in the forefront of my mind, other cerebral areas were quietly at work designing a plot, characters to enact it, a history and a culture and a political system, and all those other features that a lengthy science-fantasy novel would require. But most of my conscious attention at that point was going toward envisioning Majipoor: its climate, its native life-forms, above all its geography and topography. These things, I knew, would determine many aspects of the story itself, from the form of government to the movements of my protagonists.

All right: maps, next.

I drew some quick sketches. Three continents, each far larger than any of Earth's. One to be the center of the world government; another, less fully developed, though with some major cities and a river of phenomenal size cutting across it, to be the home of the surviving aborigines who would, I already was coming to see, play some role in the plot; the third, more obscure, a forbidding desert land in the torrid south. I gave them names: Alhanroel, Zimroel, Suvrael. The structure of these names is the same as that used for naming angels in Judaeo-Christian mythology. I don't know why I did that.

I already had my title, *Lord Valentine's Castle*. Fine: put the Castle, which I understood to be the seat of the monarch, atop a special geographical feature: a Super-Kiliminjaro, as I called it in my notes, a mountain thirty miles high in the middle of Alhanroel. Castle Mount, I called it. It would be virtually a continent in itself, albeit a vertical one, protected from high-altitude forces of wind and cold by weather-altering and atmosphere-creating machinery designed and installed when Majipoor still was in its technological era. There would be fifty spectacular cities along its slopes and a gigantic Gormenghast-like royal castle at its summit.

But, since the political structure of Majipoor and the plot of the novel now were unfolding in my mind with the same swiftness as the geographical background, I needed a second capital also, for I intended a double monarchy. In order to sustain Majipoor's huge population under a single stable government, I wanted a ruling system that would provide a long series of enlightened monarchs. Hereditary rule wouldn't do that — it gives you a Caligula or a Commodus sooner or later — and neither, as I see it, would democracy. (Hitler was a democratically elected Chancellor.) But I remembered the system of adoptive emperors that produced the most successful period in the long history of the Roman Empire, each ruler choosing the most qualified man of the realm to follow him to the throne and adopting him as his son: Nerva picking Trajan, Trajan Hadrian, Hadrian selecting Antoninus Pius and simultaneously designating the promising young Marcus Aurelius to be Antoninus' ultimate successor.

I proposed — fantasy, again — to ask the reader to believe that such a system could be kept going for thousands of years if each emperor gave proper care to his choice of a successor. But also I intended to have two rulers in office at once, much as Fifth Republic France has a President and a Prime Minister, and the later Romans operated with an Augustus and a Caesar as senior and junior emperors. The older monarch — the Pontifex, I called him, with a nod to Rome — would live out of sight, in the deepest levels of a labyrinthine underground city thousands of miles south of the Castle. The junior king — the Coronal — would be the highly visible occupant of the Castle atop the great mountain, the public figure carrying out the orders that emerged from the hidden emperor in the Labyrinth. Upon the death of the Pontifex, the Coronal would take his place in the gloomy subter-

(below)
My original sketch for the map of the continent of Alhanroel on Majipoor.
— RS

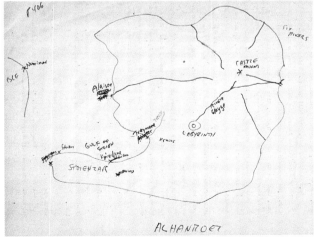

ALHANROEL

ranean capital and his designated successor, technically his adoptive son, would become Coronal at the Castle.

I saw now that I would not be writing, as my original moment-of-inspiration note had said, a "comic novel" — except in the sense that a novel that is not tragic can be classified as being comic. It would be light, yes; airy, yes; but in no way farcical, in no way satirical, in no way comic in the modern sense of that word. In its gentle way it would be a novel of quest, of internal discovery, of the attainment of responsibility.

My protagonist, I saw, would be a Coronal, Lord Valentine, who has, through some chicanery, been displaced from his throne by a usurper and set wandering as an amnesiac in the provinces, completely in ignorance of his true identity. A useful archetype: I find in my files a note that reads, "Valentine as Grail Knight — Perfect Fool — born ignorant and learns gradually." And again: "A hero suffers, comes to power as the regenerator of the world, and, if he doesn't die young, lives on to be old Tiberius and one needs a new hero." There are cryptic references on the sheet to the Tristan story, the "Perceval" of Chretien de Troyes, the Mabinogion, and books of mythic commentary by Jessie Weston, Joseph Campbell, Roger Sherman Loomis, and others. And my own final comment: "Valentine is an amiable & sunny man, though no simpleton, and people are naturally drawn to him."

Examining my gradually cohering plot in the light of my proposed governmental scheme gave me this: "Since Valentine is adopted, who is his true mother? Is she capable of detecting the impostor? (Or identifying the concealed ruler?) — She is a priestess on an island in a remote sea." Very well: put a large island between the continents of Alhanroel and Zimroel, and make it an important ritual center where the Great Mother rules.

Now I made fantasy and science fiction blend by positing that one way this giant world-state is held together is through the telepathic monitoring of dreams by this very mother-priestess and her staff, from her island fastness. She is the conscience of the world. "Dreams are significant," I wrote. "*Cf.* Tart on the Senak (?) — they guide and control society." And: "Dream interpretation a common daily practice — every morning a dream clinic — frequent public meetings to discuss/analyze dreams. 'In dreams begins responsibity.' Truths perceived more clearly by the sleeping mind." So the mother of the Coronal becomes a powerful figure in her own right, as the Lady of the Isle of Sleep, exploring the minds of all Majipoor's billions as they lie dreaming and offering advice or outright directive instruction in various metaphorical ways.

In all this, though, there was still no hint of the conflict that makes a novel work, other than the as yet unexplained usurpation that had sent Valentine into exile. Some sort of sinister player was needed. I jotted down this: "The King of Dreams is the dark adversary of the Emperor." A *second* telepathic force, this one far more stern and ominous than the benevolent Lady of the Isle: a sender of bad dreams, a planetary superego ferociously chastising those who get out of line, but also — so I realized — capable of getting out of line himself. The King of Dreams would turn out, in fact, to be connected in some way with the mysterious usurpation that thrusts the kindly Valentine from his throne. Put his headquarters, I thought, on the inhospitable desert continent of Suvrael; make him an equal partner in the government with the Pontifex, the Coronal, and the Lady — the

Powers of the realm.

My sheets of preliminary notes now fill up with all manner of archetypical references out of our world's history, literature, and myth, scooped up freely from all over and examined for their value to the developing narrative line: "Falstaff … the Malcontent figure…. Tiberius…. Caligula…. Aeneas and the descent into hell … Merlin/ Hermes … Shapeshifters … Jonah in the Whale … Darth Vader … Jason and the Fleece. . . ." All of these, and many more, would find their way in transmuted form into the plot of *Lord Valentine's Castle.*

After a few weeks of this sort of accretion of detail, virtually random at first but very quickly following a clear pattern, I was ready to set down a formal sketch of the book. It began with a statement of the general background:

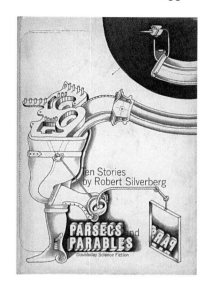

"This long picaresque adventure — the manuscript will probably run 600 pages — takes place on the huge world of Majipoor, a planet enormously bigger than Earth, but lacking most of the heavier elements, so that the gravity is only about three-fourths that of Earth. All is airy and light on Majipoor: it is a cheerful and playful place in general, although highly urbanized, bearing a population of many billions. Food is abundant, the air is fresh, the streams and oceans are clean. Majipoor was settled by colonists from Earth some fourteen thousand years ago, but also is occupied peacefully by representatives of six or seven of the galaxy's other intelligent species, as well as the descendants of Majipoor's own native race, humanoid in form, capble of physical changes of shape. These last beings are regarded with some uneasiness by the others, and this uneasiness is reciprocated.

Across the vastness of Majipoor's three colossal continents is spread an incredible diversity of cities, glittering and majestic, separated by parks, agricultural territories, forest preserves, wastelands kept deliberately barren as boundaries, and holy districts occupied by religious devotees. Such a gigantic cosmos of a planet can hardly be efficiently governed by one central authority, and yet a central authority does exist, to which all local governors do indeed pay lip-serve and on occasion direct homage. This central authority is the Pontifex, an imperial figure, aloof and virtually unknowable…."

PARSECS AND PARABLES *published by Doubleday, 1970.*

The outline goes on to describe the functions of the Coronal, the Lady of the Isle, and the King of Dreams, and the capitals from which they rule. Then it states the plot situation — Valentine's amnesia, and his affiliation with a troupe of wandering jugglers prior to his recovery of his memory and his attempt to regain his throne — and announces that "the form of the novel is a gigantic odyssey, divided into five 'books' of 35,000–40, 000 words each, during which the deposed Lord Valentine learns of his true identify, gradually and at first reluctantly resolves to regain his power, seeks successfully to obtain access to his original personality and memories, and crosses all of immense Majipoor, enlisting allies as he goes, engaging in strange and colorful adventures, finally to confront the usurper at the Castle.

There follows a synopsis of each of the five "books" — Valentine's adventures with the jugglers; his entanglement with the Shapeshifters in their jungle reservation; his sea journey to his mother's holy island, where he undergoes purification and regains much of his memory; his venture into the Labyrinth to confront his adoptive father, the Pontifex; and, finally, his ascent of Castle Mount and his war against the usurper, leading to the ultimate revelation of a usurpation within the usurpation and Valentine's successful restoration of the rule of law.

The entire outline ran to some twenty pages, and when it was presented to a number of publishers in June of 1978, it produced an enthusiastic response and brought me what was then the largest single advance in the history of science fiction publishing (a six-figure amount, impressive in its day, though it has, of course, been exceeded many times over in the intervening two decades.)

But now I had to write the book. It's one thing to sketch an outline for a world; it's another to build it line by line, page by page, for 600 pages.

The larger structures of the plot were in place, though, and I knew from past experience that I would be able to fill in necessary connective matter — minor characters, subplots, internal surprises — as I went along. What remained was for me to move Valentine across Majipoor from the west coast of the secondary continent to the heart of the primary one and up the slopes of thirty-mile-high Castle Mount, inventing the details of the terrain as I went.

In designing Majipoor it was my intent to treat my book as science fiction, not as fantasy: that is, it all would need to make sense in terms of my understanding of the phenomenological universe. Nothing could be dragged in for purely allegorical or metaphysical or symbolic purposes. Majipoor had to be as realistic as I could make it.

Here I drew on my strong suits: my knowledge of geography, archaelogy, and natural history, derived from a life of world travel, study, and experimental horticulture at home. Virtually everything that I had ever seen, read, heard about, or grown on the premises, and that includes quite a lot, went into the book. For each place to which Valentine came, beginning with the port city of Pidruid on Zimroel's northwestern coast and moving in a zigzag way toward the east, I invented an appropriate climate, a cuisine, an assortment of native wildlife, and — a matter of particular interest and amusement for me — a botanical background. All of these were, of course, derived in one fashion or another from terrestrial models; I don't believe that we science fictionists can ever really invent anything *ab initio*, but only make modifications against existing prototypes. The fiercest dragon is only *Tyrannosaurus rex* with an inner furnace; the most dreadful man-devouring Blob is just the good old amoeba writ large; and so on. The more familiar you are with a broad array of prototypes, the richer the variations you can ring on them; but true invention, I think, is Nature's own prerogative, and variations on existing themes is the best we can manage.

I managed pretty well, I feel. My garden has dozens of species of the type of plants known as bromeliads, most of which are in the form of rosettes with a cup in the center to hold a reservoir of water. Insects and plant matter fall into the cup also and decay to provide nutrients for the bromeliad. Fine: when I needed a bit of diversion I brought Valentine and his companions into a grove of "mouthplants," stemless plants that look very much like the bromeliads in my garden, except that their leaves are nine feet long and the central cups, a foot in diameter and half filled with noxious green fluid, are equipped with blade-like structures and paired grinders. The mouthplants are, in fact, carnivorous, grabbing their prey with hidden tendrils and conveying it to the cups to be chewed. There are, and let us give thanks for it, no such lovelies on our own world; but it was easy enough for me to dream them up for Majipoor, with the wealth of aechmaeas and billbergias just behind me in my garden as I wrote.

So I populated the forests and waters of Majipoor: with sea-dragons like great ichthyosaurs, with strange balloon-shaped submarine monsters that lived by filtering plankton, with glassy-fronded ferns that emitted piercing discordant sounds whenever they were approached, and — one of my particular favorites — trees whose trunks begin to atrophy with age and whose limbs inflate, until eventually their trunks have shriveled to mere guy-ropes that break at maturity, setting the limbs adrift like balloons to drift off and start new colonies elsewhere. All these things have models in real natural history, but I think I did a pretty fair job of extending and transforming those models beyond recognition to produce the distinctive flora and fauna of Majipoor.

Comic book adaptation of "Collecting Team" for Whitman Publishing Company's **STARSTREAM: Adventure in Science Fiction #2** *(series began 1976), art by Giorgio Cambiotti.*

The terrain, too — forests and jungles, mountains, rivers, a formidable desert, the mighty thrust of Castle Mount — came alive because I was working from life, depicting things I had seen myself, altering colors, shapes, forms, making everything more magical (though the originals are magical enough!) to yield the strange and extraordinarily rich landscape of my invented world. The cities were magnified versions of cities I had visited in Europe or Asia; the ruins of the prehistoric Shapeshifter capital were inspired by Roman ruins I had clambered through in North Africa; the geology was Earth-plus geology, everything writ large.

The grand scale of everything was the essential point. It would not have been enough simply to tell the old story of the disinherited prince yet again. It would not have been enough just to set a pack of wanderers loose on a gaudy planet. It would not have been enough to flange together a governmental system for that planet out of bits of Roman history and medieval archetype. It would not have been enough merely to make up a bunch of funny animals and peculiar plants.

But to do all of those things in one big book — to start with the intention of writing a "light, delightful, raffish" novel of more than usual size that delivers a "magical mystery tour" of an unthinkably huge planet — was what was needed to accomplish what I wanted to do in *Lord Valentine's Castle*. For that I needed six months of planning and research, six intense months of day-by-day writing, and some additional months of revision (in a pre-computer age that required endless retyping of the gigantic manuscript.) But the result was successful, a big, popular book that won me an audience far larger than I had ever had before.

And which gave me something to do in my autumnal years, too. Majipoor turned out to be so big that I can spend the rest of my life exploring it in book after book without ever exhausting the material.

The original "Majipoor Trilogy" — *Lord Valentine's Castle*, *Majipoor Chronicles*, and *Valentine Pontifex* — isn't really a trilogy at all. Trilogies, back in 1978, were not as automatic a concept in science fiction and fantasy as they later became, and although I was aware that I had left *Lord Valentine's Castle* open for a sequel that dealt with a resolution of the Shapeshifters' political discontent, I had no special plan at the time for writing that book. Instead I went back, all during 1980 and 1981, to write a series of stories that were essentially Majipoor afterthoughts, dealing with matters that had not been germane to the plot of *Lord Valentine's Castle* but which required examination anyway: the early days of human settlement there, the conduct of the ancient war against the Shapeshifters, the scenery of the third continent and the ocean sea (both unvisited in the novel), the nature of daily life in the big cities, and so on. Eventually I had a book of those, which became *Majipoor Chronicles*.

By then *Lord Valentine's Castle* had been published and attained its great popularity, and in 1983 I felt impelled, finally, to write the rather darker sequel, in which the gentle Valentine must come to grips with the actual problems of governing a world that has been thrust into civil war by an insurrection of the aborigines. (It was then that I discovered that much material inserted into the first novel purely for the sake of color, like the sea-dragons, retroactively came to have major importance in Majipoori history and in the plot of the new novel. It was like finding little gifts that I had left for myself.)

So the "Majipoor Trilogy" is actually two novels and a short story collection. And there I left matters for many years, until, a decade later, the urge came over

Cover illustration by John Picacio for **SON OF MAN (Pyr) 2008** .

me to find out what things were like up in the snowy northlands of Zimroel, the one place on the planet that does not have a temperate or tropical climate and is occupied by primitive roughnecks who live entirely outside the world government of the Pontifex-Coronal monarchy. So I went up there for a look, and out of that came the 1995 novella *The Mountains of Majipoor.*

And then —

Well, Majipoor is not only huge in geographical scope, but I've equipped it with 14,000 years of recorded human settlement prior to Valentine's time, and an unspecified Shapeshifter prehistory before that. The two novels deal entirely with one reign; *Mountains* goes five hundred years beyond that; the stories in *Chronicles* range across some eight or ten thousand years of history, but of necessity provide only quick snapshots here and there. There are plenty of tales to tell, when you have a civilization 14,000 years old to explore.

So I succumbed to the lure of Majipoor once more, going back a thousand years before Valentine to look into the golden age of the Coronal Prestimion, to which I had alluded in passing in one of the *Chronicles* stories. The first four Majipoor books, science-fantasy though they are, had leaned more toward science fiction than fantasy; now I saw a way to examine the other side of the equation by looking at an era when Majipoori magic had come out into the open. The long novel *Sorcerers of Majipoor* came out of that, and I see the possibility of two more before the investigation is done; and then there's something I'd like to look at in Valentine's old age, and then —

I'll be well along in my own old age by that time, though. Whether I'll go on to write all those novels is anyone's guess.

But I set out to build a world in the first of the Majipoor books, and I built better than I knew, and that world will, if I choose, keep me busy to the end of my days.

What I learned from the Majipoor experience is: Make it big. Scope counts, if you want a multi-book concept. (I wasn't looking for one, but very quickly realized that I had one anyway.) Make it ancient. Plenty of history is useful in the novel of scope, and in order to invent plenty of history, you need to know plenty yourself. See it and feel it from within: the birds and bugs, the plants, the critters large and small, the cuisine, the landscape. And, of course, the people. You're constructing a world that you and your readers are going to inhabit for a long time: give it solidity and substance. Get to know textures, detail, color, shape, above all the *purpose* of each component part of the entire invention. Everthing should fit into a logical ecological structure, and you should know what that logic is. If your invented world is a place you know extremely well, but nevertheless would like to return to again and again, your readers will feel the same way about it.

– DATE

AUTOBIOGRAPHY UPDATE II

A postscript, autumn of 1998, to a 1985 autobiographical essay for a reference book on living American writers —

"No choice but to continue," I said, back there in 1985. And that is the case, thirteen years later: I have continued to write science fiction and fantasy. Still living in California, too, at the same address, and still working at the battered old metal desk that I have used since 1956. But how much else has changed for me in those thirteen years!

I have a different agent now, a different publisher, a different wife, a different computer, even different cats. The dark Mephistophelian beard of those 1980s photographs is now bright white. The long curling dark hair of the 1972 "psychedelic" photograph is much shorter now, and very much more sparse. The out-of-print books that had returned to print and then vanished again in the closing paragraph of my 1985 essay have all returned yet again and disappeared once more, and once more I am negotiating to have them reprinted. And I have written thirteen years' worth of new books. And, finally: after all this time I still find myself caught between my decades-old desire to write complex and probing science fiction and the science fiction audience's predominant wish for easy light entertainment, despite the eternal irreconcilability of those two facts.

Things change, yes, but somehow the essences remain the same.

The cats, for instance. I find the company of cats necessary. I've had them about me my whole adult life. They make ideal writers' pets: quiet, slinky, beautiful, self-contained. I pamper my cats excessively and they generally live to fine old ages. The trouble is, though, that old age for a cat is fifteen or sixteen years, and I'm always devastated when they die. (My all-time favorite cat lived to be almost nineteen; her nearly-as-beloved predecessor lasted nearly as long.) The cycle has come around again: the cats of the 1980s finally went their way, one in 1993 and the other in 1998, and I am equipped now with successors to see me into the new century. The newest one, perhaps, will still be here when I'm gone. (I suspect that cats miss their people far less than people miss their cats.)

It used to be that one expected one's marriage to last longer than one's cats. Our culture is different now; one clings to one's pets, I gather, but spouses are discarded for the most trivial of reasons. I am of the pre-war vintage, though, raised amidst the turmoil of the Depression and then the war, and we are more retentive in our ways. Unhappy in my obviously collapsing first marriage but unwilling to take the climactic and to me gigantic step of divorce, I remained in a condition of stasis much too long. But eventually the situation became too unstable to sustain. We separated, finally, after twenty years, and I spent the next nine as a single man.

Then, while on a speaking tour in Texas in the spring of 1981, I met a bright, petite, articulate woman from New York who happened to be living just then in Houston and had decided to see what one of her favorite science fiction authors actually looked like; we exchanged a few pleasant quips, I invited her to have lunch with me, we agreed to stay in touch by mail, and eventually (to her great surprise, I think, and mine as well) she (and her cat) came to live with me in California when her Texas marriage fell apart. Her name is Karen. We were married in February 1987. She had had a background in journalism, and was a long-time reader of science fiction who had some thought of writing the stuff.

"This is how you construct a story, any kind of story," I told her, "and this is how you use a specifically science fictional story situation to generate your plot," and I gave her two or three other handy writing tips, and over the past ten years she has had eight novels and about fifty short stories published under her maiden name, Karen Haber. (It seemed to both of us that her writing as Karen Silverberg would only cause confusion in the field where one Silverberg was already so well known.) We edit each other's manuscripts; we go to each other for suggestions when a story idea refuses to gell. Over the years I had heard rumors of the existence of such things as happy marriages; it's a pleasant novelty actually to be a member of one.

A writer's relationship with his agent is much like a marriage in many important ways. My first agent, like my first wife, had many fine qualities, but there were serious things wrong with both relationships, and in both cases I overstayed them by at least a decade. I went on in 1981 to a second agent, Kirby McCauley, for whom I still feel considerable personal affection. But Kirby's working methods and mine turned out to be incompatible, and we came to a friendly parting of the ways six years later. Since then I have been represented by the formidable Ralph Vicinanza, who is (as it should be between writers and agents) not only my agent but one of my closest friends. We have known each other since the mid-1970s, when he was in charge of foreign-rights sales for my first agent and impressed me again and again with his ability to do long-range planning and to bring those plans to fruition.

His shift to the McCauley agency in 1978 to hold the same post there was

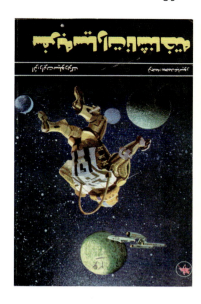

(above)
This is the (pirated) Persian edition of STEPSONS OF TERRA. I've been published all over the map.
— RS

(below)
WORLD'S FAIR 1992, Danish edition.

.

an important factor in my going to that agency a few years later; and when he left Kirby in the summer of 1987 to set up his own agency, handling domestic rights as well as overseas ones, I jumped at the chance to go with him. I was his first client, actually. Ralph's agency has grown enormously in the past decade, and by now he holds a dominant position in the science fiction and fantasy field. We remain as close as ever, despite his greatly expanded responsibilities. We stay in constant contact, seeking each other's advice on personal as well as professional matters; we anticipate each other's thoughts, we finish each other's sentences. In the areas of our lives where we are different from each other, and there are some big ones, we are as different as day and night, but where we are similar we think with one mind. I could not have hoped for a better agent.

My publishers have changed, too. I would have preferred, as John Updike has done, to have remained with a single publisher all my life, but such things are hard to manage in today's immensely transformed publishing world. Elsewhere I spoke of having "stumbled into the publishing relationship I had been looking for all my life" with the "difficult, volatile, cantankerous, brilliant" Donald I. Fine. And I would gladly have remained with Don forever, except that the small company that he founded in 1984 soon became enmeshed in financial problems, and Don, in an attempt to solve them, entered into a complicated co-publishing arrangement with Warner Books that introduced a degree of chaos into my own career which I found myself unable to abide.

In time I felt compelled to leave Don for Warner, and Warner for Bantam Books, then under the guidance of another old friend of mine, Lou Aronica. I agreed to write five novels in as many years for Lou. The year was 1988. Lou was young, and had never worked anywhere but at Bantam; I fully expected him to stay there forever, and I intended to remain there with him.

But publishing is not like that any more; to my consternation Lou abruptly moved on to another house in 1993, leaving me in the hands of people at Bantam with whom I felt no rapport, and within a couple of years I had taken myself

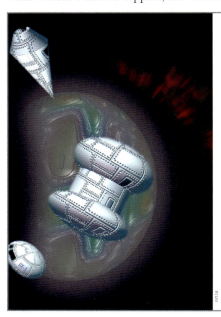

THE whole thing got arranged, with surprising ease, in short order at long range. Hanosz Prime of Prime—young again and feeling restless, beginning his new life in startling new ways, eager to travel, suddenly desirous of seeing historic old Earth while it was still there to be seen—caused word to be sent ahead by hyperwave, using diplomatic channels, in order to get himself invited to be a house-guest at the palatial home of one of the grandest and most famous of Earth's immortal aristocrats, the distinguished and celebrated Sinon Kreidge. Prime had good social connections in more than one galaxy. And so the message went forth, pretty much instantaneously across two million light-years, through an elaborate interface of official intermediaries spanning half a dozen stellar systems, and the answer came back in a trice—a favorable one. Sinon Kreidge and his daughter Kaivilda have heard a great deal about the distinguished and celebrated Hanosz Prime of Prime, or at any rate they claim that they have, and will be happy to entertain him during his stay on Earth. And so the visit was arranged. Quick, quick, back and forth across the galaxies!

It's an age of miracles, the Ninth Mandala that is the era of Prime and Sinon Kreidge. Our own accom-

HANOSZ PRIME GOES TO OLD EARTH

By
[Robert Silverberg]

51

elsewhere too. My current publishing house is HarperCollins, where I am in the hands of a couple of long-time friends, John Silbersack and John Douglas. Will I still be there by the time this postscript appears? Will they? Will HarperCollins still exist as an independent publishing house at all? Things change too fast in publishing these days for me to make any predictions about such things. *Someone* will be publishing my books five years from now, of that I'm sure. For all I know, I'll still be with HarperCollins. But there are no certainties nowadays.

I had to change computers, too. For someone as conservative as I am, that was a real ordeal. I had been one of the first science fiction writers to use a computer, back in the dark ages before CP/M, let alone MS-DOS. It was a truly fine machine for its era, but the price I paid for my innovative stance back then was to find myself left alone, after a time, on a technological island, using a splendidly versatile computer and wordprocessing program, both of which had the grave drawback of being totally noncompatible with anything used by anyone else.

One autumn day in 1991, while I was in the midst of writing a long and complex story with a serious deadline attached to it, my computer suddenly decided not to speak to its printer any more, and there was no one left on the

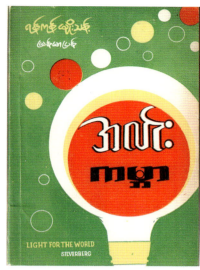

And this is the Burmese edition of a nonfiction book of mine, LIGHT FOR THE WORLD. I think it's the only book of mine to have been published in Burma (Myanmar).—RS

(bottom)
AT WINTER'S END, *Warner Books, NY; 1988, first Edition. Cover art by Michael Whelan.*

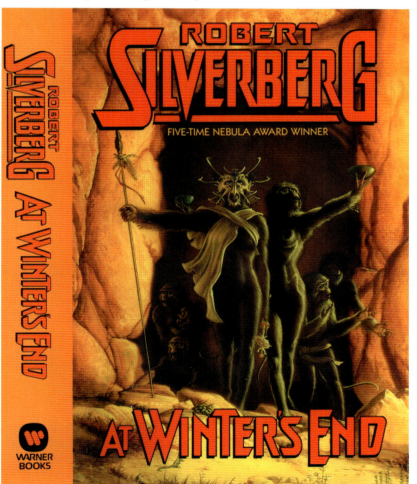

Art by Bob Eggleton for
THE ALIEN YEARS.

planet who understood how to restore the link between those two pieces of obsolete equipment. By heroic measures that constitute an epic in themselves, my unfinished story was rescued from digital form; I keyed it into a newly purchased MS-DOS-based computer, employing a DOS variant of my word-processing program, and have used that machine ever since. Of course, it's pretty much obsolete too, now — the triumphant arrival of Windows swept MS-DOS into the wastebins of computer antiquity — but, in my doggedly conservative way, I still use it for my daily work, because my beloved old word-processing program can't be installed through Windows. (I have a Windows-based computer too, modem and all, but I use it only for e-mail and the Internet.)

My writing output has diminished gradually, here in the fifth decade of my career. Still, I remain a fairly prolific writer, though of course I have never returned to the tremendous, virtually unthinkable productivity of the fifteen years beginning in 1956. I hew pretty closely today to the pattern I set for myself in 1971, which is keyed to the California seasons: usually I begin work in October or November, when our rainy season begins, and carry on through to April or May. This leaves the six dry, sunny months of the California summer for gardening, swimming, travel, or whatever else I please.

Nevertheless, given my habit of intense concentration on my work and ferocious daily application to the task, a working year of five or six months is ordinarily enough to produce a novel and two or three shorter pieces. And thus it has gone over these thirteen years. 1985 saw *Tom O'Bedlam*, a character-driven novel set in the relatively near future — a book that I thought never received the attention it was due. A year later I tried something completely different in *Star of*

Gypsies, which I intended as a rich, rollicking space story narrated by a Rabelaisian gypsy king very much unlike the author who created him. That book, too, failed to cause much of a stir, which I ascribe not to any deficiency on its part but to the confusions in my career that the collapse of the Donald Fine publishing company was beginning to cause.

I emerged from that debacle to enter a relationship with Warner Books, a company run by good-natured and well-intentioned people who didn't seem to know much about publishing science fiction. By the time I discovered that, though, I had expended an enormous effort in the creation of what was meant as a vast and visionary epic trilogy set in the unimaginably distant future. I intended the books as a way of showing my love for the sort of fiction that escorts readers through a wholly imaginary world realized with such richness of detail that it would remain part of their mental landscapes forever. But the first two novels in the trilogy — *At Winter's End*, published in 1988, and *The New Springtime*, which appeared in 1990 — sold so poorly that the publisher made only a token offer for the rights to the third book, which would have been called *The Summer of Homecoming*. I did not have the heart to undertake so long and punishing a task for so little in the way of financial recompense, particularly at a time when the cost of my too-long-postponed 1986 divorce from my first wife was hitting me hard, and so I refused the offer and the third book has never been written. Which I greatly regret, because it was to have been the summation of the entire grand vision. But I see no way now that I can ever finish the trilogy, since it would be necessary to find someone to republish the first two books before bringing out the third, and I see no likely chance of that.

Four books in a row had failed commercially, although I had found each, in its very different way, personally rewarding to write. And I had, at least, been well paid during this difficult time, since each book carried a healthy guarantee in advance of publication. I would rather see my publishers make money on my books rather than lose it, but I always see to it that they, not I, carry the economic risk of publication. There's no other way for a writer to guard against the usual gloomy fate of most publishing deals, which always begin with high hopes, warm feelings, and glowing promises, and generally end with catastrophic bungling on the publisher's part and disappointment for the writer.

So I banked my big Warner checks and went trundling on to the next publisher, who was Lou Aronica of Bantam Books: a man for whom I felt great personal affinity and one whose innovative publishing ideas had shot him to a lofty executive post at a preternaturally early age. We had had a brief publishing flirtation in 1981, which was thwarted by the odd contractual fluke that swept me off to Arbor House; but now Aronica lost no chance to tie me up for years, offering me not only a five-novel contract to write any sort of books I pleased, but also a lucrative three-book deal for collaboration with, of all people, Isaac Asimov.

Isaac had been, of course, one of my boyhood heroes when I was discovering science fiction, and later, after I launched my own professional career, we had become good friends. He was fifteen years my senior, but our lives had had much in common: two bright Jewish boys from Brooklyn, bratty and precocious when young, both educated at Columbia, prolific careers in science fiction afterward, troubled first marriages and expensive divorces followed by happy second marriages.

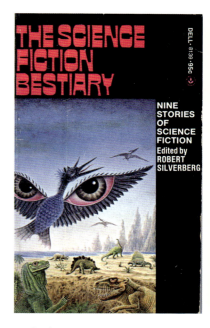

(top)
THE SCIENCE FICTION BESTIARY,
Dell paperback, 1974.

(bottom)
CAPRICORN GAMES,
Pan Books, paperback, 1979.

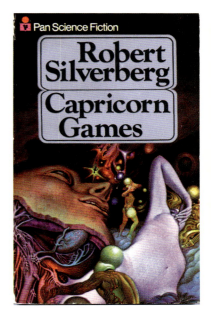

I think THE TIME HOPPERS *was the best book I had written up till then, or at least one of the two or three best. But that was in 1965.*

BOOK OF SKULLS *was done with four different first-person narrators. A stunt, in other words. I was trying all sorts of stunts in those days. That experiment worked out successfully, but it's not the sort of thing you ought to try more than once.—* RS

THE TIME HOPPERS *cover art by Don Ivan Punchatz.*

In 1988, when our collaborative deal surfaced, Isaac's health was beginning to weaken. He felt certain he had just a few years to live, and there were some big books on science he wanted to write, but his publisher — Doubleday — wanted him to write sf. Since Doubleday now was affiliated with Bantam Books, Lou Aronica arranged a compromise: I would transform three famous novellas of Isaac's into novels under his close direction for Doubleday and Bantam, thus leaving Isaac himself free to write the nonfiction he yearned to do.

The arrangement was that we would plan the expansions of the stories together, but that I would write the first drafts myself, and that meant I needed to absorb and replicate Isaac's own literary style. His prose always was simple, lucid, straightforward. My own tone, somewhat more baroque, had to be suppressed. His narrative method relied almost entirely on dialogue and bare-bones exposition; he had little interest in evoking sensory images, particularly visual ones, whereas I have always strived toward rich descriptive impact. But I found it was surprisingly easy to drop into the low-key Asimovian mode of storytelling, especially since I had his original stories ("Nightfall," "The Ugly Little Boy," and "The Bicentennial Man") to use as templates.

"Nightfall" was the first one I did, and it was a strange experience for me to find myself working with a story I had revered since I was twelve years old, adding new sections before and after it and even, to some degree, rewriting the original classic novella itself. But my expansion met with Isaac's enthusiastic bless-

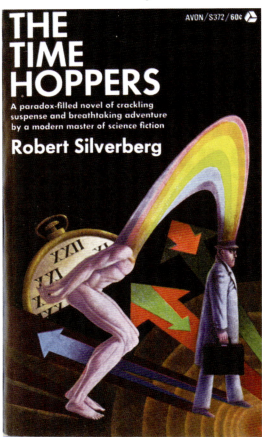

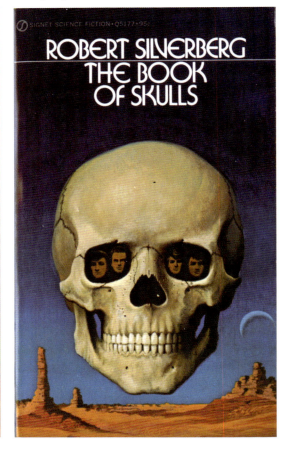

ing. He made relatively few revisions in my text, and the following year I went on to "The Ugly Little Boy."

For this one I was virtually on my own, because Isaac now was seriously ill, and he had neither time nor energy to contribute much to the book, though he did read my draft and give it unqualified approval. I think it was the most successful of the three, greatly extending and illuminating the existing story-line and the character of the protagonist and adding to it a whole layer of background material set in Neanderthal times.

As for the third book, which ultimately appeared under the name of *The Positronic Man*, I believe my work was an important extension of Isaac's moving original story, but I will never know what he thought of it, because he had been

(left)
art by Joe Brozowski done for Whitman Publishing Company's **STARSTREAM: Adventure in Science Fiction,** *(unpublished), c. 1977, adapting "Birds of a Feather."*

hospitalized by the time I finished the book and was in no condition to read my draft. The book appeared soon after his death in 1992. (A few years later it was purchased for filming by Disney, with Robin Williams starring in the movie.)

Meanwhile, alternating with the three Asimov books, I was writing novels of my own for Bantam: *The Face of the Waters* in 1990, *Kingdoms of the Wall* in 1991, *Hot Sky at Midnight* in 1992. The first was a hearkening-back to one of my big themes of two decades before, an isolated and alienated man's complicated quest for submergence in some kind of vast communal entity. It did quite well, going into several printings, my most commercially successful book in some years. The second, diametrically opposed in its conclusions, sent the primitive people of an alien land on a disillusioning search for their gods. Its sales were not quite as good. The third book, a kind of techno-thriller with a greenhouse-effect world as its setting, had, I thought, an excellent chance of reaching an audience that went far beyond the usual sf readership, but the publisher wrapped the book in a vivid, sensationalistic genre-fiction jacket that doomed any such hope, and the book did poorly.

I was beginning to understand by now that the modern science fiction reader, weaned on television series and movie sequels, did not greatly want standalone novels. Such singleton items as *Tom O'Bedlam* and *Face of the Waters* and *Hot Sky at Midnight*, whatever their qualities might be, stood little chance of gaining public attention when they had to compete with the latest *Dune* novel, or the newest *Rama* book, or the current sequel to *2001*, or whatever. The series book dominated the marketplace utterly. So I began to plot a return to Majipoor, the world of *Lord Valentine's Castle*, my best-selling book. Bantam owned the paperback rights to *Castle* and its two sequels, *Majipoor Chronicles* and *Valentine Pontifex*. I hatched the idea of kindling new interest in Majipoor by writing a very short novel, *Mountains of Majipoor*, to catch the attention of new readers; Bantam would, at the same time, reissue the original trilogy.

It was another mistake. Very short novels, even if they are connected with well-known series, don't usually sell well either. Today's readers want fat books. *Mountains* did very poorly indeed and provided no help whatever for a reissue of the trilogy.

With two books left on my main five-book Bantam contract, I was in com-

Silverberg c. 1990.

mercial trouble. And about this time, Lou Aronica left Bantam Books, and I was bereft of his invaluable counsel and support. I wrote the fourth Bantam book, *Starborne*, without much hope that the new administration at Bantam would get behind it. And then, even before *Starborne's* inevitable failure in the marketplace, I bailed out once more, buying back the fifth book in the Bantam contract and taking myself over to HarperCollins, the successor to Harper & Row, which was the company for whom I had written *Lord Valentine's Castle* sixteen years before.

The plan was to write new Majipoor novels for them — full-length ones, big books in the modern mode that would appeal not to the science fiction audience but to the far larger one that doted on fantasy. Through an intricate contractual maneuver I was able to bring the paperback rights of the previous Majipoor novels along with me, so that HarperCollins would be able to reissue *Lord Valentine's Castle* and its companions in paperback format along with the new books, giving me renewed visibility in this era of multi-volume series.

And so it happened. They put out *Castle* and *Chronicles* and *Pontifex* in handsome new reprint editions using Jim Burns' elegant cover art from the decade before, and I wrote *Sorcerers of Majipoor* in 1996 and its sequel, *Lord Prestimion*, two years later, with possible further Majipoor books to follow.

The Majipoor concept is essentially inexhaustible — a world ten times the size of Earth, with 14,000 years of history since the arrival of the first human settlers and a lengthy prehistoric period besides — and I could easily use it as a source for books for the rest of my life. But that's not what I want to do, however eager the readers are for more and more and more. It's not my intention to let the Majipoor books eclipse everything else I've done.

And so the book that immediately followed *Sorcerers of Majipoor* was not its sequel, though I already had that in mind, but rather a wholly unrelated science fiction novel, *The Alien Years*. In that book I take the grand old H. G. Wells *War of the Worlds* theme and give it a post-modern spin, telling a tale of Earth's conquest that ends not with Hollywood heroics but with an unexpectedly anticlimactic resolution, quite deliberately intended. Some readers evidently were baffled by my apparent failure to finish the book with a pyrotechnic display and were annoyed, but in general *The Alien Years* has had an enthusiastic reception both critically and commercially. It appeared in the summer of 1998, just as I was finishing *Lord Prestimion*. And in the month I write this I am in negotiations both for the third novel in the current Majipoor sequence and for a new stand-alone science fiction novel that's unlikely to win wide sales but which will satisfy whatever's left of my urge to write the kind of science fiction that I would admire if I were simply a reader of the stuff, not a professional writer with one eye on the royalty charts.

Not that I'm indifferent to the sales figures even now, of course. But my finances are in good order and I'm under no pressing need these days to aim my work for the mass audience, something I was never consistently able to do very well anyway. There's enough income coming in from my existing books, and from such peripheral projects as the best-selling fantasy anthology *Legends* (1998), a collection of eleven big new novellas by the likes of Stephen King, Robert Jordan, Ursula K. Le Guin, and Anne McCaffrey that I edited for Tor Books, to see me through any likely expenses, leaving me free to write just the books I feel like writing. (There has also been a surprising and welcome burst of Hollywood interest in my work in recent years: the short story "Amanda and the Alien" has already been filmed, movies of *The Book of Skulls, The Man in the Maze, The Positronic Man*, and the short stories "Passengers" and "Needle in a Timestack" are in various stages of becoming reality, and a number of further deals for stories and books of mine are approaching fruition.)

What I wanted, long ago back there in my Brooklyn boyhood, was simply to write a few science fiction stories that someone would want to publish. After what seemed at the time like an endless period of travail and frustration, but which I now can see in retrospect was an eyeblink moment that led to overnight success, I did indeed accomplish that. And went on from there to spend decade after decade — I am halfway through the fifth of them now — achieving goal after goal, not merely getting published but building a significant career, attaining fame and fortune, winning awards, even writing some stories that I felt were on a par with the great works of science fiction that had drawn me inexorably into this field in the first place half a century ago. If I were looking at my own career from the outside, no doubt I'd envy myself tremendously. Why not? A long life of enormous and seemingly effortless productivity, financial success, and critical acclaim — what more could I have wanted for myself?

Here on the inside it seems a little different. The productivity was enormous, yes, but since the early 1960s, when I put the cheerful churning-out of anonymous hackwork behind me, the sentence-by-sentence job of writing has been by no means effortless for me, however others looking at my great output might think, and some projects have been downright agonizing. This problem has intensified as I grow older and the normal and natural decline of physical energy and imaginative vitality has set in. (Shakespeare did all his work before he reached 50; Dickens died at 58, Hemingway at 61. I'm older than that now. Among my own more immediate colleagues, Robert Heinlein and Isaac Asimov and Ray Bradbury had all produced most of the work for which they are known by the age of 45 or so.) And there has also been the ongoing and insoluble problem of the conflict between my literary ambitions and the fact that science fiction is primarily a species of mass-audience entertainment, an issue that has consumed no little quantity of my ingenuity and from time to time sapped my willingness to write at all.

So my career, marked as it has been by triumph after triumph, has often seemed to me like nothing but a formidable struggle. On half a dozen occasions in my life I have felt that it was a struggle in which I was no longer willing to engage; at least twice I have given it up entirely, only to find myself returning, willy-nilly, to contend against the often maddening forces that keep drawing science fiction back to its pulp-magazine roots. It seems impossible for me to walk away from science fiction entirely, despite my dissatisfactions with the way it is published and my lack of any financial pressure to go on writing here in my sixties.

And so this postscript ends where my original essay does, a dissonant chord resolving itself into an acceptance of an inescapable destiny. I suspect that if I am lucky enough to be asked to provide yet another autobiographical report thirteen years hence, I will once again be found grumbling about the deficiencies of the readership and the deplorably low level of publishing integrity in these modern times — and talking also about my two or three most recent books.

1998

FOUR: MISCELLANY OF A LIFE

Silverberg c. late 1980s.

TIPTREE

The critic John Clute, in his introduction to the wonderful collection of stories by "James Tiptree, Jr." that Arkham House published in 1990 under the title of *Her Smoke Rose Up Forever* and which you should certainly buy immediately and read, because Tiptree was one of the great masters of modern science fiction, has this to say about a certain much-discussed introduction to a previous Tiptree collection that I wrote nearly two decades earlier:

"In 1975, in his introduction to Tiptree's *Warm Worlds and Otherwise*, Robert Silverberg gave voice to a biocritical speculation about the author which has since become famous. 'It has been suggested that Tiptree is female,' he wrote, 'a theory that I find absurd, for there is to me something ineluctably masculine about Tiptree's writing.' Given human nature, it's unlikely many of Silverberg's readers could have failed to enjoy the discomfiture he must have felt in 1977 when Tiptree's identity was uncovered, and there is no denying that what he said was both inapposite in its self-assurance and culture-bound in its assumption that an artifact of language … was inherently sexed, so that only a biological male could utter it. This was surely careless of Silverberg."

What this is all about, for those who come in late, is the revelation in 1976 that the mysterious person who for the previous eight or nine years had been writing superb science fiction under the name of "James Tiptree, Jr." — and whose easy familiarity with such "masculine" matters as guns, airplanes, the interior workings of automobile engines, and the military/espionage world seemed to indicate that he was, as I put it in my celebrated introduction, "a man of 50 or 55, possibly unmarried, fond of outdoor life, restless in his everyday existence, a man who has seen much of the world and understands it well" — was, in fact, a 61-year-old retired psychologist named Alice B. Sheldon, very much female.

Well, I certainly looked silly, didn't I! But — contrary to my good friend John Clute's assertion — I felt very little 'discomfiture,' only surprise, and some degree of intellectual excitement. For what the Tiptree affair had done was to bring into focus the whole issue of whether such things as "masculine" and "feminine" fiction existed. This is what I had to say in an unabashed afterword to my Tiptree introduction when *Warm Worlds and Otherwise* was reissued four years after Alice Sheldon had confessed to being the author of those "ineluctably masculine" Tiptree stories:

"Just before Christmas, 1976, came a letter in the familiar blue-ribbon typing, hesitantly confessing that 'Tiptree' is the pseudonym of Dr. Alice B. Sheldon, and hoping I would not be too upset about having gone so far out on a limb with my insistence on 'Tiptree's' maleness. Quite a surprise package....

"Okay: no shame attaches. She fooled me beautifully, along with everyone else, and called into question the entire notion of what is 'masculine' or 'feminine' in fiction. I am still wrestling with that. What I have learned is that there are some women who can write about traditionally male topics more knowledgeably than most men, and that the truly superior artist can adopt whatever tone is appropriate to the material and bring it off. And I have learned — again, as if I needed one more lesson in it — that Things Are Seldom What They Seem. For these aspects of my education, Alli Sheldon, I thank you. And for much else."

I never met the woman who wrote the Tiptree stories, though as the editor of the *New Dimensions* series and other projects of the 1970s I published a number of her finest stories. We corresponded, on and off, for about fifteen years. Since "James" is a male name and the Tiptree stories were not only crisp, tough, conventionally "male" in voice but also indicated a much deeper knowledge of machinery and politics and the military world than many unquestionably male writers (Robert Silverberg, for instance) have, I had no reason to think that this reclusive, much-traveled, knowledgable Tiptree person was anything but what "he" seemed to be.

Alli Sheldon herself, be it noted, *never* in any way claimed to be a man to any of her many correspondents. She simply never said she wasn't, and left us to draw our own conclusions. And occasionally dropped in an artful half-truth to keep us bamboozled.

For example, in a letter to me of June 8, 1974, she noted that I had written my last letter to her on the back of a piece of my wife's stationery, and so, she said, "I read the first part of your letter under the impression I was hearing from her. In fact, I shaved and applied lotion before continuing."

Very tricky. Men, of course, are not the only members of the human species who shave; but shaving is, nevertheless, an act that is more commonly associated with men than with women, perhaps because the part of the body that men customarily shave is more visible than the parts women shave.

But notice also that Tiptree talks about feeling that it would be appropriate *to shave and apply lotion* before continuing to read a letter that seemed to come from my wife, which could easily be construed as a macho male's amiable way of saying that he would want to look his best in the presence of such an attractive woman as he understood my wife to be. (In the same paragraph, though, "Tiptree" provided, if I had only had the wit to see it, a huge hint in the other direction. My wife in 1974 was not the Karen of modern times but Barbara, an electronics engineer with a training in physics, very much the prototype of the liberated woman; and Tiptree, citing Barbara's reputation as a formidable scientist who also happened to be female, said, "She is, if you want to know, one of my chief inducements to forsake anonymity, the other being U. K. Le Guin." I was free to interpret that as meaning that if Tiptree came out of hiding he would have the chance to meet those two remarkable women — something a man might very well want to do; but in hindsight it also appears to be saying that the success of those two women in attaining intellectual achievement and public acclaim despite the handicap of belonging to the "second sex" was almost inspiring enough for the author of the Tiptree stories to admit that she, too, was a woman.

I assume that Alli Sheldon felt she would somehow be at a disadvantage if she submitted her stories with a female byline. In fact she was wrong about that: such women as Kate Wilhelm, Joanna Russ, Ursula Le Guin, Anne McCaffrey, and Marion Zimmer Bradley were already quite prominent in sf when the first Tiptree stories began to appear. But also, I think, the masquerade in false whiskers was a kind of stimulating game to her, a facet of her complex, quirky personality. And certainly she carried it off brilliantly.

Eventually a Baltimore fan named Jeffrey D. Smith, through clever sleuthing, uncovered the Sheldon identity behind the Tiptree stories. In December 1976, she admitted the truth to a small group of people like me whom she felt she might have offended by allowing them to persist in their error. ("Honour, or

ISAAC ASIMOV SF MAGAZINE *July, 1987 with "The Fascination of the Abomination".*

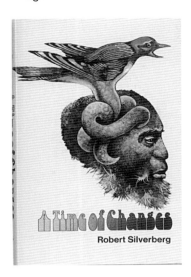

A TIME OF
CHANGES, *Nelson
Doubleday, Inc., 1971,
cover art by Brad Holland.*

something, compels me to do something after which I fear I may have lost a deeply valued friend," she wrote me, and confessed the truth about herself, saying, "It hasn't been a put-on or attempt to take advantage, it just grew and grew until 'Tip' became me.") And when I replied that I was more amused than angered, she wrote back to say, "Thank God. Jesus with what trepidation I opened your letter.… When I saw how thick it was I thought, Here it goes. 2 pages of telling me what a shit I am; all gone forever.")

I suppose I *could* have been annoyed. She had seen my infamous introduction proving that she was male before it was published, and let it appear in print. (Her comment to me on it after reading the manuscript was, "Just read your intro for that Ballantine thing. Jesus god, man. I won't go on about looking over my shoulder to see who in hell he's *talking* about.… The organization and clarity of the thing is a bit boggling. It conveys the picture of a mind so lucidly, effortlessly informed that on request it turns out indifferently a flawless essay on the lepidoptera of Mindanao or the political theories of Apollinaris Sidonius." Not a hint from Tiptree there that my lucid and well-informed mind was completely in error about the writer I was discussing.)

After all this time, one basic issue remains: Was Alice Sheldon/James Tiptree a writer who was so well informed about traditional man-stuff like guns and armies and machinery that she crossed the boundary that separates men's fiction from women's fiction, or is that boundary in fact nonexistent? As you form your own opinion, bear in mind that we are talking about a woman who was born in 1915, and that even in the world of the 1970's, not all that long ago, men were the ones who did most of the rough, tough things that Alli Sheldon wrote about with such apparent expertise. The lines have blurred since then; the stereotypes have begun to break down.

I *still* think that Ernest Hemingway wrote like a man and that Jane Austen like a woman, and that there are discernible differences both in style and in content. (Don't tell me about the yearnings toward androgyny that have surfaced in Hemingway's posthumously published work: he still sounds like a man to me.) So, the Tiptree episode notwithstanding, I suppose I still haven't fully learned my lesson.

In the very collection that I prefaced was the powerful feminist story "The Women Men Don't See." The title tells it all. I chose to interpret it as the work of a man with great insight into the difficulties women face in our culture. Stupid of me, in retrospect. I let myself be snookered by the first-person-male narration and forgot to listen to what was really being said.

Or consider, if you will, Tiptree's classic "Houston, Houston, Do You Read?," which was published after I wrote my introduction and won all the awards in sight. It's a superb story. The male sex has become extinct and the women are doing just fine by parthenogenesis, and then three men out of the past turn up out of a time-warp. They act like boobs, generally. They can't help it, poor things: they're men, after all. And the cool, competent women of that future world know what to do with them. I like to believe that if I had been able to read that cruel, magnificent story before I had written that 1975 piece on Tiptree, I would have thought twice about proclaiming the "ineluctable masculinity" of its author. Maybe a man *could* have written "Houston, Houston." But certainly I don't think so. Am I in trouble all over again?

1993

AGBERG, LTD; EST. 1981

For the first time in my life I'm an employee, after more than twenty-five years as a self-employed freelance writer. Of course, I own the company that employs me, so you might argue that not a whole lot has changed, but so far as the bureaucracy of the United States Government is concerned there has been an immense transformation indeed. Details of this momentous transition a little later on.

It was around 1958 or so that I gave my mimeograph machine to Lee Hoffman and thereafter depended on the good offices of other people to reproduce my fan publications, which have appeared steadily if not exactly frequently since then. Boyd Raeburn did the work for a long time, and then Susan Wood handled it, and for a time Bill Rotsler, and probably there have been a few others along the way who did the work for me too. I could look it all up, but what the hell, some nitpicker is bound to take care of that on my behalf, probably the same nitpicker who ran off the mag and collated it for nine issues back in the 1960s, or so.

But now I actually have reproductive equipment of my own again after all those dreary decades without it. It isn't any grubby old mimeograph machine this time, kid. (This isn't 1949, kid.) I've got my own little photocopy machine sitting on the floor a dozen feet from me, and the wonder of it is how I got along without a copier all these years. I do regret it, just as I regret not having sold myself out to a corporation long ago. But at least I've made up for past omission lately. My role model in all of these experiments in modern living is none other than the fabled Harlan Ellison of Sherman Oaks, CA., who has pioneered the way. Time was when I was the one who taught Harlan stuff, like how to put that cute little wave in his hair and which end of the sheet of paper to stick into the typewriter first. But the dear little bugger is a fast study, and somewhere along the way he picked up some tricks of his own, and then he began to do things that would never have occurred to me.

Like getting a photocopier. I always thought copiers were things that huge corporations owned, or else that people with Heavy Responsibilities rented. I recall that when Damon Knight was president of SFWA he rented a Xerox machine, and under the terms of the rental he had to make umpty copies a

Harlan Ellison, Larry Shaw, and RS at the 1984 Worldcon. Photo by Jay Kay Klein.

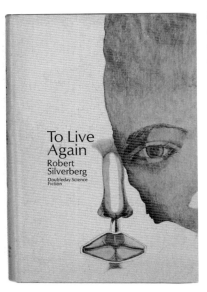

TO LIVE AGAIN,
Doubleday & Company,
Inc., 1969.

month or else each copy would be prohibitively expensive, so Damon ran off copies of every goddamn thing imaginable that might be relevant to the officership of the Science Fiction Writers of America and sent it around in umptiplicate. That struck me as a damn silly thing to be doing with your own money, so I didn't do it.

Then one day about nine years ago I noticed a bulky machine sitting in a corner of Harlan's office. He had rented a Xerox too. And behold: he began sending around copies of every goddamn thing too, running off whatever struck his fancy. I calculated the cost of all of that and decided that I could get along without one, even as today I have decided, quite firmly for the moment, that I can get along without a home computer and word processor.

But I started to notice how useful Harlan's gadget was.

You know, when you get a story published, the editors of the magazine generally muck it up somehow. They change your punctuation, they deflower your prose, they stick little spaces between scenes that aren't scenes and they ignore your own scene breaks. Then, when the story becomes a deathless classic and gets reprinted by a bunch of anthologists, you have only the tearsheets of your mutilated magazine version to let the anthologists use. (Or else you can send the first one your carbon copy, and hope he doesn't lose it, and if he gets the story straight you can let the reprinters use his edition of it after that.)

But then I noticed that whenever I used a story of Harlan's in one of my anthologies, he sent me a photocopy of his original manuscript — which, whatever its flaws, was at least the story as he had conceived and punctuated and scene broken it. Gradually it dawned on me that he never sent his manuscripts anywhere, only photocopies, and didn't have to rely on tearsheets of over-edited versions when his stuff was reprinted.

I noticed also that when it was necessary to pass some document along to my agent, I had to waste a lot of time typing it all out for him, or else risk losing it in the mails — letters from foreign publishers, stuff like that. When I unretired in 1978 and started writing again, I began to feel uncomfortable about the fact that the first draft manuscript of *Lord Valentine's Castle* existed only in a single copy, but I didn't want to fool around making carbons of a rough draft, so I went out every hundred pages or so and had them photocopied.

And gradually it dawned on me that it might be handy to have a copier around the office.

So I bought one, last fall — a nifty Sharp, the any-paper kind, not suited to giant instantaneous runs but pretty good for what I needed it for. I told the salesman I would probably be running off 150–200 copies a month, but I notice that the counter is currently at 4150, and I've had the thing eight months, so I suppose I've found more uses for it than I suspected. I've even found one use that Harlan hadn't thought of. Now when I write a short story, and I've been writing quite a few lately, I immediately run off six extra copies of the manuscript and send them to my agent. (My new agent. There have been quite a number of changes around here lately.) And he sends one to Germany, one to France, one to Japan, etc. In the past, the only way I could get a foreign sale on a short story was to wait until it had been published and collected in a book of my stories, a process that takes several years; now the manuscripts go out simultaneously in the U.S.A. and in the half dozen other countries that publish sf short stories, and the results — in terms of immediate overseas sales — have in fact paid for the copying machine already. I told Harlan about that angle, figuring he had been going about his business that way for years, but it hadn't occurred to him. And so it goes. It's not exactly cheap, but I'm more solvent than I was in the days when I was turning mimeo cranks. And there are some infinitely juicy advantages. I hated mimeography. I did it terribly at first, and after two or three years I learned how to do it more or less adequately, but it was a nerve-wracking job for me at best, and I think it was my loathing of the mimeo machine that caused me to abandon active fandom in 1955 and become a professional writer. With the photocopier, all I do is stick the typed sheet on top and push the button. I don't know what's going on underneath and I don't need to know, and I don't fool around with black glop that gets indelibly into my fingers (I think I'm still carrying some around from the pre-1955 days) and whenever the stuff that the copier uses, a ghastly black metallic powdery substance, needs replenishment, I call the service and they come out and replenish it. My hands stay clean.

Of course, sometimes the copier chews up a page. In mimeo, that would have been disastrous: I would have to fish out the foul, gooey stencil of the page and run off, with great distaste, as many replacement copies as I needed. (Or else run extras to begin with.) Now I just pop the master copy back into the machine, push the button, and get my replacements, no futzing around with used stencils.

About that business of being an employee, now —

You know, I've never held any sort of job, except for being a counselor in a summer camp in West Cupcake, New York, almost thirty years ago, and a quickie thing in a furniture warehouse between my graduation from high school and my entry to college. But in 1955 I went into business for myself as a freelance writer, and for the past quarter of a century I've been self-employed.

I did pretty well at it. Very well, in fact. I lived long and prospered, and grumblingly paid my pound of flesh to the IRS every April. But then came inflation and around the same time I sold a book called *Lord Valentine's Castle* for a fairly hefty sum, and between one thing and another my income vaulted into quite improbable zones. And suddenly the amount of tax I was paying amounted to more than my entire income for, say, 1975, and in 1975 I'd been in a good high bracket. The situation became critical: the government was reaching too deep into my pockets.

Meanwhile, down at Ellison's Wonderland, somewhere in 1978 Harlan transformed himself into The Kilimanjaro Corporation, at the advice of his tax man. I knew about it because I was named a director of The Kilimanjaro Corporation, a role carrying no duties except to sign my name to a document now and then. I figured that Harlan, who likes to be the first kid on the block to get the newest toy, was incorporating just because it was a trendy Hollywood thing to do, and — although I was roughly in the same tax bracket — there wasn't any great need for me to follow his example.

But then the *Lord Valentine* moolah began to pour in, and my tax burden got heavier and heavier, and it became more and more complicated to set aside earnings to pay Uncle, and less and less acceptable to do it. And one day I was complaining bitterly to Harlan about my tax problems and he said, "How much do you actually have to pay them this year?"

"Umpty-ump thousand and umpty cents," I said mournfully.

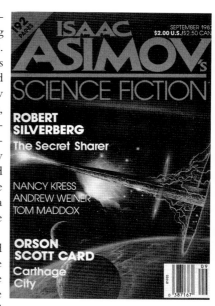

ISAAC ASIMOV SF MAGAZINE *September, 1987 with "The Secret Sharer".*

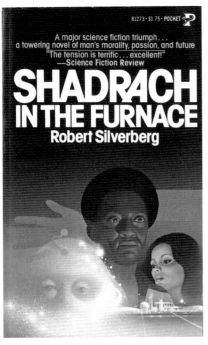

SHADRACH IN THE FURNACE *Pocket Book paperback.*

And he said, "You sucker, why don't you incorporate? You know how much I paid in taxes this year?"

"How much?"

"Practically zilch," said he. "Wait a second, I'll look it up. Here: federal taxes, zilch and a half bucks. State taxes, half a zilch."

"But how much did you make?"

And he told me, and I moaned into the phone and asked him to send me photocopies — ah, that wonderful machine — of his personal and corporate tax returns. Which he did, and I studied them with care, and it became apparent that on his quite healthy income he was quite legally paying very much less in taxes than I on an also quite robust income was paying, and the next thing I knew I was on the phone talking to Harlan's tax man, a genial Los Angeles type who is fond of helping writers preserve their income from the jaws of the bureaucracy. And he asked me to send him a photocopy of my last tax return, and I did, and behold he called back and said it is truly unnecessary for you to be contributing quite so much toward the wellbeing of your fellow citizens, and in very short order I contacted a Bay Area lawyer who guided me through the required steps that turned me into AGBERG, LTD.

Being a corporation instead of a self-employed writer is not exactly a license to steal. But it has remarkable tax-reduction qualities, because a good many things that are not deductible for the ordinary free-lancer become deductible to me. Health insurance, for instance. If a writer gets sick, really sick, and can't turn the product out, his income is likely to diminish drastically. At the same time his medical bills are apt to increase notably. Given the ugly potential of that situation, you'd think that Joe Freelance would at least be able to deduct the cost of his medical insurance from his taxes, but no go: he can take $150 off as a personal deduction, but anything above that comes out of after-tax dollars.

Not so with a corporation. Corporations are permitted to insure their employees against crushing medical expenses. It stands to reason, doesn't it? So my medical insurance plan — currently running at $800 a year and getting more expensive annually — is converted abruptly into a deductible corporate business expense. The corporation is also allowed to reimburse its employees for any medical expenses that they might incur that are not covered by insurance — that $34 dentist bill, let's say. Again, deductible. But these goodies are not regarded as taxable income for the employee.

You see the drift? All kinds of little things suddenly get written off. And some big things. As a self-employed person I was entitled to set up a Keogh Plan pension arrangement for myself, and put $7,500 a year of deductible dollars into it. That isn't bad, but corporate pension arrangements are a lot more liberal, and I can now stash away about five times as much, if I choose, in the Agberg, Ltd. pension plan. It all accumulates tax-free, compounding like crazy, until the age of 55, when I can begin drawing it out. (Paying regular income taxes on it then, of course. But it's been earning tax-free compound income all that time.)

This may sound hideously unfair to those who aren't incorporated. Well, sure; but it's a lot more hideously unfair for a writer whose only assets are his wits to be turning over something like 61% of his income to the state and federal governments, which is where I was. The corporate scheme is altogether legal and very welcome. I gather that every sf writer who earns a living at all is busily getting himself incorporated these days — Asimov does business now as Nightfall, Inc., and Roger Zelazny is Amber Industries, and Frank Herbert is probably Dune Enterprises, and Greg Benford is talking to the lawyers, and —

Why Agberg, you ask? If you're a trufan you shouldn't need to ask, because you'd know that that was Richard Eney's Besterization of my name, a couple of decades back. If you're at all familiar with the periodic table, you're aware that "Ag" is the chemical symbol for silver, nicht wahr?

I was going, by the way, to appoint Harlan a director of my corporation, just to be fraternally corporate about things. But my lawyer pointed out that under current California law I don't have to have any outside directors, or any officers other than myself, for that matter. I am the board of directors. I am also president, treasurer, chief financial officer, and secretary of the corporation. I made Harlan a vice-president. Vice-presidents don't have to sign the corporate resolutions.

I also executed an employment contract with myself — part of the legal formalities. (You have to be very formal and proper about all this, or it won't be kosher.) My contract, which is a pretty standard one, specifies that I'm to work for Agberg, Ltd. for a year, the contract renewable by mutual consent after that. If for any reason I find it necessary to fire myself, I have agreed not to go to work for any competing companies for a period of some years, and not to divulge any of my company's trade secrets to a competitor. I also get four weeks of paid vacation a year and various other little benefits from my kindly employer. It's a somewhat Kafkaesque document, but it's a very proper one.

So much for the intimate financial details of the lives of great sf stars. So far as the other aspects of my career go, you'll be pleased to know that I continue to use an Olympia manual typewriter, never having gotten as far as the electric typewriter, let alone the superfuturistic gadgets on which the literary masterpieces of X and Y and Z are now being composed. Interesting, trendy old Harlan has also always used an Olympic manual — the only other writer I know for certain to consume no power while turning out his stuff. (Though I think Lester del Rey still uses an antiquated East German portable typewriter when he writes, which probably isn't very often.)

So I got a new agent (I had been with the old one 27 years and I felt restless) and I changed my typewriter ribbon and I bought a photocopier and then I became a corporation and I sold a new book, a companion but not a sequel to *Lord Valentine's Castle* called *Majipoor Chronicles*, and now I'm a writer again.

And a lot of people who, during my retirement, told me that it was a damn shame that somebody with my talent had walked away from such a wonderful career, are now telling me that I'm taking up too much space in the high-powered markets and crowding them out, and will I please try to be a little less prolific? And so it goes, I guess.

1981

THE OAKLAND FIRE

Thinking fast is a good idea when disaster comes, but sometimes the best thing is not to think too much at all. And so when the sky turned black over Oakland midway through a lovely golden autumn morning, just five days ago as

I write this, I didn't spend a lot of time pondering which of my possessions I preferred to save if the fire that had suddenly begun to rage five or six miles north of me should reach my neighborhood, as was beginning to seem altogether possible.

Of course, I've had some practice at this kind of thing. In 1968, when I still lived in New York City, fire came from nowhere at four in the morning on a February night and drove me out into 12-degree weather. I had very little time that night to gather things, or even my wits; so just about all I took with me was the manuscript of the book I was working on and one little ancient Roman glass bowl that I found particularly precious. I didn't even bother to grab the ledger in which I keep irreplaceable business records. Instead of trying to pack up the four cats and various kittens of the household, I chased them all down to the basement, four stories below the fire itself, and shut them into a room where I thought they'd be safe. That turned out to be dumb, because one of the first things the firemen did was to open that room, letting cats loose into the house. As it happened, all the cats survived the fire anyway, and so did many of the possessions that I had left behind, though the house itself was a total wreck. And I found the ledger a few days later in the ruins of what had been my office.

This time, when the alarms began to go off in the distance and that terrible plume of smoke fouled the sky, the *first* thing I did was corral the cats — different ones, 23 years later — and pack them into their carriers. Then I got the business ledger, with 23 more years of notations in it, and the little box of backup disks containing my current story and the financial records I had just finished transferring to my new computer. The computer itself I left behind, along with a houseful of treasures. My wife Karen and I loaded what we had chosen to take into the car, turned the car around in the driveway to be aimed outward for quick departure, and spent the next hour and a half hosing down the roof of the house while the fire drew closer. At half past three in the afternoon the helicopters came overhead, bellowing evacuation orders for our entire neighborhood, and we joined the outward migration. As I passed through the house and the separate building that is my office, locking things and setting burglar alarms, I did find myself wondering whether I would ever see any of this again. But that was as much speculation as I allowed myself. There are times when it's best not to do a lot of thinking.

We took refuge over the hills, ten miles away (it seemed like worlds away) at the home of our friend Jim Benford, Gregory Benford's twin brother, and his wife Hilary. And there we stayed through the frightful night of October 20, compulsively watching the terrible scenes on television as the lovely hillside town where I have lived for the past twenty years underwent trial by fire.

Conditions couldn't have been better for a major conflagration. Not only has Northern California undergone a drought for the past five years, but the *normal* climate of the California coast gives us long rainless summers, and we had had virtually no measurable precipitation for six full months. There had been an atypical hard frost the previous December, leaving many trees in the eucalyptus forests of the high ridges with clusters of dry dead leaves. And October is usually the warmest month of the year for us: the temperature that morning was in the high eighties. A weird and troublesome easterly wind was blowing out of the hot, dry interior of the state instead of the cool ocean breeze that usually sweeps across the Bay Area.

So when a brush fire that somehow had begun in the hills the day before — and supposedly had been extinguished — came back to life Sunday morning and got out of hand, disaster was inevitable. The parched trees and dry grassy meadows of the hills went up immediately; the lovely wooden houses in the initial fire zone were ignited within minutes; and then, as trees exploded into flame, great firebrands were lifted aloft and carried hundreds of yards by that deadly east wind, down into the heavily populated residential regions below the hill area itself. You probably know the rest of the story, though not as well as we do. By daybreak at least two thousand homes had been destroyed; whole neighborhoods had been obliterated; an enviably beautiful landscape had been transformed into a thing of horror.

Karen and I were among the lucky ones. The fire was brought under control a mile north of our house. At nine the next morning the evacuation area for our immediate neighborhood was lifted, and we said goodbye to Jim and Hilary Benford and set out, badly shaken but immensely relieved, for our house. Because the fire zone blocked the ten-minute direct route between the Benford house and ours, we came home the long way around, a trip of more than an hour; but eventually we were there to see that the place had gone untouched. We unpacked our bewildered cats, wandered around thankfully to visit our possessions, and tried to put some of the nightmare behind us.

Silverberg c. 1995.

Most other members of the Oakland hills science fiction community came through, as we did, with nothing more than a bad scare. Charles Brown's hilltop house, where *Locus* is published, was well outside the danger zone. The canyon-side house that Jack Vance built with his own hands and where he and his wife

**THE DESERT OF
STOLEN DREAMS,**
*cover art by Steven Fabian;
Underwood Miller, 1981.*

Norma have lived for more than forty years was closer to the blaze, but went unharmed; Jack's son John defied the evacuation order and spent the night in the house to guard it, and when I spoke to him by phone that evening he said that glowing embers were floating by but that no fires had started nearby. Poul and Karen Anderson, who live on the other side of the hill in Orinda — also menaced in the early hours of the fire — were all right also. The most remarkable story involved the house on Broadway Terrace where Terry Carr and his wife Carol lived for many years, and which Carol still occupies. The fire came as far south as Broadway Terrace, wiping out everything along the north side of the street. But Carol's house is on the south side; and the next day we discovered that it was still there, utterly unscathed along with five or six of its neighbors in the midst of the awesome destruction. And on the Berkeley side of the fire, where the Hotel Claremont (site of the 1968 World Science Fiction Convention) was threatened but ultimately was saved, the house known as Greyhaven, inhabited by Marion Zimmer Bradley's brother Paul, agent Tracy Blackstone, and writers Diana Paxson and Jon DeCles, also came through, despite early rumors that it had been lost. On the other side of the ledger was the destruction of the house where my first wife Barbara — who had suffered through that 1968 fire with me — lived. It was in the zone where the blaze broke out, and must have been incinerated in the first moments of the event. (Barbara herself was out of town at the time or her life might well have been in danger.)

Now a few days have passed, and things slowly return to normal for those of us who escaped with nothing more than a few hours of fright, while those who were more closely touched by calamity begin the long, numbing process — which will take a year or more, and in some senses will never be at an end, if my 1968 experience is any guide — of rebuilding their interrupted lives. Already new utility poles are being erected in the disaster area, electric and telephone service is being restored, and crews with chainsaws and jackhammers are starting to haul away debris. In a few weeks wildflowers will begin to bloom atop the ashes; by spring the first new houses will be under construction.

The area where we live is one of the most beautiful in the world. We have the sea nearby; we have hills and mountains; we have a vast blue sky above us most of the year, clear air, months on end of brilliant sunshine. The winters are mild and the summers are gentle, so that our weather is a kind of perpetual springtime. Few of us are talking about moving away, despite all that we have been through in recent years.

But we have been through a great deal here. There has been a drought, in an already dry climate, for the past five years. There was a terrifying earthquake in 1987. 1990 brought us a hard frost, which wiped out cherished gardens decades old and harassed our fertile agricultural regions. And now this fire, which has left so frightful a scar on our lovely hills. It makes one uneasy about what may come next; it eats into one's reserves of resilience. Our friends back east ask us why we don't move to some safer place.

And yet — and yet —

A day or two after our fire there was a great earthquake in India. Last sum-

mer the Philippines struggled to cope with the effects of a huge volcanic eruption. Just yesterday I read a newspaper account of another eruption, in the
Chilean Andes on August 12, that has buried a section of Patagonia five times the
size of Connecticut in volcanic ash, threatening the economic welfare of an enormous region of Argentina. And of course I could go back through the roster of
historic eruptions, floods, earthquakes, hurricanes, and all the rest.

So what is the lesson to derive from the fire that roared through my pretty
neighborhood last Sunday? That the San Francisco Bay Area, lovely as it is, is too
dangerous for human habitation, and that we should all move somewhere else,
someplace safer?

No. The real conclusion to draw from what has happened here is something
that we already know in the abstract from having read about Pompeii or the
Bangladesh floods or the San Francisco earthquake of 1906, but which does not
become completely real until it strikes closer to home. And that is that there may
be safer places than this one, but that no place is really safe. We who inhabit the
planet Earth live on the shoulders of an indifferent giant. At any moment he may
choose to shrug or even simply twitch, and hurl us to destruction. It's a wonderful planet, and I don't know of a better one to live on. But even its most beautiful regions are places of peril, and though we like to think of ourselves as the masters of the world, we need to remember that we are only its tenants and the terms
of the lease can be altered, without our consent, at any time.

1992

GOING TO CONVENTIONS

There's been a certain elegiac tone to these columns this summer, a harken-
ing back to earlier times, old memories of the science-fiction field that used
to be. Undoubtedly the deaths last year of those two colossi of our genre, Isaac
Asimov and Fritz Leiber, were factors that aroused much of that feeling of nostalgia in me; and, as I noted a couple of months ago, 1993 is also the fortieth
anniversary of my own first sale to a science-fiction magazine. Fortieth anniver-
saries do have a way of getting one to look toward the past.

And now another fortieth anniversary is upon me. For this is September, the
month of the World Science Fiction Convention; and this year's Worldcon will
be the fortieth convention I have attended.

The Worldcon is the great annual family gathering of the science-fiction
clan, an assemblage of thousands and thousands of people who care passionately
about this strange stuff that we choose to read and write. *Everyone* is there: writers, editors, artists, publishers, book dealers, and, of course, readers — the fans,
who are actually the people who organize each year's Worldcon and do the brutal work that makes it happen. In the course of my forty years of Worldcon attendance, I've had a chance to meet and get to know virtually the entire roster of
science fiction's great creative figures, from Frank R. Paul, Edmond Hamilton,
and E. E. "Doc" Smith of the earliest days of our field down to the promising
novices who will evolve into the supernovae of twenty-first century sf. I can't
imagine missing a convention. Through all the ebbs and flows of my career, the
thought of *not* going to a Worldcon has never entered my mind.

There aren't many who have attended as many as forty Worldcons. Forrest J Ackerman, that survivor from the dawn of sf fandom, is one who has, I know: Forry was at the first one in 1939, and has been at virtually every one since. Probably Fred Pohl (who was excluded from that 1939 convention for political reasons by fiat of its organizers, a notable moment in fan history) has been to more than forty, too, out of the fifty that have been held up to this year. Perhaps there are three or four others. But I must be high up on the list of perennial attendees.

This year's convention is in San Francisco, just across the bay from my home. Ironically, the last time I missed a Worldcon, it was in San Francisco also, in 1954: but I lived on the East Coast then, and as a 19-year-old college student I simply couldn't come up with the funds to take me on that vast journey of 3000 miles across the country. I often wonder what that young Bob Silverberg would say, if he could be told that forty years later he would be driving twenty minutes from his home to attend another San Francisco Worldcon — or that he would be writing about doing it in his regular *Amazing Stories* column.

Images of Worldcons past come floating up out of the memory bank as I look back over those astonishing forty years.

Your first one, of course, is always unforgettable. For me that was the Philadelphia convention of 1953, at the glorious Bellevue-Stratford hotel. I was eighteen; I had just made my first professional sale (and would be paid for it, all thirty dollars, at the convention.) And now, at last, I would attend my first Worldcon! Staying in a three-room suite, no less.

A suite, you say? How did an impecunious college kid manage that? Where did I ever find the money — a suite at the Bellevue-Stratford must have cost all of twelve or fifteen dollars a night, in 1953 — to manage such stately lodgings?

Through entrepreneurial zeal, of course. I teamed up with a fellow fan, a kid from Cleveland, one Harlan Ellison, with whom I agreed to split the bill. Then we offered crash space — couches, chairs, the floor, whatever — to our numerous friends in the fan community, at $5 per night. At least twenty of them signed up. The result was a kind of convention within the convention: our three rooms were packed every night, a stellar array of 1953's great fan figures holding an intense round-the-clock party. As the organizers of the commune, Harlan and I not only got to be the ones who slept in the beds (when we slept at all, an hour or two a night) but wound up paying nothing for our suite and turning a profit of forty or fifty dollars each, besides.

It was a wondrous weekend. I stared in awe at the writers and editors I had revered all through my adolescence — Theodore Sturgeon, John W. Campbell, Willy Ley, Frederik Pohl, Lester del Rey, L. Sprague de Camp, and dozens more — moving like ordinary mortals through the throngs in the lobby. I looked with envy on the hot young writers like Robert Sheckley and Frank M. Robinson, whose names were on the tables of contents of all the magazines, and earnestly prayed to join them there some day. (Which I did; and I formed lifelong friendships with them both, besides.) I mingled with fan friends I had known only through correspondence, and worked hard to live up to my postal reputation for acute wit and erudition. I blurted out my literary ambitions to editors like Harry Harrison and Larry T. Shaw, and was encouraged by what they had to say, though probably they were just being nice to the lanky, crew-cutted tyro that I was. I watched the very first Hugos being handed out, not even daring to suppose that

Joe Haldeman and I are enjoying a sober moment at a recent convention, perhaps San Jose or perhaps the 2004 Nebula weekend.
— RS

some day I would be a winner myself. And I went home (by bus, Philadelphia to New York) in a daze of excitement and fatigue, my life forever transformed in a single weekend.

I swore never to miss a Worldcon again. But the next year's convention, I discovered, was in far-off San Francisco, the other side of the continent from me. It might just as well have been on the moon.

By the time of the 1955 convention in Cleveland, though, I was a prosperous young writer who had made at least a dozen sales to the sf magazines, on my own and in collaboration with the somewhat more experienced writer Randall Garrett, whom I had met in New York. (At the 1953 Worldcon, Garrett had shown up one night, drunk and disorderly, at the perpetual party in the Ellison-Silverberg suite, and I had shut the door in his face. "Do you know who that is?" Harlan had asked me, aghast. "That's *Randall Garrett*. He's a *pro!*" But I didn't care: we had enough loudmouths in the room as it was. Garrett had no recollection of the incident a couple of years later, when we met, and we hit it off beautifully as collaborators.) Now my stories were all over the magazines. I had graduated with lightning swiftness into the professional ranks. It all seemed pretty much like a dream to me as Garrett led me around the convention, introducing me to the writers who were now my colleagues.

I met Isaac Asimov at that convention, and Fritz Leiber, and James E. Gunn, and Fred Pohl, and Anthony Boucher, and the legendary Bob Tucker, and I don't know how many others of the great. It was an awesome thing to be in their presence, actually chatting with them virtually as an equal at a party where only the inner circle of writers and editors was present. The 1953 convention had been my initiation into the tribe; the 1955 one marked my debut among the pros. I was a figure of some interest to them, I could see: the field then was very small, and *any* prolific new writer was immediately conspicuous. (The total attendance at that 1955 convention, fans and pros together, was all of 380 people, so everyone quickly knew everyone else. Modern Worldcons are ten to twenty times as big.)

I remember the trip home from Cleveland, too: six or seven of us, including Harlan, and Ian Macauley (who would become an editor with the *New York Times*), and jolly Karl Olsen (who still comes to conventions, jolly as ever) and some others, crammed into what I think was Macauley's car for an all-night turnpike drive to New York. I didn't have a driver's license, then, but everyone else took turns at the wheel, including Karl, who *also* didn't have a license but didn't tell us that until he had run the car up on the center median. We survived.

And went on to 1956, a vast Worldcon in New York. I had sold so many stories by then that my colleagues were looking at me not with curiosity, now, but with uneasiness and a bit of horror. That was the year I won my first Hugo — the award for Most Promising New Author. (I beat out two fellows who were still pretty obscure that year: Harlan Ellison, whose professional career had barely begun, and a guy named Frank Herbert, who had had two or three stories published.) It seemed a very long way from that Philadelphia convention, just three summers earlier.

I vividly remember the sweaty, exciting time just after the Hugo ceremony, as I stood there clutching my shiny trophy and accepting congratulations. Betty Farmer, Philip Jose Farmer's irrepressible wife, came up to me and gave me a hug;

1977 French edition of **THORNS** *with DJ art by Philip Caza.*

HOMEFARING,
Phantasia Press, 1983

and then she said, "You know, Phil won the same Hugo in 1953. And he hasn't been able to sell a story since.") She was just joking, of course. And he and I both managed to keep our careers afloat thereafter, as did Brian W. Aldiss, the third and final winner, a couple of years later, of the Hugo in the Most Promising New Author category.

I could fill a book, I think, with Worldcon anecdotes. (Some of them would get me sued, I suspect.) The 1957 convention was the first overseas one, in London, and I made my first trip to Europe to attend it. The hotel room cost $2.40 per night, and seemed a little overpriced at that, but we had a wondrous time, all 268 of us from both sides of the Atlantic. (The hotel dining room staff would put out the breakfast cereals in open bowls every night, and would urge us please not to take short-cuts through the room on our way to the bar because it would get dust into the corn flakes.)

1958, and Los Angeles: I got to see California at last, the palm trees and the freeways, little imagining that I'd live there some day. Among those I met for the first time at that convention were Poul Anderson and William Rotsler, now friends of decades' duration; I met Terry Carr there too, and watched him meet the beautiful woman who would become his first wife. (The marriage didn't last long, and, sadly, neither did Terry; but he and I had some wonderful times together before his too-early death at the age of 50.)

1959, 1960, Detroit, Pittsburgh.... It was at one of those conventions, I forget which, that I was roaming the halls of an afternoon and came upon Gordie Dickson, Poul Anderson, and Ted Cogswell sitting in a hotel room with the door open, contemplating an entire case of tequila. I was never a drinker on the heroic Dickson-Anderson-Cogswell scale, but I do touch a drop now and then; they invited me in and I helped them dispose of some of it. Quite an afternoon.

And Seattle, in 1961: the con was at a little motel near the airport that year. Robert A. Heinlein was the guest of honor, and gave a party in his room *for the entire convention*, the entire roster of 300 attendees, holding court in his bathrobe, pouring drinks himself, greeting dozens of people by name, an astonishing performance. I began to understand why Heinlein was such a mesmerizing writer: his irresistible fiction was an extension of his own magnetic personality. An extraordinary man; it was a privilege to have known him, and if there had been no Worldcons, I might never have had the chance.

Heinlein was the star again in 1962 in Chicago, materializing unexpectedly as though out of hyperspace in a white dinner jacket to collect his Hugo for *Stranger in a Strange Land*. Conventions were starting to get bigger, now: there were 550 people at the Chicago con, in a two-tower hotel of confusing layout. (One night Harlan Ellison and I somehow missed connections with our friends and found ourselves with no way of discovering where the party we were supposed to be attending was located. We didn't even know which building it was in. So we sat quietly by ourselves on a back staircase for an hour or two, reviewing in wonder the dizzying six-year-evolution of our writing careers, until at last someone we knew came by and told us where to find the gathering we were looking for.)

There was the crazed episode in 1967, another New York Worldcon, where dozens of writers waited forever in the hotel dining room for service, and an angry Lester del Rey dumped an overdue salad on the floor while at the same moment Harlan flung a plate of popovers against the wall. And the next night I led many of the same people to a favorite restaurant of mine where we wound up in a back room next to a garbage can, and waited again for our dinners, waited so very long this time that people whose names would be recognized by you all started to go berserk, and I thought I would be lynched by my own friends. Anne McCaffrey had to quell the raging mob, finally.

I no longer regarded myself as a callow novice amidst a band of demigods, by then. I had been around for a dozen years, and plenty of writers junior to me had entered the field — Roger Zelazny, Larry Niven, Samuel R. Delany, Thomas Disch, and more. I watched them arrive one by one, and remembered how the old-timers had watched me do the same.

Still, I was startled in 1968 when the chairman of that year's Worldcon (it was to be in Berkeley, California) phoned and asked if I would serve as Toastmaster at the Hugo Awards ceremony. The toastmastership is one of the Worldcon's most significant responsibilities, and in those years it seemed invariably to rotate exclusively among a small group of our most distinguished citizens — Isaac Asimov, Anthony Boucher, Robert Bloch. Boucher was to have been toastmaster again at that year's convention, but he had died that spring; and suddenly I found myself promoted into that little group. To me it marked a rite of passage in the Worldcon subculture. (My toastmaster stint at the 1968 convention was exhausting and exhilarating, and I loved every moment of it. In the years that followed I ran the awards ceremony on four or five other occasions, and, I hope, lived up to the standard set by my impressive predecessors.)

That 1968 convention was a bizarre event — marked by widespread drug use, the convention debut of weird 1960s clothing and rock bands, riots near the hotel, all the craziness of that strange era erupting all at once. No one who was there will ever forget that dreamlike weekend.

Nor will I forget the more prosaic convention in St. Louis the following year, but for different reasons. Again, I found myself ascending into realms of sf achievement that would have sent my adolescent self into paroxysms of disbelief. I delivered the keynote address at that convention; a couple of days later, I was handed another Hugo, for my novella "Nightwings"; and then I was told, right at the end of the weekend, that I was to be Guest of Honor at the following year's convention in Heidelberg, Germany.

To be Worldcon Guest of Honor is, I suppose, the summit of the science-fiction writer's course of accomplishment. I was only 35 years old when my turn came, making me one of the youngest ever — along with Heinlein and Asimov, who were 34 and 35, respectively. What amazed me even more, and left me a little abashed as well, was that at the time of my elevation to the Guest of Honorship, such writers as Clifford D. Simak, Frederik Pohl, Jack Williamson, Ray Bradbury, Alfred Bester, and Jack Vance had never been chosen. (They all got their turns, eventually. But they should have preceded me.)

So many stories to tell, so little space for them ....

The 1964 convention in Oakland, where I rose to place a mock bid for a convention the following year at some posh resort in the Virgin Islands, and discovered, to my chagrin, that the attendees were taking the bid seriously and had given me a majority vote on the spot. (I withdrew in favor of London, the genuine bidder.) The 1975 convention in Australia, where I rose to address Australian

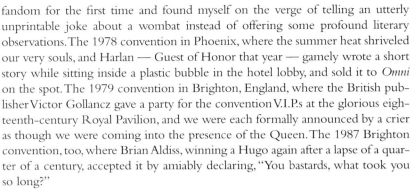

fandom for the first time and found myself on the verge of telling an utterly unprintable joke about a wombat instead of offering some profound literary observations. The 1978 convention in Phoenix, where the summer heat shriveled our very souls, and Harlan — Guest of Honor that year — gamely wrote a short story while sitting inside a plastic bubble in the hotel lobby, and sold it to *Omni* on the spot. The 1979 convention in Brighton, England, where the British publisher Victor Gollancz gave a party for the convention V.I.P.s at the glorious eighteenth-century Royal Pavilion, and we were each formally announced by a crier as though we were coming into the presence of the Queen. The 1987 Brighton convention, too, where Brian Aldiss, winning a Hugo again after a lapse of a quarter of a century, accepted it by amiably declaring, "You bastards, what took you so long?"

(Which brings to mind the grotesque 1983 Hugo ceremony in Baltimore, which was preceded by a ketchupy crab luncheon where thousands of impatient fans began to bang their spoons on the table, after which everything else that could possibly go wrong did. The winners went away happy, anyway.)

Heinlein once more, presiding over a Red Cross blood drive in Kansas City in 1976: you wanted a Heinlein autograph, you had to donate a pint of your blood. Or Fred Pohl, resplendent in tuxedo, performing tirelessly and brilliantly at four or five functions a day in his capacity as master of ceremonies at the 1989 Boston Worldcon. Or the evening I spent with Isaac and Janet Asimov at the same convention — the last time, as it turned out, that I would ever see Isaac. Or the post-Hugo party at the 1990 con in Holland, where I stood around in a crowded room in the heat of an almost tropically humid evening wearing jacket and tie while accepting congratulations for my newest award until I felt myself beginning to melt, and ran off to my hotel room two blocks away to change into fresh clothing....

The 1991 convention in Chicago, where the glittering block-long bar of the Hyatt Hotel offered grappa at $350 a shot, and where I met Kim Mohan of *Amazing Stories* for the first time. (He bought me a drink. But our first meeting happened to take place in the hotel next door, so I didn't get a chance to put a shot of that grappa on his expense account. Just as well, I suspect.)

And last year, in Orlando, where the elite of science fiction gathered twice a day in the lobby of the elegant Peabody Hotel to watch a parade of ducks....

Forty years. The stories I could tell would fill a book and a half.

And now this year, in San Francisco. Another Worldcon, a new collection of wondrous memories to add to the rich store already laid by. If this is going to be your twentieth or twenty-fifth convention, well, it'll be good to see you again, old friend. And if it'll be your first Worldcon: welcome, stranger! You're in for the experience of a lifetime.

1993

Taken at the 2004 Nebula awards in Seattle — Karen on one side of me and the Grand Master trophy on the other.— RS

GRAND MASTERS, THE SEQUEL

Long-term readers of this column with long-term memories may remember the following nine paragraphs, which were published here exactly four years ago, and which I am going to reprint here now for reasons that I'll make clear very shortly for those who haven't already figured it out from the heading above:

The Grand Master award of the Science Fiction Writers of America is one of the two highest distinctions our field confers — the other being the Guest of Honor designation at the World Science Fiction Convention. These awards recognize a lifetime of significant work; and anyone who wants to understand the history of science fiction in the twentieth century need only look at SFWA's list of Grand Masters.

It was Jerry Pournelle, when he was President of SFWA nearly thirty years ago, who dreamed up the idea of the Grand Master award. Since 1965 SFWA had been giving its Nebula trophy annually to the authors of the best novels and short fiction of the previous year; but Pournelle felt that the accomplishments of some of our greatest figures were being slighted, because they had done their outstanding work in the years prior to the Nebula's inception. So he proposed a special award — an oversized version of the handsome block of Lucite that is a Nebula — to be awarded by vote of SFWA's officers and past presidents in acknowledgment of the significant work those writers had done over the long term. And, to avoid cheapening the value of the award, Pournelle stipulated that it should be given no more often than six times every decade.

Pournelle's suggestion was eagerly accepted by the membership, and in 1975 the first Grand Master Nebula was given to Robert A. Heinlein, surely one of the defining figures of modern science fiction. Heinlein's recent work had come under attack by critics who found fault with it on literary and even political grounds, but no one questioned the greatness of the man who had written *Methuselah's Children*, *Double Star*, *The Moon is a Harsh Mistress*, and the Future History stories. (And, in fact, his career was far from over even in 1975: he would go on to produce such well-received novels as *Friday* and *The Cat Who Walks Through Walls* in the years following his receiving of the award.)

In those days nearly all the writers who had clustered around the great editor John W. Campbell of *Astounding Science Fiction* to create the so-called "Golden Age" period of the 1940s were still alive, and they were the obvious choices for grand-masterhood in the next few years. And so Jack Williamson, who had given us *The Legion of Space* back in the 1930s, and such Golden Age Campbell-era classics as the Seetee and Humanoids books, became the second Grand Master in 1976. Clifford D. Simak, of *City* and *Way Station* fame, joined the group the following year.

Because the original rules, since amended, stipulated only six awards per decade, no Grand Master was chosen in 1978; but in 1979 another golden-age favorite, L. Sprague de Camp, he of *Lest Darkness Fall* and *The Incomplete Enchanter* and ever so much more, was honored. Another year was skipped, and then in 1980 Fritz Leiber (*Conjure Wife*, *The Wanderer*, *Gather, Darkness!*) was the pick.

Under the rules then in effect no further award could be given until 1984, when Andre Norton became the first female Grand Master (a designation that created certain grammatical problems that have never been adequately resolved) and also the first who had not been associated with the Campbell editorship.

You may be wondering, at this point, why the name of Isaac Asimov has not yet been included in the list. As it happened, Isaac was wondering the same thing, since he, too, had been a key member of the John Campbell team, and by the 1980s the name of "Asimov" was virtually synonymous with science fiction, as the magazine that bears his name will testify. And so, in his goodnaturedly self—promoting way, Isaac was given to observing, far and wide, that a certain conspicuous figure of the era had not yet been given his due. He said it playfully, of course, and made it clear that he was just joking — but in fact there was no small degree of seriousness beneath his clowning. He privately suspected that he was not going to live many more years, and he wanted to win that award before he died.

It is quite true that one of the considerations involved in nominating people for the award is an actuarial one. Even great writers don't live forever, and we have always tried to honor our oldest ones first. Heinlein and De Camp had been born in 1907, Williamson in 1908, Leiber in 1910, Norton in 1912, Simak all the way back in 1904. Isaac — born in 1920 — was a veritable youth by comparison. No one was aware in the 1980s of how quickly Isaac's health was weakening, though. So, despite his otherwise quite valid claim and all his yelps, he simply had to sit by and wait, even while his great friend and rival, Arthur C. Clarke (born 1917) carried off the 1986 trophy.

But of course a group of Grand Masters of Science Fiction that did not include Isaac Asimov was plainly incomplete; and his torment came to an end in 1987 at a ceremony in New York. I went up to him afterward to congratulate him as he stood there cradling the trophy in his arms; and as I put out my hand he feigned a look of great alarm, as though I were trying to take it away from him, and cried, "You can't have it! You can't have it! You have to wait another fifteen years!"

Well, lo and behold, etc., the fifteen years predicted by Isaac went by, and two extra by way of lagniappe, as they say in New Orleans, and then in the spring of 2004 the Science Fiction Writers of America named its latest Grand Master, and indeed the award went to the writer of these very words.

I thus become the twenty-first of the Grand Masters, and although I am not the youngest to have been chosen (not only Isaac Asimov but also Heinlein and Williamson were younger at the time of winning than I am now) I am the first of the winners who was born in the 1930s, a significant generational shift. An award whose winners were, in the beginning, exclusively drawn from that gifted crew who created the John W. Campbell Golden Age of science fiction in the 1940s (Heinlein, Williamson, Simak, de Camp, Leiber), has begun to pass to the innovative figures that built on the achievements of those titans to create the science fiction of our own day.

Since the rules of the award stipulate that it can be given only to living writers, the pool of eligible Golden Age authors eventually was used up, as Lester del Rey, Alfred Bester, A.E. van Vogt, and Hal Clement joined the ones I've mentioned above. (Theodore Sturgeon and L. Ron Hubbard, two other conspicuous figures of the Campbell era, did not live long enough to be named.) Then came a group of writers who established their claims to the Grand Master trophy in the period immediately following World War II: Ray Bradbury, Arthur C. Clarke, Jack Vance, Philip Jose Farmer, Damon Knight, Frederik Pohl, and Poul Anderson. More recently, two writers who came to prominence a little later than that group joined the roster: Brian Aldiss and Ursula Le Guin, both of them a few years older than I am. And now it is my turn. Though my own writing career goes back to the middle of the 1950s, I didn't hit my full stride as a writer until 1966 or so, which makes me part of the Aldiss–Le Guin group rather than of the Knight–Farmer–Anderson–Pohl contingent. And within the next few years we will see winners drawn from the great pool of writers who entered the field in the last thirty years, as the great generational wheel keeps turning.

And how do you feel, Mr. Silverberg, about winning this majestic award?

On the most obvious level, I feel terrific about it. I regard it as confirming that I did actually succeed in what I set out to do many decades ago: to write science fiction that would be as important to other readers as the science fiction of the writers I've listed above was to me in my own formative years. Since I've put in half a century of hard work at that goal, I'm not going even to make a pretense of modesty here: I think that much of what I wrote over those decades was pretty damned good, and the fact that I've now received the Grand Master award indicates that I'm not the only one who feels that way.

But — but — there is this generational issue —

The eerie thing for me, because I *am* the first Grand Master who was born in the 1930s, is that I find myself swept up into a pantheon populated almost entirely by writers whose work I read with awe and reverence when I was twelve and thirteen and fifteen years old. I'm talking primarily about Heinlein and Asimov and van Vogt, about Vance and Leiber and Anderson, about de Camp and Bradbury and Clarke and Williamson, about — well, just about the whole bunch of them, other than Aldiss and Le Guin. (Fine writers that those two are, they began their writing careers after I had already become an adult, and I can't look upon them in quite the same way as I do the idols of my childhood and adolescence.)

My shiny new trophy tells me that I am now regarded as the peer of all those people. But somewhere within me is what remains of my inner adolescent self, who warns me to walk humbly among them, making the proper gestures of respect, and remembering to speak softly and say "Yes, sir" when spoken to. There's something to that. A Grand Master I may indeed be, now, but in the company of Robert A. Heinlein and Jack Williamson and L. Sprague de Camp and Frederik Pohl and Clifford D. Simak I'm always going to feel like the new kid on the block.

2004

ROBERT SILVERBERG
SCIENCE FICTION BIBLIOGRAPHY

Due to space limitations and the nature of this book, the titles of the author's numerous works of soft-core erotica, written between 1959 and 1966, have not been listed here. Other omissions include many stories in mystery and men's magazines, which are also beyond the scope of this book.

Finally, any bibliography for a writer as prolific as Robert Silverberg will always remain a work-in-progress. With this in mind we would appreciate hearing of any additions or corrections. Please contact us through the publisher. — *Editors*

Robert Silverberg's pseudonyms: Gordon Aghill, Robert Randall, & Richard Greer (used in collaborations with Randall Garrett); Robert Arnette, Alexander Blade, E.K. Jarvis, & Warren Kastel, Clyde Mitchell, Ivar Jorgenson (all Ziff-Davis house pseudonyms used by several authors); Ralph or Robert Burke, S.M. Tenneshaw, & Leonard G. Spencer (sometime in collaborations with Randall Garrett); Ralph Spencer; Ellis Robertson (for collaborations with Harlan Ellison); Calvin M. Knox; Dan Malcolm; Webber Martin; David & George Osborne.

Abbreviations: BCE - book club edition; ca - cover art; ed – editor; HC w DJ – hardcover with dust jacket; illo - illustration; PB – paperback; pp – pages; sf – science fiction; ss – short story; tr - translation

Italicized blocks of text represent blurbs from books or magazines, or comments by RS as indicated.

NOVELS

ACROSS A BILLION YEARS
- The Dial Press, Inc., NY; 1969; 1st Edition; HC w DJ; Cover art by Emanuel Schongut
- Victor Gollancz, London, United Kingdom; 1977; 1st UK Edition; HC w DJ; ca: Terry Oakes
- Magnum/Methuen, London; 1979; PB; 249 pp; wraparound cover art: Peter Elson
- NACH ALL DEN JAHRMILLIARDEN; Moewig, Munich, Germany; 1982; 240 pp
- Tor, NY; 1983; PB; 249pp; ca: Dell Harris

ALIENS FROM SPACE
Osborne, David (pseudonym for RS).
- Avalon Books/Thomaas Bouregy & Company, NY; 1958; HC, 1st edition.

THE ALIEN YEARS
- Morrow/Avon, New York, NY; 1998; HC w DJ; 428 pp; illustrator: Michael Herring
- Voyager, London, United Kingdom, 1999; PB
- HarperCollins; 1999; PB

AT WINTER'S END
- Warner Books, NY; April, 1988; HC w DJ; 1st Edition; 404

pp; Cover art by Michael Whelan
After 26 million years of vibrant civilization, the great world ended, locked in an ice age. But one small band of people had survived in an underground cocoon where they and their descendant's descendants waited for 700,000 years. Now the long winter is over and it's time to come out. Time to inherit, to claim and take charge of their world…but… they are not alone, Because other beings — some not human — are coming forth from the ice. Other tribes with other gods.
- Victor Gollancz Ltd., London; 1988; HC w DJ; 404pp; DJ art: by Shay Barsabe
- University of Nebraska Press, Bison Book; 2005; PB

THE BOOK OF SKULLS
- Charles Scribner's Sons, NY; 1972; 1st Edition; tan and red HC with gold colored lettering text on spine; HC; DJ design by Robert Aulicino; 222 pp.
- Signet/NAL [Q5177]; 1972; PB; 190 pp
- ROC; 1976; PB
- Victor Gollancz, London; 1978; HC w DJ
- Berkley Publishing Corporation, NY; 1979; PB; Cover by Alexander
- Coronet Books, London; 1981; PB; 222 pp
- Bantam Books, NY (Bantam 23057-3); 1983; PB; Cover Art by Jim Burns
- BRUDERSCHAFT DER UNSTERBLICHKEIT; Moewig, Munich, Germany; 1980; PB; 239 pp
- EL LIBRO DE LOS CRÁNEOS; Ediciones B, Barcelona; 1987; PB; 304 pp
- MacMillan, London; 1999; Soft Cover
- Orion Publishing Co, UK; 1999; PB 222 pp
- Del Rey; 2006; PB

BORN WITH THE DEAD
First magazine appearance in special RS tribute issue of *The Magazine Of Fantasy And Science Fiction*, April 1974.
Novella won the 1974 Nebula and 1975 Hugo awards.
- Random House, NY; 1974; HC w DJ, states "First Edition"; 267 pp; Cover art by Carl Berkowitz
  Collects: Born with the Dead, Thomas the Proclaimer, and Going.
- Vintage Books, NY; June 1975; 1st PB Edition; 257 pp; ca: Shields
- Victor Gollancz, London; 1975; HC w DJ; 267pp
- Hodder & Stoughton Ltd, Coronet, London; 1977; PB; 224 pp
- Berkley Pub., NY; 1979; PB
- Bantam, NY (#24103); 1984; PB; ca: Jim Burns
- Tom Doherty Associates, NY, Tor Books, NY [Tor Double Novel No. 3]; 1988; PB; bound w THE SALIVA TREE by Brian W. Aldiss; cover: Ron Walotsky

CHILD OF TIME
See THE UGLY LITTLE BOY.

COLLISION COURSE
- Avalon Books, NY; 1961; HC w DJ; 1st edition; 224 pp; ca: Ed Emshwiller
- Ace Double, [F-123]; PB, 1961; bound with THE NEMESIS FROM TERRA By Leigh Brackett

CONQUERORS FROM THE DARKNESS
- Holt, Rinehart and Winston, NY; 1965. HC w DJ
- Dell Publishing/Mayflower, NY [#1456]; Sept. 1968. PB. 1st PB edition; 156pp; ca: Paul Lehr
  A thousand years in the future, the earth has been conquered by an alien race and covered by a single sea. Dovirr Stargan, who is disgusted with the servility of his life; longs to become one of the Sea-Lords, who roam the sea as powerful protectors of the cities. Dovirr gets his wish, but the return of the alien race brings unexpected and critically dangerous crises to this new life as he learns the real, sometimes terrible, significance of power.
- Ace Double Novel; 1979; PB; bound with MASTER OF LIFE AND DEATH; 386pp
- Tor Books, New York, NY, USA; 1986; PB
  … [this] book was written for readers between the ages of 10 and 14…. I wrote the underlying novella in 1957, I think, for a magazine that published simple action-adventure stories, and expanded it into a book around 1964.— RS

THE DAWNING LIGHT
First magazine appearance in *Astounding Science Fiction* March, April, May 1957
Sequel to THE SHROUDED PLANET.
RS and Randall Garrett writing as Robert Randall.
- Gnome Press, Inc., Publishers, NY; 1959; HC w DJ; 1st edition; 191 pp
- Mayflower-Dell, [#1678]; 1964; PB; 189 pp; ca: Richard Powers
- Donning/Starblaze, Norfolk, VA; 1981; PB; ca: Barclay Shaw
- Ace, NY; 1982; PB; 216 pp; ca: Walter Velez

THE DESERT OF STOLEN DREAMS
- Underwood Miller, San Francisco; 1981; HC; 1st Edition; 96 pp
  Trade state was limited to 780 copies; Signed state limited to 200 specially bound copies; 1st edition, numbered and signed by RS; DJ & interior illustrations: Stephen E. Fabian.

DOWNWARD TO THE EARTH
First magazine appearance in *Galaxy* Dec. 1969, Jan., Feb., March 1970.
- Doubleday; 1970; HC w DJ; 180pp; DJ art: Frank Frazetta
- New American Library/NAL, Signet, (#T4497); 1971; 176 pp; Cover by Gene Szafran
- DIE MYSTERIEN VON BELZAGOR; Heyne, Munich; 1973; PB
- Victor Gollancz, London; 1977; PB; cover art Jim Burns
- Pan Science Fiction, London England; 1978; PB
- Berkley Books, New York, NY; 1979; PB
- REGRESO A BELZAGOR; Ediciones Martínez Roca, Barcelona (Colección Super Ficción); 1985; PB; 167 pp;

tr into Spanish by Margarita González

DYING INSIDE
First magazine appearance in *Galaxy*,
- Charles Scribner's Sons; 1972, 1st edition; DJ design by Jerry Thorp; 245 pp.
- Ballantine Books, NY, 1973. PB. First PB edition
- Easton Press; 1990; HC; 245 pp; illustrator: Freas RS signed 5000 copies for a "limited" edition
- Ibooks; 2002; PB

THE FACE OF THE WATERS
- Bantam Books, NY; November 1991; HC w DJ; 363 pp Limited Edition of 350 copies, signed, numbered, with page edges silver all around in mint-green cloth, slipcased
  On the waterworld planet of Hydros, the human colonists are exiled by the amphibious natives from the few habitable land masses and set off in a desperate search for refuge in the shadowy mystical land of the Face of the Waters.
- Grafton, London, A Division of HarperCollinsPublishers; 1991; HC w DJ; First UK Edition
- Bantam Dell Pub Group; 1991; PB

THE GATE OF WORLDS
(Juvenile)
- Holt, Rinehart and Winston, NY; 1967; HC; 1st edition
- Victor Gollancz Ltd., London; 1978; HC w DJ; 244 pp

GILGAMESH THE KING
- Arbor House, NY; 1984; HC w DJ; 1st edition; 320 pp; Cover art by Loretta Trezzo

THE KING OF DREAMS
- Eos, NY; 2001; HC w DJ; 1st edition; 451 pp Volume 7 in the "Majipoor" series
- EOS/HarperCollins, NY; 2002. PB; 480 pp.
- Voyager, London, UK; 2002; PB; 514 pp

HAWKSBILL STATION
Original publication of novella in *Galaxy* Vol.25 No.6, August 1967
1967 Nebula and 1968 Hugo nominee
- Doubleday & Company, Inc., Garden City, NY; 1967. 1st edition; HC; book club are not usually firsts but this is a true 1st edition; 166 pp; Pat Steir (illustrator)
- THE ANVIL OF TIME; Sidgewick and Jackson; 1969; First UK; HC with DJ; 192 pp
- Avon Books, New York, NY, USA (#S411); 1970; PB; 176 pp; Cover art by Don Ivan Punchatz
- Tandem, London (#04124); 1969; PB; 192 pp
- Ballantine, NY; 1972; PB
- Berkley Publishing Corporation, NY; 1978; PB; 185 pp
- Universal/W. H. Allen, Britain, (Universal Book Club), 1978; PB; 192 pp
- W. H. Allen, London; 1982; PB; 192 pp
- LES DÉPORTÉS DU CAMBRIEN; J'ai lu, France; 1984;

PB; tr in french by Guy Abadia
- Warner Books, New York, NY; 1986;
- TOR BOOKS, [TOR SF Double, # 26]; Bound with PRESS ENTER by John Varley; 1990; PB; 192 pp
- ESTACIÓN HAWKSBILL; Plaza & Janes Editores, Barcelona; 2000; 223pp; Introduction by Frederik Pohl; translated by Antonio Prado
- HAWKBILL TIMES TWO; Fox Acre Press; 2002; PB; Both version of Hawksbill Station – the novella and the novel – in one volume. Includes an intro. and afterword by RS. *Hawksbill Station was very different in its novella and novel forms, and I felt it was worth reprinting in the original version.— RS*
- LES DÉPORTÉS DU CAMBRIEN; Livre de Poche, France; 2002; 192 pp

HOMEFARING
- Phantasia Press, Michigan ; 1983; Signed, limited, slipcase edition of 450 copies; 102 pp

HOT SKY AT MIDNIGHT
Sections first appeared in *Playboy* 1986
- Spectra Bantam, NY; Feb.,1994; HC w DJ; 1st US edition, 327 pp
- Easton Press, 1994, Norwalk, 1994; HC Full-Leather; 327pp; Illus by Fred Mayo
- Bantam Books, NY; 1994; HC w DJ
  A tale of Earth on the brink of ecological collapse - and humanity on the edge of extinction.

IN ANOTHER COUNTRY
- TOR Double #18; 1990; PB; bound with VINTAGE SEASON by C.L. Moore; ca: Wayne Barlow
  RS novelette written as sequel to Moore's story.

INVADERS FROM EARTH
First publication in *Science Fiction Quarterly* as We, the Marauders.
- Ace Books [#D-286] Ace Double, bound with ACROSS TIME by Don A. Wollheim writing as David Grinnell; 1958; 169 pp
- Avon Books, New York, NY U.S.A; 1968; PB

INVISIBLE BARRIERS
RS writing as David Osborne
Expander version of And The Walls Came Tumbling Down first published in *If* magazine.
- Avalon Books, NY; 1958; 1st edition: HC w DJ; 223 pp

KINGDOMS OF THE WALL
- Spectra Bantam, NY; 1993; HC w DJ; 1st edition; 307 pp

LEST WE FORGET THEE EARTH
RS writing as Calvin M. Knox three part novel first published in *SF Adventures*
- Ace Double, [D-291]; bound with PEOPLE MINUS X by R. Gallun; 1958; PB; 126 pp; ca: Ed Valigursky

LION TIME IN TIMBUCTOO
- Pulphouse Publishing, Eugene, OR. 1990., 1990. Also a edition of 75 numbered copies bound in full blue leather.

LORD OF DARKNESS
- Arbor House, NY; 1983; HC w DJ; 558 pp; DJ art: Paul Bacon
- Bantam; 1984; PB; 613 pp
- Victor Gollancz, Ltd., London; 1983; HC w DJ
  An exotic, vivid recreation of a life lived to the brim in the zenith of the Elizabethan age as a young British seaman confronts the Lord of Darkness.

LORD PRESTIMION
- HarperCollins Publishers, Prism; 1999; HC w DJ; DJ art: Jim Burns
- Voyager, London; 1999; HC w DJ; 434 pp

LORD VALENTINE'S CASTLE
- Harper & Row, Publishers, NY; 1980; 1st edition; Numbered state limited to 250 numbered & signed copies also produced
- Pan Books, UK; 1981; PB; 504 pp

THE LONGEST WAY HOME
- Eos Books; 2002; HC w DJ; 304 pp
  A *New York Times* Notable Book for 2002.
  The Folk were first to arrive on this faraway planet, pushing aside the docile, intelligent aboriginal races they encountered. The 'Masters' followed to subjugate the careless, complacent fellow humans who preceded them here. And so it has remained for ages…
- LE LONG CHEMIN DE RETOUR; Laffont, France; 2003; PB

LOST RACE OF MARS
(Juvenile)
- John C. Winston Company, Philadelphia: 1960. HC w DJ; Illustrated by Leonard Kessler; 120 pp
- Scholastic Book Services, SBS NY; [#TX 535]; 1964; PB; 123 pp; Illustrated by Leonard Kessler

MAJIPOOR CHRONICLES
Second book of the Majipoor series.
- Arbor House, NY; 1982; HC; 1st edition
- Arbor House, Priam Books; 1982; PB; 314 pp; maps by Palacios

THE MAN IN THE MAZE
Serialized in *Worlds of If* magazine.
- Avon; 1969[V2262]; PB; 192 pp; ca: Don Punchatz
- Sidgwick & Jackson, London; 1969; HC; First British edition
- Ibooks; 2002; PB; 224 pp; intro by Neil Gaiman

THE MASKS OF TIME
- Ballantine Books, NY [U6121]; May 1968; PB; 252 pp
- Retitled VORNAN-19; Sidgwick & Jackson, London; 1970;

HC; First British edition; 252 pp
• LAS MÁSCARAS DEL TIEMPO; Ultramar, Spain; 1990; PB; 303 pp

MASTER OF LIFE AND DEATH
• Ace Double, D-237, (with James White's THE SECRET VISITORS); 1957; ca: Ed Emshwiller
• Avon [S329]; PB; Mar. 1968; 144 pp; ca: Hector Garrido
• Sidgwick & Jackson, London; 1977; HC w DJ
• Ace Books, New York, NY, USA; 1979; PB
• Panther, London; 1979; PB.
• Foxacre Press, Takoma Park; 2001; PB; 149 pp

THE MOUNTAINS OF MAJIPOOR
• Bantam/Spectra: 1995; 1st Edition HC w DJ; 225 pp
It is now a thousand years after the time of Lord Valentine, hero of the earlier Majipoor books, and one of his descendants, young Harpirias, accidentally kills a rare and valuable animal belonging to another nobleman. By way of punishment, Harpirias is sent to the snow-covered mountains to ransom an archaeological expedition from the local inhabitants. He is accompanied by a shape-shifting interpreter ....
• Easton Press; 1995; HC; 225 pp
• Pan; PB; 240 pp
• DIE MAJIPOOR-CHRONIKEN: DIE BERGE VON MAJIPOOR; Lübbe; PB; German edition; 234 pp; ca: Jim Burns
• LES MONTAGNES DE MAJIPOOR; Livre de Poche, France; 1999; PB; 188 pp

THE MUTANT SEASON
With wife Karen Haber.
• Doubleday Foundation; Nov. 1989; Trade PB; 289 pp; ca: Dean Motter
• Bantam; 1990; PB; 289 pp; ca: Jim Burns

THE NEW SPRINGTIME
See THE QUEEN OF SPRINGTIME

NIGHTFALL
With Isaac Asimov
• Doubleday, NY; 1990; HC w DJ; 1st Edition; 339 pp
This novel is based on the ss "Nightfall" by Isaac Asimov, which first appeared in *Astounding Science Fiction* in 1941.

NIGHTWINGS
Hugo Award winner novella, 1969.
First magazine publication in *Galaxy* magazine Sept. 1968
• Avon Books, NY [#V2303]; Sept. 1969; PB; 190 pp; ca: Don Ivan Punchatz
Book dedication: *For Harlan/to remind him of open windows/the currents of the Delaware River/quarters with two heads/and other pitfalls*
• Walker and Company, NY, 1970; HC w DJ; First HC Edition; ca: Jack Gaughan
• Sidgwick & Jackson, London [SF Special 10]; 1972; 1st British edition; 190 pp

• ACI DELLA NOTTE; Editrice Nord, Milan, Italy; 1973; First Italian edition HC
• Sphere, UK; 1974; PB; 192 pp
• LES AILES DE LA NUIT; J'ai lu, Paris [#585]; 1975; PB; 212 pp
• ALAS NOCTURNAS; Edhasa. Nebulae Ciencia Ficcion, Barcelona; 1976; 227 pp
• Avon/Equinox; 1976; PB; 190 pp; ca: Gene Szafran
• DC Comics graphic novel; 1985; adapted by Gary Bates, interior art: Gene Colan; ca: Bill Sienkiwicz
• Ibooks; 2003; PB; 240 pp
• IDW; 2008; PB; ca: Michael Parkes

ONE OF OUR ASTEROIDS IS MISSING
As Calvin M. Knox
• Ace Double, [F-253]; bound with THE TWISTED MEN by A. E. van Vogt; 1964; PB; 124 pp; Cover Ed Emsh

THE PLANET KILLER
First published in *SF Adventures*.
• A.A. Wynn/Ace Book, Inc., Ace Double, D-407(bound with WE CLAIM THESE STARS by Poul Anderson); 1959; PB; 255 pp; ca: Ed Valigursky

PLANET OF DEATH
(Juvenile)
• Holt, Rinehart, Winston, NY, NY; 1967. stated 1st edition; HC w DJ; 124 pp; ca: Lawrence Ratzkin

THE PLOT AGAINST THE EARTH
Written as Calvin M. Knox
• Ace Double, [D-358]; bound with RECRUIT FOR ANDROMEDA by Milton Lesser; 1950; PB; 138 pp

THE POSITRONIC MAN
With Isaac Asimov,
• Doubleday NY, Published 1993; HC 1st edition; 259 pp

PROJECT PENDULUM
• Walker & Co, NY; 1987; HC w DJ; 1st edition; 200 pp; Illustrator: Moebius
Project Pendulum, the first practical experiment in time travel, launches paleontologist Sean Gabrielson into the age of dinosaurs and his twin brother Eric, a physicist, ninety-five million years into the future.
• Bantam; Nov. 1989; PB; 210 pp; wrap-around ca: Mark Harrison

THE QUEEN OF SPRINGTIME
Second book of "The New Springtime" trilogy, preceded by At Winter's End (1988). Published later in the U.S. as THE NEW SPRINGTIME (1990).
• Victor Gollancz Ltd, London; 1989; HC w DJ; 416 pp; DJ art: Nicholas Rodgers
Forty years have passed since the events of AT WINTER'S END, and many changes have overtaken the People since Hresh and Taniane led their tiny band out of the marvellous half-ruined city of

Vengilboneeza to found a new community far away. Old tribal identities, fostered in isolation of the cocoons, have begun to break down. Others of the same species as the People have come forth from their cocoons by the thousands, tribe upon tribe bursting out into the world; a vigorous new civilization is thriving upon the Earth, the world's greatest age is beginning anew. But there are still many problems to overcome - most notably the threat of the mysterious, almost incomprehensible hjjk-folk, which brings before the People the spectre of an apocalyptic war. This second volume of Robert Silverberg's brilliantly inventive far-future trilogy confirms that this is his most colourful and popular work since Lord Valentine's Castle.

- THE NEW SPRINGTIME; Warner Books Inc, NY; 1990; HC w DJ; 358 pp
  Hundreds of thousands of years in Earth's future, as the planet slowly wakes from centuries of deep freeze, various tribes vie for supremacy — until the Hjjks, a bizarre insect-like species, threaten to vanquish all other creatures.
- THE NEW SPRINGTIME; Warner Books Inc, NY; 1991; PB; 472 pp
- Arrow, UK; 1991; PB; 519 pp; ca: Kevin Tweddell
- DER NEUE FRÜHLING; Heyne, Germany; 1992; PB; 652 pp
- Univ. of Nebraska Press, Bison Books; 2005; PB; 368 pp

RECALLED TO LIFE
First magazine appearance in *Infinity* - Vol. 3, # 5, 6 – June, July, Aug. 1958
- Lancer Books, NY; 1958; PB
- Lancer Books, NY, [#74-810]; 1962; PB; cover: Ed Emsh
- Avon Books, NY; 1967; PB
- Doubleday, Garden City, NY; 1972; HC w DJ; ca: Emanuel Schongut; First printing of the revised text with printing code "N24" in the gutter on page 184.
- Gollancz, London; 1974; HC w DJ
- Panther, UK; 1975; PB
  When a nervous scientist from Beller Laboratories approached James Harker, asking him to introduce a new scientific discovery to the world, Harker had his own reasons for agreeing. The discovery was a reanimation process - bringing the recently dead back to life. But Harker hadn't anticipated treachery within the ranks of the scientists working on the process, nor on the consternation and mounting hysteria when the news broke….
- Ace Books, New York, NY; 1977; PB; New intro by RS

REGAN'S PLANET
Revised as WORLD'S FAIR 1992
- Pyramid Books, #F-986, March,1964; PB; 141 pp; ca: Ed Emshwiller
  The story of how Claude Regan built a whole new world for the World's Fair…

REVOLT ON ALPHA C
(Juvenile)
- Thomas Y. Crowell Company, NY;1955; HC w DJ; 1st edition of author's first book; 148 pp
- Tab Books, Inc./Scholastic Book Services, NY [TX137];

1959; PB; 118 pp; cover & interior illustrator: William Meyerriecks
- LA PATTUGLIA DELLO SPAZIO; Editrice Milano, Italy; 1960
- Warner Books, NY; 1989; PB; "Not for Sale" printed in red letters on cover
  For RS' 35th year as a pro writer, Warner Books offered copies of this book free to purchasers of AT WINTER'S END. The special edition of REVOLT has a new introduction, explaining the history of the book, by RS.

A ROBERT SILVERBERG OMNIBUS
- Sidgwick & Jackson, 1970. 1st edition; HC w DJ; 182 pp
  Contains: Master Of Life And Death (1957), Invaders From Earth (1958), And The Time Hoppers (1967). First HC publication of the last 2 novellas.
- Harper & Row, NY, 1971. HC w DJ.
  Contains: The Man In The Maze, Nightwings, & Downward To The Earth

SAILING TO BYZANTIUM
Hugo and Nebula Awards winning novella.
- Underwood & Miller, Grass Valley, CA, USA; 1985; HC w DJ, 1st edition [trade issue]; 114 pp
  Limited edition with suede cloth slipcase; 250 numbered copies specially bound and SIGNED by the author
- Tom Doherty Associates, LLC, NY, [Tor Double Ser., No. 1]); 1989; PB; bound with SEVEN AMERICAN NIGHTS by Gene Wolfe; Cover Art (RS novel): Brian Waugh
- IBooks; 2004; PB

THE SECOND TRIP
First magazine appearance in *Amazing Stories* - Volume 45, number 2, 3 - July 1971
- Nelson Doubleday, Inc., Garden City, NY; 1972; 1st edition; HC w DJ; First printing with code "39N" on page 181; 185 pp; Cover Sculpture by Gene Szafran
  In the 21st century, society has developed a new way of dealing with dangerous criminals. Their memories and identities are expunged and a new personality is built up in their place.
- New American Library, Signet, NY; 1973; PB
- L'HOMME PROGRAMMÉ; Éditions Opta, collection 'Nébula (dirigée par Alain Dorémieux)', Paris; 1976; 253 pp; tr into French by Bruno Martin.
- Gollancz, Uk; 1979; HC
- Pan Science Fiction, UK; 1980; PB; Cover art by Peter Gudynas
- Avon Books, New York, NY, USA; 1981 PB
- Morrow/Avon, New York, NY, USA; 1981; PB
- Gollancz, London; 1991; PB; Cover Image Bank stock image

THE SEED OF EARTH
Expanding of the ss The Winds of Siros published in *Venture* magazine; Sept. 1957; Novella version first published in *Galaxy*: June 1962; Vol. 20, No. 5.

- Ace Double [F-145]; 1962; PB backed with NEXT STOP THE STARS (*Exciting stories of wonders in new worlds*) by RS; PB; 1st edition (Stated); ca: Valigursky
- Ace Books, New York, NY, USA;1977; PB; First separate edition; Cover art by Don Ivan Punchatz
- Hamlyn, UK; 1978; PB; First UK Edition; 167 pp; ca: Tony Roberts
- LA SEMENCE DE LA TERRE; Librarie des Champs Elyses (France); 1960; PB

SEVENTH SHRINE
- LEGENDS: Short Novels by the Masters of Modern Fantasy Vol. 1; Harper Collins Publishers; 1998; HC w DJ; ed. by RS
- Image Comics; 2005; PB
- Marvel Comics; 2007; PB

SHADRACH IN THE FURNANCE
- The Bobbs-Merrill Co., Indianapolis/New York; 1976; HC w DJ

THE SHROUDED PLANET
RS and Randall Garrett writing as Robert Randall.
- Gnome Press, NY; 1957; HC w DJ; 1st edition; 188 pp
- Mayflower-Dell, [#7881,]; 1963; PB; 188 pp; ca: Richard Powers

THE SILENT INVADERS
- Ace Double F195 (Backed with BATTLE ON VENUS By William F. Temple); 1963; RS story is 1st book publication; Cover art to RS side by Ed Emshwiller
- Ace 76390, [76390]; 1973; PB; 2nd printing
- Ace Books; 1977; PB; New introduction by the RS
- Dennis Dobson, London, England: 1979; HC w DJ; DJ art: Richard Weaver

SON OF MAN
- Ballantine [#02277]; June1971; PB; 1st printing; ca: Gene Szafran; 213 pp
- Del Rey Book-Ballantine Books; 1977; PB; 213 pp; ca: Murray Tinkleman
- Panther/Granada, UK; 1979; PB; ca: Jim Burns
- Warner Books, NY; 1984; PB; 212pp; ca: Don Dixon
- Victor Gollancz Ltd., UK; 1991; PB; 192 pp
- Gollancz, UK; 2003; PB
- Pyr/Prometheus Books, Amherst, MA; 2008; PB; 225 pp

SORCERERS OF MAJIPOOR
- Harper Prism, NY; 1996; HC w DJ; 1st Edition; 462 pp
  A prequel to Silverberg's earlier Majipoor novels.

STAR OF GYPSIES
- Donald I. Fine, Inc., NY; 1986. HC W DJ; 1st edition; 397 pp
  Star of Gypsies tells the story of the rise to prominence of the ancient Gypsy people in the year 3159.

STARBORNE
- Bantam/Spectra, NY; 1996; HC w DJ; 1st edition; 291 pp

STARHAVEN
As Ivar Jorgenson (pseudonym)
- Avalon Books, NY;1958; HC, 1st edition; DJ art: Ric Binkley

STARMAN'S QUEST
- Gnome Press, Hicksville, NY; 1958; HC w DJ; 1st edition; 185 pp; DJ art: Stan Mack

STEPSONS OF TERRA
- Ace Double,; D-311; 1958; PB; bound with A MAN CALLED DESTINY by Ian Wright
- SCHATTEN UBER DEN STERNEN (Shadow on the Stars), Moewig, Verlag, Germany; Terra, Utopiache Romane, Science Fiction; 1959; PB
- Ace Books, New York, NY, USA; 1976; PB; new introduction by RS; ca: Don Ivan Punchatz
  In over 500 years the distant Terran colony of Corwin had no communications with earth. Now they need help. But earth had nothing to offer, and no ability or desire to fight.
- Ace, [0-441-78600-6]; [date not indicated]; PB
- Sphere, UK; 1979; PB; 158 pp

SORCERERS OF MAJIPOOR
- Harper Prism, NY; 1996; HC w DJ; 1st edition; 462 pp

STOCHASTIC MAN
- Harper&Row; 1975; 1st edition, HC
- Fawcett Gold Medal #13570; Aug. 1976; PB, 1st printing
- Gollancz, London; 1976; First UK Edition; HC w DJ;
- Orion Publishing Co; 1992; PB

THEBES OF THE HUNDRED GATES
- Axolotl Press, Pulphouse Publishing, Eugene, OR [AXOLOTL PRESS SERIES BOOK #22]; 1991; First, limited in an edition of 75 numbered copies bound in full dark brown leather leather, also, 300 numbered cloth-bound copies numbered and signed by RS from total of 900 HC copies produced; also, Soft Cover, in wrappers, Signed by the RS, Limited edition of 525 copies; 110 pp; Illustration By Donna Gordon
- Bantam Books/Spectra, New York, NY; 1992; PB
- HarperCollins, London; 1993; HC w DJ; 120 pp

THREE SURVIVED
(juvenile)
First appearance in *Super SF*, Aug. 1957, Vol. 1, # 5
- Holt, Rinehart & Winston, NY; 1969; HC; 1st edition; 117 pp

THE 13TH IMMORTAL
- Ace Books, A. A. Wynn Inc., (Ace Double D-223); 1957; bound with THIS FORTRESS WORLD By James E. Gunn; covers by Ed Valigursky and Emsh
- DER 13. UNSTERBLICHE; Moewig, Verlag, Germany;

Terra, Utopiache Romane, Science Fiction; date; PB
• Wildside Pr; 2004; PB; 145 pp

THORNS
Nominated for Nebula (1967) and Hugo (1968)
• Ballantine Books, New York, NY, USA (#U6097); Aug. 1967; PB; ca: Robert Foster; Phil Kirkland art on Canadian edition
  Duncan Chalk was a vulture that fed on other people's pain. As he became more powerful and rich he also became more monstrous. Lona Kelvin and Minner Burris were to be two of his puppets— but they were also Ultra-Woman and Non-Man.
• DER GESANG DER NEURONEN; Lausanne, Editions Rencontre (Germany); 1967; PB; 199 pp
• Walker & Co, NY; 1969; HC w DJ, 1st Edition; 222 p.
• Rapp & Whiting, UK; 1969; HC w DJ; First UK; 222 pp
• UN JEU CRUEL; Editions J'ai Lu N°800 (French); 1977; HC w DJ; 214 pp; DJ art by Philip Caza
• New English Library, London; May 1977; PB; wrap-around ca: Keith Laban
• Futura (Orbit); 1987; PB; 224 pp
• DER GESANG DER NEURONEN; Heyne, Munich; 1989; PB; 253 pp
• Victor Gollancz, Great Britain, (Orion Books Ltd); 2000; PB (Part of the Gollancz SF Collectors' Edition Series. This is the first type with matching bright all yellow covers with French fold-ins, and no cover art); 224 pp

THOSE WHO WATCH
• The New American Library, Signet Books, NY [P3160]; 1967; PB; 143 pp
  Only three humans would ever know that the blinding flash in the sky on that night in 1982 was an exploding flying saucer. Only they would learn the truth about Those Who Watch – about the alien beings who came into this world in a crash landing from the stars….
• Roc; 1971; PB
• New English Library (NEL), London: 1977; PB
• BEOBACHTER AUS DEM ALL; Wilhelm Goldmann Verlag, Munich. Germany; 1981; Softcover

A TIME OF CHANGES
First serialized in *Galaxy* Magazine March, April, May 1971. Winner of Nebula Award for best novel, 1971
• Nelson Doubleday, Inc., NY; 1971, HC w DJ; 183 pp; ca: Brad Holland
• New American Library/ Signet, NY [Q472]); 1971; PB
• The New American Library of Canada Limited, Scarborough, Ontario; 1971; PB; ca: Szafran
• Victor Gollancz, London; 1973; HC w DJ; 1st UK edition; 221pp
• Panther Books, UK; 1971, 1975; PB; ca: Bruce Pennington
• Granada, London; 1975; PB
• TIEMPO DE CAMBIOS; Tiempo Cero, Argentina (Col. Ciencia Ficción); 1976; 230 pp
• Berkley Books, NY [04051-8];1979; PB; new introduction by RS; ca: Paul Alexander

"Under the gold-green sun of Velada Borthan, mankind had found peace, but at a terrible price. For it was a peace without love, without self, where even the mention of the word 'I' was taboo…"
• Bluejay Books; 1983; HC
• Warner Books, NY; 1986; 214 pp; PB; ca: Jim Burns
• Gollancz, London [SF Classic 3]; 1986; PB; ca: David Jackson
• Easton Press, Norwalk, Connecticut; Easton Press Collector's Edition Masterpieces of SF; 1988; bound in blue leaf with gold gilt pattern to front and back boards, and gilt print on spine; gilt page edges; bound-in ribbon place marker; Introduction by Joe Haldeman; frontispiece by Randy Lagana

THE TIME HOPPERS
• Pyramid; 1963; PB
• Doubleday and Company, NY; 1967; HC w DJ; 182 pp
  Joseph Quellen is a man for whom the year 2490 is suddenly the wrong time to live. In a vastly overpopulated world, one of the more unusual diversions for an utterly bored populace is time-hopping— an escape, via time travel, away from the crush of the twenty-fifth century and back to the tranquil past.
• Belmont Tower; 1967; PB
• Avon Book, NY[#S372]; 1968; PB; ca: Don Punchatz
• Fontana, London: 1979; PB

TIME OF THE GREAT FREEZE
• Holt, Rinehart and Winston, NY; 1964; 1st edition; HC w DJ; 191 pp; DJ art: Brinton Turkle
• Dell, Laurel-Leaf Mayflower, New York, NY; 1966; PB; ca: Schare
• Ace Books, NY; 1980; PB; 195 pp; ca: Paul Alexander
• DIE STADT UNTER DEM EIS; Tosa publishing company, Vienna; 1981; PB; 153 pp
• Tor Books; 1988; PB
  "The Fourth Ice Age is ending; will mankind reclaim the Earth?"

TO LIVE AGAIN
• Doubleday, Garden City, NY, USA; 1969; 1st edition (stated); HC w DJ; 231 pp; ca: Pat Stier
• Dell NY [#8973]; Jan. 1971; 1st PB printing; 207 pp
• Sidgwick & Jackson, GB; 1975; PB; 231pp
• Fontana/Collins, London; 1977; PB; ca: Jim Burns
• Berkley, NY; 1978; PB; 208 pp
• NOCH EINMAL LEBEN; Moewig, Munich, Germany; 1981; PB; 285 pp

TOM O'BEDLAM
• Donald I Fine, NY; 1985; HC w DJ; 1st edition; 320 pp
• W.Paul Ganley; 1985; PB; 191 pp; Illustrated by Stephen E. Fabian
• Dutton Adult; 1985; HC w DJ
• Warner Books, Boston, Massachusetts, U.S.A; 1986; PB; 374 pp
  It is 2103 and Tom O'Bedlam, madman, prophet, and visionary,

wanders through California, dwelling place of the last humans on a continent decimated by radioactive dust. Tom, caught up in a living vision of distant worlds ruled by godlike beings, is the herald of a new age, a herald no one wants to hear until others too begin to dream of salvation beyond the stars.

- Victor Gollancz Ltd, UK; 1986; HC w DJ; First British edition; 320 pp
- Futura Orbit, UK; 1987; PB; 320 pp
- Heyne book, Munich; 1987; PB; German first issue
- Editions J'ai Lu (French); 1991; 381 pp
- Olmstead Press; 2001

TO OPEN THE SKY
Shorter version first appeared in *Galaxy* Magazine Vol 24, No 5 (June 1966) as Open the Sky
- Ballantine Books [U6093]; 1967; PB; ca: Richard Powers; 222 pp
- Sphere Books Ltd., London; 1970; PB; 202pp
- Gregg Press, Boston; 1977. Octavo, cloth. First HC edition. Text offset from the 1967 Ballantine Books edition. New introduction by Russell Letson; 222 pp; b/w frontis by Richard Powers
- Berkley Medallion; 1978; PB
- ÖFFNET DEN HIMMEL; Moewig, Munich, Germany (Moewig: Science Fiction; 3537); 1981; PB; 255 pp
- LE CHEMIN DE L'ESPACE; Editions J'ai Lu [N°1434]; 1983; 249 pp;. Tr into French by M. Deutsch; ca: Steve R. Dodd.
- Bantam, NY [#24502]; 1984; PB:

TOWER OF GLASS
First publication in *Galaxy*: Vol. 30; April, May, June 1970
- Charles Scribner's Sons,, NY; 1970; HC w DJ; 1st ed; 247pp
- Bantam Books, Inc., NY; 1971; PB
- LA TOUR DE VERRE; Bibliotheque Marabout, Paris; 1972, 246 pp; tr into French by Simone Hilling
- Panther SF, London England; 1976, PB; 206 pp
- Granada Publishing; 1976; PB
- Bantam Books, NY; 1980. PB; Second Bantam Edition, Bantam 12641-5; Cover Art by Lou Feck
- Warner Books, Boston, Massachusetts, USA; 1987; PB
- Futura Publications, London/Sydney (Orbit); 1987; PB; 207 pp
- Victor Gollancz, LTD, United Kingdom; 2001; Trade PB, yellow cover

THE UGLY LITTLE BOY
From a novella by Isaac Asimov, first published in *Galaxy* 1958.
Isaac's original novella is embedded within the novel just about in complete form, so if you want to figure out who wrote what, go through the book and highlight everything that comes from the original story. The rest is mine. Isaac read and approved it, but he was too ill at that point to do any of the writing himself.— RS
- Doubleday; 1992; 1st Edition HC w DJ;
- CHILD OF TIME; Victor Gollancz, London; 1991; HC w DJ; 302 pp; First UK Edition; ca: David Farren

A children's nurse is hired as part of a scientific project aimed at bringing a living being from the past to the present. A four-year-old Neanderthal boy is snatched from his home and hurled 40,000 years into a terrifying future.
- CHILD OF TIME; Pan Books, Great Britain; 1992; PB

UP THE LINE
Original publication in *Amazing Stories*: July & August, 1969
- Ballantine Books [#01680]; 1969; PB
- Sphere Books, London; 1975; PB; 208 pp
- Ballantine / Del Rey, NY; 1978; PB; 250 pp; ca: Murray Tinkelman
- Victor Gollancz, U.K; 1987; PB
- Ibooks, New York, NY, USA; 2002. Trade PB; 298 pp

VALENTINE PONTIFEX
- Morrow/Avon, NY; 1983; HC w DJ; 347 pp

VORNAN-19
See THE MASKS OF TIME.

THE WORLD INSIDE
- Doubleday & Co;1971; HC w DJ; 184 pp
  Man had attained Utopia. War, starvation, crime and birth control had been eliminated. Life was totally fulfilled and sustained within mammoth skyscrapers hundred of floors high.
- Signet; 1972; PB; 174
  The Throwbacks, We Are Well Organized, The World Inside, The World Outside, All the Way Up, All the Way Down, A Happy Day in 2381
- LES MONADES URBAINES; Laffont, France; 1974; HC; 251 pp
- Bantam; 1983; PB; 167 pp
- Gollancz (UK); 1990; PB; 174 pp

WORLD'S FAIR 1992
- Follett Publishing Co., Chicago; 1970; HC w DJ; 1st edition, (stated); 248 pp; DJ art: Jack Endewelt
- Ace SF; 1982; PB; 240 pp; ca: Atilla Hejja

STORY COLLECTIONS

ANDROLDS, TIME MACHINES AND BLUE GIRAFFES
- Follet Publishing Company; 1973; ss The Mutant Weapon become The Mutant Season in later reprintings

BEYOND THE SAFE ZONE
- Donald I Fine; 1986; HC w DJ; Collection of 27 tales

THE BEST OF ROBERT SILVERBERG
- Pocket Book; 1976; PB; intro by Barry Malzberg contains: Road to Nightfall; Warm Man; To See the Invisible Man; The Sixth Palace; Flies; Hawksbill Station; Passengers; Nightwings; Sundance; Good News from the Vatican
- Gregg; 1978; HC; 288 pp

THE BEST OF ROBERT SILVERBERG
VOLUME 2
• Gregg; 1978; HC
  contains: Born with the Dead; Breckenridge and the
  Continuum; Caliban; Capricorn Games; The Dybbuk of
  Mazel Tov IV; A Happy Day in 2381; In Entropy's Jaws;
  Schwartz Between the Galaxies; Trips

THE CALIBRATED ALLIGATOR
• Holt, Rinehart and Winston, New York, NY; 1969;
  HC w DJ; 224 pp
  Contains: The Calibrated Alligator, Blaze Of Glory, The
  Artifact Business, Precedent, Mugwump Four, Why?, His
  Head In The Clouds, Point Of Focus, Delivery Guaranteed

CAPRICORN GAMES
• Random House, New York, NY; 1976; HC W DJ; 1st edi-
  tion (stated); Cover art by Jack Ribik
  contains: Ship-Sister, Star-Sister, The Science Fiction Hall of
  Fame; A Sea of Faces; The Dybbuk of Mazel Tov IV;
  Breckenridge and the Continuum; Capricorn Games; Ms.
  Found in an Abandoned Time Machine; Getting Across
• Victor Gollancz, London; 1978; HC w DJ; 1st British
  contains: Capricorn Games; The Science Fiction Hall
  of Fame; Ms. Found in an Abandoned Time Machine;
  Breckenridge and the Continuum; Ship-Sister, Star-Sister; A
  Sea of Faces; The Dybbuk of Mazel Tov IV; Getting Across;
  Ishmael in Love
• Donning Starblaze; 1979; PB; 176 pp; ca: Kelly Freas
• Pan, UK; 1979; PB; 191 pp

COLLECTED STORIES OF
ROBERT SILVERBERG: VOL. 1 SECRET SHARERS
• Bantam Dell Pub Group/Spectra: 1992; PB; 568 pp

THE COLLECTED STORIES OF
ROBERT SILVERBERG
VOL. 1: TO BE CONTINUED
• Subterranean Press, Burton, MI; 2006; 1st edition, HC with-
  out DJ
  *First in a projected eight volumes collecting all of the short stories
  and novellas. Collects 24 stories from the prolific first five years of
  his career (1953-1958).*
  Vol, 1 Contains: Gorgon Planet, The Road to Nightfall, The
  Silent Colony, Absolutely Inflexible, The MacAuley Circuit,
  The Songs of Summer, To Be Continued, Alaree, The
  Artifact Business, Collecting Team, A Man of Talent, One-
  Way Journey, Sunrise on Mercury, World of a Thousand
  Colors, Warm Man, Blaze of Glory, Why?, The Outbreeders,
  The Man Who Never Forgot, There Was an Old Woman,
  The Iron Chancellor, Ozymandias, Counterpart, Delivery
  Guaranteed.

THE COLLECTED STORIES OF ROBERT SILVER-
BERG: VOL. 2: TO THE DARK STAR
• Subterranean Press, Burton, MI; 2007; 1st edition, HC
  without DJ

21 stories from 1959 to 1968.
Contains: To See The Invisible Man, The Pain Peddlers,
Neighbor, The Sixth Palace, Flies, Halfway House, To The
Dark Star, Hawksbill Station, Passengers, Bride 91, Going
Down Smooth, Fangs of the Trees, Ishmael in Love, Ringing
the Changes, Sundance, How It Was When the Past Went
Away, A Happy Day in 2381, Now + n, Now - n, After the
Myths Went Home, The Pleasure of Their Company, We
Know Who We Are.

THE COLLECTED STORIES OF
ROBERT SILVERBERG
VOL. 3: SOMETHING WILD IS LOOSE
• Subterranean Press, Burton, MI; 2008; 1st edition, HC with-
  out DJ.
  16 Fictions from 1969 to 1972.
  Contain: Something Wild is Loose, In Entropy's Jaws, The
  Reality Trip, Going Caliban, Good News from the Vatican,
  Thomas the Proclaimer, When We Went to See the End of
  the World, Push No More, The Wind and the Rain, Some
  Notes on the Pre-Dynastic Epoch, The Feast of St.
  Dionysus, What We Learned from This Morning's
  Newspaper, The Mutant Season, Caught in the Organ Draft,
  Many Mansions.
  *The world that these stories sprang from was the troubled, bewilder-
  ing, dangerous, and very exciting world of those weird years when
  the barriers were down and the future was rushing into the present
  with the force of a river unleashed. But of course I think these stories speak to our times, too, and that most of them will remain valid
  as we go staggering onward through the brave new world of the
  twenty-first century. I am not one of those who believes that all is
  lost and the end is nigh. Like William Faulkner, I do think we will
  somehow endure and prevail against increasingly stiff odds. — RS*

COLLECTED STORIES OF
ROBERT SILVERBERG, VOL. 4, TRIPS 1972-1973
• Subterranean Press, Burton, MI; 2009; 1st edition, HC with-
  out DJ

THE CONGLOMEROID COCKTAIL PARTY
• Arbor House, NY; 1984; HC w DJ; 1st edition; 284 pp
• Bantam Books; July 1985; 1st PB printing; 317pp
• Gollancz; 1984; 1st UK ed

CRONOS
• Ibooks, New York; 2001; PB; 1st edition; 438p
  Contains: Letters From Atlantis, Project Pendulum, The
  Time Hoppers, w new introduction by RS.
  Three complete novels that embody the concept of time travel.

THE CUBE ROOT OF UNCERTAINTY
• The Macmillan Company, NY; 1970; HC w DJ; 239 pp; DJ
  art by Anthony Sini
  Contains: Passengers, Double Dare, The Sixth Palace,
  Translation Error, The Shadow Of Wings, Absolutely
  Inflexible, The Iron Chancellor, Mugwump Four, To The
  Dark Star, Neighbour, Halfway House, Sundance

DIMENSION THIRTEEN
• Ballantine, #01601; 1969; 215 pp

EARTH'S OTHER SHADOW
• Signet/NAL, NY; June 1973; PB; 207 pp
• Millington Books, London; 1977; 214pp
  Contains: Something Wild Is Loose; To See the Invisible Man; Ishamael in Love; How it Was When the Past Went Away; To the Dark Star; The Fangs of the Trees; Hidden Talent; The Song the Zombie Sang; and Flies.

THE FEAST OF ST. DIONYSUS:
FIVE SCIENCE FICTION STORIES
• Scribner's, N.Y; 1975; HC w DJ; 255 pp;
  DJ art: David Lunn
  collects: title story, Schwartz Between the Galaxies, Trips, In the House of Double Minds
• Gollancz, UK; 1976; HC w DJ
• Coronet, London; 1976; PB; 255 pp
• Berkley Book, NY; 1979; PB; 210 pp
• Hodder and Stoughton, UK; 1987; PB; 260 pp

GODLING, GO HOME!
• Belmont, (#L92–591); 1964; PB; 157 pp
  Contains: Godling, Go Home!, Why?, The Silent Colony, Force Of Mortality, There's No Place Like Space, Neutral Planet, The Lonely One, Solitary, The Man With Talent, The Desiccator, The World He Left Behind

IN THE BEGINNING
• Subterranean Press, Burton, MI; 2005; HC w DJ; 1st Edition; 335 pp; ca: Bob Eggleton
  Contains: Yokel with Portfolio (1955), Long Live the Kejwa (1956), Guardian of the Crystal Gate (1956), Choke Chain (1956), Citadel of Darkness (1957), Cosmic Kill (1957), New Year's Eve—2000 A.D. (1957), The Android Kill (1957), The Hunters of Cutwold (1957), Come into My Brain (1958), Castaways of Space (1958), Exiled from Earth (1958), Second Start (1959), Mournful Monster (1959) Vampires from Outer Space (1959), The Insidious Invaders (1959)

LETTERS FROM ATLANTIS
• Atheneum, NY; 1990; HC W DJ; 1st edition; Robert Gould (illustrator)
  A Byron Press Book in the Dragon Flight series.
• Atheneum; 1990; HC; 136 pp

MOONFERNS AND STARSONGS
• Ballantine Books, NY [02278]; 1971; 245 pp;
  ca: Gene Szafran
  Contains: A Happy Day In 2381, After The Myths Went Home, Passengers, To Be Continued, Nightwings, We Know Why We Are, The Pleasure Of Their Company, The Songs Of Summer, A Man Of Talent, Collecting Team, Going Down Smooth

NEEDLE IN A TIME STACK
• Ballantine, [U2330]; Nov. 1966; 190 pp; ca: Richard Powers
• Sphere; 1967; PB; 190 pp
  Contains: The Pain Peddlers, Passport To Sirius, Birds Of A Feather, There Was An Old Woman, The Shadow Of Wings, Absolutely Inflexible, His Brother' Weeper, The Sixth Palace, To See The Invisible Man, The Iron Chancellor
• Revised Sphere edition; 1979; PB; 180 pp
  …not quite the same book that was published under that title a decade and more ago. About half of the original stories have been retained; the other stories, subsequently made available in other books, have been erased here and replaced with a group of stories of about the same length, vintage, and quality….[this] is a ploy calculated to drive bibliographers insane…— from RS' introduction. Collection now includes: The Iron Chancellor, The Reality Trip, The Shrines Of Earth, Black Is Beautiful, Ringing The Changes; Translation Error, The Shadow Of Wings, Absolutely Inflexible, His Brother's Weeper.
• Ace Science Fiction Books (Berkley Pub. Group), NY; Nov. 1985; PB; ca: Don Dixon; 180 pp

NEXT STOP THE STARS
• Ace Double [F-145]; 1962; PB backed with THE SEED OF EARTH; 114pp
  RS' first collection of short fiction; Contents: The Seed Of Earth; Slaves Of The Star Giants; The Songs Of Summer; Hopper; Blaze Of Glory; Warm Man.
• Dennis Dobson, London; 1979; HC w DJ; new introduction by RS

PARSECS AND PARABLES
• Doubleday, Garden City, NY;,1970. HC w DJ;
  1st edition; 203 pp
  Collects ten stories: Sunrise on Mercury; The Man Who Never Forgo; Ishmael in Love; Flies; The Fangs of the Trees; Counterpart; Road to Nightfall; The Outbreeders; One-Way Journey; Going Down Smooth
• Hale, London; 1970; HC; First English Edition

THE REALITY TRIP AND
OTHER IMPLAUSIBILITIES
• Ballantine Books, NY; 1972; PB; 210 pp
  Contains: In Entropy's Jaws, The Reality Trip, Black Is Beautiful, Ozymandias, Caliban, The Shrines of Earth, Ringing the Changes, and Hawksbill Station.

THE ROAD TO NIGHTFALL: The Collected Stories of
Robert Silverberg Volume 4
• HarperCollins UK; 1996; PB; 347 pp.
  Contains: Road to Nightfall; Gorgon Planet; The Silent Colony; Absolutely Inflexible; The Macauley Circuit; The Songs of Summer; Alaree; The Artifact Business; Collecting Team; A Man of Talent; One-Way Journey; Sunrise on Mercury; World of a Thousand Colors; Warm Man; Blaze of Glory; Why?; The Outbreeders; The Man Who Never Forgot; There Was an Old Woman…; The Iron Chancellor; Ozymandias

RINGING THE CHANGES: The Collected Stories of Robert Silverberg Volume 5
- HarperCollins UK; 1997; PB; 359 pp; To See the Invisible Man; The Pain Peddlers; Neighbor; The Sixth Palace; Flies; Halfway House; To the Dark Star; Passengers; Bride Ninety-One; Going Down Smooth; The Fangs of the Trees; Ishmael in Love; Ringing the Changes; Sundance; How It Was When the Past Went Away; After the Myths Went Home; The Pleasure of Their Company; We Know Who We Are; Something Wild Is Loose; The Reality Trip

ROMA ETERNA
Contains: A.U.C. 1203. Prologue, With Caesar in the Underworld, A Hero of the Empire, The Second Wave, Waiting for the End, An Outpost of the Empire, Getting to Know the Dragon, The Reign of Terror, Via Roma, Tales from the Venia Woods, & To the Promised Land.
- EOS HarperCollins, NY; 2003; HC
- EOS HarperCollins, NY; 2003; PB; 464 pp
- Morrow/Avon, New York, NY, USA; 2003; HC w DJ; DJ art: Chris Moore
- Orion Publishing Co; 2003; PB; 400 pp
- Victor Gollancz Ltd, London; 2004; PB; 385 pp; ca: Emma Wallace
- ROMA ÆTERNA; Laffont 2004; French tr by Jean-Marc Chambon
- Ediciones Minotauro, Colección: Ucronia, Barcelona; 2006; 397pp

THE SECRET SHARER
- Underwood and Miller; 1988; HC w DJ; also slipcase edition limited to 250 copies that are signed and numbered by the author.

THE SHORES OF TOMORROW
- Thomas Nelson; 1976; HC
  Contains: Sound Decision by RS and Randall Garrett; The Silent Colony; Stress Pattern; Quick Freeze; Deadlock by RS and Barbara Silverberg; The Day the Founder Died; The Final Challenge; The Isolationists

THE SONGS OF SUMMER AND OTHER STORIES
- Victor Gollancz Ltd., London, 1979; HC w yellow DJ; first UK edition; 173pp
- Pan, London; 1981; PB
  Contains: The Songs of Summer; To Be Continued; Double Dare; A Man of Talent; Dark Companion; Halfway House; By the Seawall; The King of the Golden River; Bride Ninety-One; We Know Who We Are

SUNDANCE AND OTHER SCIENCE FICTION STORIES
- Thomas Nelson; 1974; HC
- Abelard-Shuman; 1975
- Corgi, UK; 1976 174 pp
  Contains: Something Wild Is Loose; Sundance; The Overlord's Thumb; The Pain Peddlers; Passport to Sirius;

Caught in the Organ Draft; Neighbor; Neutral Planet; The Outbreeders

SUNRISE ON MERCURY
- Thomas Nelson, Inc Publishers, Nashville; 1975; HC w DJ; Cover art by Fred Sampiri
- Pan Books Ltd., 1983; PB; British edition

TO THE LAND OF THE LIVING
- The Easton Press, Norwalk, Connecticut; 1990; Limited Edition; black leather with gold decoration, gold gilt page edges, silk moiré endpapers, ribbon bookmark.; illustrator: Bob Eggleton

TOMORROW'S WORLD: TEN STORIES OF SCIENCE FICTION
- Meredith, NY, 1969. HC w DJ

A PAIR FROM SPACE
- Belmont; 1965; HC; 159 pp
- Belmont Double [#92-612]; Jan. 1965; 1st printing, PB Contains: We, The Marauders by RS; Giants in the Earth by James Blish.

PHASES OF THE MOON: STORIES OF SIX DECADES
- IBooks; 2004: Short Stories; PB; 624 pp

UNFAMILIAR TERRITORY
- Charles Scribner; 1973; 1st edition; HC w DJ; 212 pp The thirteen stories by RS collected in this book are: Caught In The Organ Draft, Push No More, Now + n, Now −n, The Mutant Season, Some Notes On The Pre-Dynastic Epoch, When We Went To See The End Of The World, In The Group, What We Learned From This Morning's Newspaper, Caliban, In Entropy's Jaws, Many Mansions, The Wind And The Rain
- Berkley Medallion Book, NY, NY; Dec. 1978; PB

VALLEY BEYOND TIME
- Dell [#9249]; 1972; PB; 223 pp Reissue of four stories published in the 1950's: Spacerogue, The Flame and the Hammer, The Wages of Death, & Valley Beyond Time.

WORLD OF A THOUSAND COLORS
- Arbor House Pub Co, New York, NY; 1982, 1st ed; HC w DJ; Cover art by Loretta Trezzo Contains: En Route to Earth; Going Down Smooth; Passport to Sirius; Prime Commandment; Solitary; Something Wild Is Loose; To the Dark Star; The Man Who Never Forgot; The Outbreeders; One-Way Journey; The Pain Peddlers; The Four; How It Was When the Past Went Away; Introduction (World of a Thousand Colors); Journey's End; Counterpart; Neighbor; World of a Thousand Colors; Neutral Planet; The Fangs of the Trees
- Priam; 1983; PB; 329 pp
- Bantam; 1984; PB; 331 pp

EDITED ANTHOLOGIES

THE ALIENS
• Thomas Nelson; 1976; HC w DJ

ALPHA 1
• Ballantine Books, NY; 1970; PB; 278 pp;
  ca: John Lindner

ALPHA 2
• Ballantine Books, NY; 1971; PB

ALPHA 3
• Ballantine Books, NY; 1972; PB

ALPHA 5
• Ballantine Books, NY; 1974; PB

ALPHA 6
• Berkley/Ballantine #3048; 1976; PB; ca: Richard Powers

THE ANDROIDS ARE COMING
• Elsevier Nelson Books; 1979; HC; 183 pp

THE ARBOR HOUSE TREASURY OF GREAT
SCIENCE FICTION SHORT NOVELS
• Arbor House; 1980; HC & DJ; eds RS & Martin H
  Greenberg; 754 pp

THE ARBOR HOUSE TREASURY OF MODERN
SCIENCE FICTION

THE BEST OF NEW DIMENSIONS
• Pocket Books; 1997; PB

BETWEEN WORLDS
• Science Fiction Book Club, Garden City, NY; 2004;
  HC w DJ; 1st edition; 398 pp.

BEYOND CONTROL
• Thomas Nelson, Nashville; 1972. HC w DJ
• Dell, #2112; 1974; PB; 236 pp

BEYOND THE GATE OF WORLDS
• Tor; 1991; PB; 280 pp; short novels including title by RS,
  John Brunner, Chelsea Quinn Yarbro

CAR SINISTER
• Avon; 1979; PB 253 pp; eds RS, Martin H. Greenberg &
  Joseph D. Olander; ca: Wilkes

THE CRYSTAL SHIP
• Nelson; 1976; 1st ed; HC w DJ; introduction by RS

CHAINS OF THE SEA:
Three Original Novellas Of Science Fiction
• Thomas Nelson; 1973; HC; intro. By RS

• Dell; PB; 208 pp

DANGEROUS INTERFACES [TIME GATE]
• Baen; 1990;PB; 296pp; ca: David Mattingly

DARK STARS
• PB; introduction by RS; ca: Ron Walotsky

DAWN OF TIME: Prehistory through Science Fiction
• Thomas Nelson; 1979; HC; intro. By RS; w Martin H.
  Greenberg & Joseph Olander; 224 pp

DEEP SPACE
• Doubleday; 1973; HC
Include ss The Sixth Palace & Introduction by RS

EARTH IS THE STRANGEST PLANET
• Thomas Nelson; 1977; HC
  Includes ss When We Went to See the End of the World by
  RS
• Wildside; 2000; PB; 192 pp

EARTHMAN & STRANGERS
• Duell, Sloan, & Pearce/Meredith; 1966; HC w DJ
• Dell, #2206; 1966; PB; ca: Jeff Jones
• Manor; 1977; 240 pp
  Include ss Alaree and introduction by RS

THE ENDS OF TIME
• Hawthorne; 1970; HC
• Wildside Press; 2000; PB; 240 pp
  Includes ss At the End of Days by RS

THE EDGE OF SPACE: THREE ORIGINAL
NOVELLAS OF SCIENCE FICTION
• Elsevier/Nelson Books, NY; 1979; HC w DJ

EPOCH
• Berkley Publishing Company; 1975; HC w DJ; ed. w Roger
  Elwood; ca: Richard Powers
• Berkley; 1975; PB; ed. w Roger Elwood; ca: Richard Powers
  The state of the art of science fiction now.

EXPLORERS OF SPACE
• Thomas Nelson; 1975; HC w DJ; 253pp; DJ art:
  Frank Alois

THE FANTASY HALL OF FAME

FAR HORIZONS: THE GREAT WORLDS
OF SCIENCE FICTION
• Avon; 1999
• Little Brown/Orbit; 1999

FAR HORIZONS: ALL NEW TALES
FROM THE GREATEST WORLDS OF
SCIENCE FICTION

- Eos; 2005; PB; 484 pp; ca: Bob Keck
  includes ss Getting to Know the Dragon by RS

FOUR FUTURES
- Hawthorne; 1971; HC
  Includes ss Going by RS

GALACTIC DREAMERS : SCIENCE FICTION AS
VISIONARY LITERATURE
- Random House, NY, 1977. 1st edition; HC w DJ

GREAT SCIENCE FICTION OF THE
20TH CENTURY

THE GREAT SCIENCE FICTION: 1964
2001

GREAT SHORT NOVELS OF SCIENCE FICTION
- Ballantine Books, NY; July, 1970; PB; 373 pp; cover art
  Donna Violetti

THE HORROR HALL OF FAME
1991

INFINITE JESTS
- Chilton; 1974; HC w DJ; 231 pp; DJ art by Freas
  The Lighter Side of Science Fiction

THE INFINITE WEB
- Dial; 1977; PB
  Includes ss The Wind and the Rain by RS

INVADERS FROM SPACE:
TEN STORIES OF SCIENCE FICTION
- Hawthorn Books; 1972; HC

LEGENDS
- TOR; 1998; First American edition; HC w DJ

LEGENDS: SHORT NOVELS BY THE
MASTERS OF MODERN FANTASY
- Tom Doherty Associates, N .Y.; 1998; HC w DJ

LEGENDS II: NEW SHORT NOVELS BY
THE MASTERS OF MODERN FANTASY
- Del Rey Ballantine; 2004, HC w DJ

LEGENDS II: DRAGON, SWORD, AND KING
- Del Rey Ballantine; 2003, HC w DJ

LEGENDS II: SHADOWS, GODS, AND DEMONS
- Ballantine Books, New York; 2004

LOST WORLDS, UNKNOWN HORIZONS
- New English Library; 19978; PB
  Include ss Trips by RS

MEN AND MACHINES: TEN STORIES OF
SCIENCE FICTION
- Hawthorn; 1968 HC w DJ (Book Club
  [BCE/BOMC]/First HC Edition));
  cover art Barry Martin
  Include The Macauley Circuit by RS

MIND TO MIND
- Thomas Nelson; 1971; HC
  Include Something Wild Is Loose by RS
- Dell; PB

THE MIRROR OF INFINITY
- Harper & Row, NY; 1970; HC w DJ;

MURASAKI
- Spectra Bantam Books, NY; 1992; HC w DJ; 290 pp
  A novel in six part with contributions by Poul Anderson,
  Greg Bear, Gregory Benford, David Brin, Nancy Kress, and
  Frederik Pohl

MUTANTS
- Thomas Nelson Inc.; 1974; HC w DJ, BC; 182 pp
  includes: The Man Who Never Forgot by RS

NEBULA AWARDS SHOWCASE 2001
2001

NEANDERTHALS: ISAAC ASIMOV'S
WONDERFUL WORLDS OF SCIENCE FICTION
- Signet; 1987; PB; eds RS, Isaac Asimov, Martin H
  Greenberg, & Charles G Waugh; (The sixth book in the
  Isaac Asimov's Wonderful Worlds of SF series)

THE NEW ATLANTIS AND
OTHER NOVELLAS OF S.F.
- Hawthorne; 1975; HC w DJ
  First publication of: Silhouette by Gene Wolfe, The New
  Atlantis by Ursula K. Le Guin, & A Momentary Taste of
  Being by James Tiptree, Jr.
- Warner Books; 1976; PB; 190 pp; ca: Di Fate

NEW DIMENSIONS 1
- Doubleday;1971; HC w DJ

NEW DIMENSIONS 2
- Doubleday;1972; HC w DJ

NEW DIMENSIONS 3
- Doubleday;1973; HC w DJ
- Signet; 1973; PB; 183 pp
NEW DIMENSIONS 4
- Signet; 1974; PB; 237 pp

NEW DIMENSIONS 6
- Harper & Row, NY; 1976; HC w DJ; First edition

NEW DIMENSIONS 10
• Harper & Row, NY; 1980; HC w DJ; First edition

NO MIND OF MAN
• Hawthorn Books, UK; 1973; HC w DJ
  contains: This is the Road by RS

OTHER DIMENSIONS: Ten Stories Of Science Fiction.
• Hawthorn Books: NY; 1973; HC w DJ

ROBERT SILVERBERG'S WORLDS OF WONDER
• Warner; 1987; HC w DJ
  RS collects 13 sf stories that affected him, and helped him
  learn his craft, and annotates each with a discussion analyz-
  ing virtues and faults, forming a virtual primer on the writing of sf. Includes a long introductory memoir.

SCIENCE FICTION: 101
• 2001

THE SCIENCE FICTIONAL DINOSAUR
• Avon/Flare,; 1982; PB; eds. Charles G. Waugh, Martin H.
  Greenberg, RS; 224pp; ca: Hildebrand

STRANGE GIFTS
• Thomas Nelson; 1975; HC
  Includes ss To Be Continued by RS

SUNRISE ON MERCURY: AND OTHER
SCIENCE FICTION STORIES
• T. Nelson & Sons, Nashville; 1975; HC w DJ; 175 pp
• Pan Books, UK; 1986; PB; 176 pp

THREE TRIPS IN TIME AND SPACE: Original Novellas
of Science Fiction.
• Hawthorn Books, NY; 1973. HC w DJ; 1st ed; Foreword by
  RS; 193 pp
  Original short novels by three Hugo award-winning writers:
  Flash Crowd by Larry Niven, You'll Take the High Road by
  John Brunner, Rumfuddle by Jack Vance
• Dell Laurel Leaf, NY; 1973; PB; 235 pp

THREADS OF TIME
• Thomas Nelson Inc; 1974; HD w DJ
  Three original novellas of science fiction. Contents: Threads
  of Time by Gregory Benford, The Marathon Photograph by
  Clifford D. Simak, Riding the Torch by Norman Spinrad

TIME GATE
• Baen; 1989; PB; 277 pp
  Includes ss Enter a Soldier. Later: Enter Another by RS
TO THE STARS: EIGHT STORIES OF
SCIENCE FICTION
• Hawthorn Books, NY; 1971; HC w DJ; 1st edition

TOMORROW'S WORLDS
• Meredith; 1969; PB

Includes ss Sunrise on Mercury by RS

TO WORLDS BEYOND: STORIES OF
SCIENCE FICTION
• Chilton Books; 1965; HC w DJ
• Sphere, UK; 1969; PB

TRIPS IN TIME
• Nelson Doubleday, NY; 1973; HC w DJ
• Thomas Nelson Inc; 1977; HC; BCE; 174 pp
  Contains: Mugwump 4 by RS; An Infinie Summer by
  Christopher Priest; The King's Wishes by Robert Sheckley;
  Manna by Peter Phillips; The Long Remembering by Poul
  Anderson; Try & Change the Past by Fritz Leiber; Divine
  Madness by Roger Zelazny; Secret Rider by Marta Randall;
  The Seesaw by A.E. van Vogt

THE SCIENCE FICTION BESTIARY:
NINE STORIES OF SCIENCE FICTION
• T. Nelson, NY; 1973; HC w DJ; 256 pp
• Dell [8139]; 1971; PB; 251 pp; ca: Gallardo
  Includes Collecting Team by RS.

THE SCIENCE FICTION HALL OF FAME, VOL. I

STRANGE GIFTS: EIGHT STORIES OF
SCIENCE FICTION
• T. Nelson, NY; 1975; HC w DJ

THE TIME TRAVELERS: A Science Fiction Quartet.
Edited by RS & Martin H. Greenberg
• Donald I. Fine, Inc., NY; 1985; HC 1st ed; 284 pp
  A collection of four classic novellas on the theme of time
  travel: The Ugly Little Boy by Asimov, Sidewise In Time by
  Marray Leinster, Consider Her Ways by John Wyndham, and
  Vintage Season by Henry Kuttner and C.L. Moore, with an
  introduction by RS
• Donald I. Fine, Inc., Primus: May 1986; PB; 284 pp

TRIAX
• Pinnacle; 1977; PB

TRIPS IN TIME
• Thomas Nelson; 1977; HC
Includes ss Mugwump Four by RS

THE ULTIMATE DINOSAUR
• Bantam; 1991; 336 pp
• iBooks; 2000; 429 pp

UNIVERSE 1
Terry Carr's UNIVERSE series of anthologies is continued
after his death by editors RS & Karen Haber.
• Doubleday Foundation; 1990; HC w DJ; 449 pp; DJ art:
  Kriegler
• Doubleday; 1990; PB; 449 pp

• Broadway Books; 1990; PB; 468 pp
The revival of UNIVERSE under Karen and me was a sentimental attempt by Lou Aronica of Bantam to create a monument to the recently dead Terry Carr; it lasted three issues and lost quite a pile of money for Bantam.— RS

UNIVERSE 2
With Karen Haber
• Bantam Books; 1992; HC

UNIVERSE 3
With Karen Haber
• Spectra/Bantam; 1994; PB

WINDOWS INTO TOMORROW
• Hawthorn Books; 1974; HC w DJ; 197 pp
• Pinnacle Books; 1975; PB; 197 pp

WORLDS IMAGINED
• Avenel Books; 1989;HC w DJ; ed with Martin H. Greenberg; 704pp; DJ art: Jean Krulis

WORLDS OF MAYBE
• Thomas Nelson; 1970: HC
• Dell; 1974; PB; 208 pp
Contains; Poul Anderson's "Delenda Est", Isaac Asimov's "Living Space", Miriam Allen deFord's "Slips Take Over", Philip José Farmer's "Sail On, Sail On", Murray Leinster's "Sidewise in Time", and Larry Niven's "All the Myriad Ways".

VOYAGERS IN TIME: TWELVE STORIES OF SCIENCE FICTION
• Hawthorn Books, Inc., NY; 1967; HC w DJ; 243 pp

NON-FICTION

AKHNATEN THE REBEL PHARAOH
• Chilton Book Co., Philadelphia; 1964; 1st edition; HC, Green cloth, gold lettering in blue spine panel, w DJ; 16p b/w photos; 234 pp

THE AUK, THE DODO AND THE ORYX: VANISHED AND VANISHING CREATURES.
Study of birds and beasts which have become extinct by reason of the spread of human civilization, and a few which have escaped extinction.
• Thomas Y. Crowell Co; 1967; HC; 246 pp; Illustrator: Jacques Hnizdovsky
• Thomas Y. Crowell Co; 1967; PB; Illustrator: Hnizdovsky
• Penguin Puffin Books, UK; 1973; PB; 232 pp

BEFORE THE SPHINX: EARLY EGYPT
• Thomas Nelson Inc. NY; 1971; HC w DJ; 176 pp

BRUCE OF THE BLUE NILE
About explorer James Bruce.
• Holt, Rinehart & Winston; 1969; 1st edition. HC w DJ

THE CHALLENGE OF CLIMATE
• Meredith Press, NY; 1969; 1st edition; 326 pp

THE DAWN OF MEDICINE
• Putnam; 1967; 191 pp

DAWN OF TIME: PREHISTORY THROUGH SCIENCE FICTION
• Elsevier/Nelson Books; 1979; HC w DJ; Martin Greenberg, Joseph Olander, RS editors; 224 pp

EMPIRE IN THE DUST: ANCIENT CIVILIZATIONS BROUGHT TO LIGHT
• Chilton Books, Philadelphia, PA; 1963; HC w DJ; 1st edition; Illustrated, Bibliography. Index; 247 pp
A study of the major archaeological discoveries of our time including Howard Carters work in Egypt at the tomb of Tutankhamen, Hiram Binghams journey to the lost city of the Incas, Flinders Petries explorations of the pyramids.

FIRST AMERICAN INTO SPACE
• Monarch Books [#Sp1]; May 1961; PB
The first American is back from outer space, safe, sound, and ready for further adventures which, a few years back, would have been considered the pipe dreams of a science fiction addict. Here is the spine-tingling, true story of that blast into the realm of the stars, of the men who underwent the rigorous training for that epic mission and of the one man who made the safe journey. Here is a factual account of the history of rocketry, its triumphs and its failures, our shame in the neglect of it and our pride in later accomplishments.

IF I FORGET THEE O JERUSALEM:
American Jews and the State of Israel
• William Morrow, NY; 1970. HC w DJ; 1st edition

INTO SPACE: A YOUNG PERSON'S GUIDE TO SPACE
With Arthur C. Clarke
• Harper & Row, NY; 1971; HC w DJ; 129 pp

JOHN MUIR, PROPHET AMONG THE GLACIERS.
• G.P. Putnam's Sons, NY; 1972; HC w DJ; 1st edition

LIGHT FOR THE WORLD: EDISON AND THE POWER INDUSTRY
• Van Norstrand Com., Princeton NJ; 1967; 1st Edition; HC w DJ; 281 pp. 4 pages of b&w illustrations
A biography of Edison as well as an account of his success at promoting electricity as a practical and safe industry.

LOST CITIES AND VANISHED CIVILIZATIONS
• Chilton, Philadelphia; 1962; HC; 1st edition
• Bantam Book, NY (Bantam Pathfinder Edition); Aug. 1963; PB; 152 pp

MAN BEFORE ADAM: THE STORY OF MAN
IN SEARCH OF HIS ORIGINS
• Macrae Smith Co; 1964; HC w DJ;

MEN AGAINST TIME: SALVAGE
ARCHAEOLOGY IN THE UNITED STATES
MacMillan, NY; 1967; HC; illus b/w

MOUND BUILDERS OF ANCIENT AMERICA:
THE ARCHAEOLOGY OF A MYTH
• NY Graphic Society, Conn.; 1968; HC w DJ; 369 pp
• Ballantine; 1974; PB; 184 pp
• Ohio University Press, (North America, Native
  Americans);1986; 369 pp
  Reprint of the NY Graphic Society printing

THE REALM OF PRESTER JOHN
• Doubleday; 1972; HC w DJ; 344 pp
  *For five centuries the legend of Prester John- priest-king of a fabu-
  lous paradise of the east - haunted the hearts and minds of Western
  Christians.*
• Ohio Univ Press; 1996; PB; 334 pp
• Phoenix Press; 2001; PB

REFLECTIONS AND REFRACTIONS: THOUGHTS
ON SCIENCE FICTION, SCIENCE, AND OTHER
MATTERS
• Underwood Books, Grass Valley, California; 1997; HC; 1st
  edition; 300 edition signed by the author in slipcase

SCIENTISTS AND SCOUNDRELS : A Book of Hoaxes
• Thomas Y. Crowell Company, New York, NY, U.S.A; 1965;
  HC; 1st edition; illustrations: Jerome Snyder
• University of Nebraska Press, Bison Book (Extraordinary
  World series); 2007; PB; 251 pp

SOCRATES
• G.P. Putnam, NY; 1965; first edition; HC w DJ

STORMY VOYAGER:
THE STORY OF CHARLES WILKES
• J.B. Lippincott, Philadelphia; 1968; HC w DJ; 192pp; Index,
  biblio, Maps and 7 drawings
  History of the Wilkes expedition.

SUNKEN HISTORY
• Bantam; 1964;PB

THREE SURVIVED
• Holt Rinehart, NY; 1969; HC w DJ;

TREASURES BENEATH THE SEA
• Whitman; 1960; HC; 92pp; Norman Kenyon (Illustrator)
  Tells the stories of treasure hunters and difficult salvage
  operations from 1687 to 1947 and describes treasures which
  have never been recovered.

WORLD OF THE OCEAN DEPTHS
• Meredith Press, NY; 1968; 1st edition; 156 pp
  Contents include: The Depths of the Ocean; Man Explores
  the Sea; Man Invades the Depths; Life in the Sea; Dwellers
  in the Abyss; Deep-sea Fishes; Sea Serpents and Other
  Monsters; The Uses of the Sea. With a bibliography.

THE WORLD WITHIN THE OCEAN WAVE
• Weybright & Talley, NY;1972; HC; 113 pp;
  illustrator: Bob Hines

SHORT FICTION
First appearances.

1950
• The Invader Star; as Bob Silverberg; *Space Magazine*;
  Published by Clyde Hanback and the American Rocketry
  Association, Washington D.C; vol. 1, #3; summer 1950
  *Amateur magazine, of course. The story is, ah, of very modest
  quality. — RS*

1952
• The Sacred River; as Bob Silverberg; *The Avalonian*

1954
• Gorgon Planet; *Nebula (Scotland)*; Feb. 1954 / as The Fight
  with the Gorgon; *Super SF*; Oct. 1958
• The Silent Colony; *Future*; Oct. 1954

1955
• The Martian; *Imagination*; June 1955
• Yokel with Portfolio; *Imaginative Tales*; Nov. 1955

1956
• A Woman's Right; *Fantastic Universe*; Feb. 1956
• A World of His Own; *Amazing*; Dec. 1956
• Absolutely Inflexible; *Fantastic Universe*; July 1956
• Alien Dies at Dawn, The; as Alexander Blade; *Imagination*;
  Dec. 1956
• Always; *Nebula (Scotland)*; Mar. 1956
• Battle for the Thousand Suns; as Calvin M. Knox & David
  Gordon *SF Adventures*
• Beast with Seven Tails, The; as Leonard G. Spencer (with
  Randall Garrett); *Amazing*; Aug. 1956; ca: Edward Valigursky
• Calling Captain Flint; as Richard Greer (with Randall
  Garrett); *Amazing Stories* Aug. 1956; b&w illo: Llewellyn
  *An alien life form with all the arts of makeup and camouflage at its
  command, is required to walk among human beings and not be sus-
  pected. A tough problem. What manner of impersonation should the
  alien attempt? Why, the obvious one, of course.*
• Catch a Thief; as Gordon Aghill (with Randall Garrett);
  Amazing; July 1956
• Catch 'Em All Alive!; alt. title: Collecting Team
• Choke Chain; *Fantastic*; Dec. 1956
• Chosen People, The; as Robert Randall *Astounding SF*; June
  1956

- Collecting Team; *Super SF*; Dec. 1956; alt. title: Catch 'Em All Alive!
- Desiccator, The; *SF Stories*; May56
- Deus Ex Machina; as Robert Randall; *SF Quarterly*; Nov. 1956
- Double Dare; *Galaxy*; Nov. 1956
- Dream Girl; *Fantastic*; June 1956; ca: Ed Valigursky
- Entrance Exam; *Amazing Stories*; June 1956
- False Prophet; as Robert Randall (with Randall Garrett); *Astounding SF*; Dec. 1956
- Final Challenge, The; *Infinity*; Aug. 1956
- Gambler's Planet; as Gordon Aghill (with Randall Garrett); *Amazing*; June 1956

  Step into a world where the gambling den instead of the church is sanctuary for the criminal; where gambling is a religion; where murderers may stand shoulder to shoulder with saints. Where Chance is All and the words 'I'll bet my life!' are taken literally.
- Girl from Bodies, Inc., The; as Leonard G. Spencer (with Randall Garrett); *Fantastic* Oct. 1956
- Great Kladnar Race, The; as Richard Greer (with Randall Garrett); *Amazing*; Dec. 1956
- Guardian of the Crystal Gate; *Fantastic*; Aug. 1956; story written around ca: Ed Valigursky
- Hole in the Air; *Amazing Stories*, Jan. 1956 / *SF Greats*; Winter 1969 (all RS issue of reprints); b&w illo: Virgil Finlay
- Hopper; *Infinity*; Oct. 1956
- Hunted Heroes, The; *Amazing Stories*; Sept. 1956
- The Judas Valley; w. Randall Garrett; *Amazing Stories* Oct. 1956
- Lair of the Dragonbird; *Imagination*; Feb. 1956
- Lonely One, The; *Original SF Stories*; July 1956; b&w illo Orban

  Why couldn't these final men depart from a dying Earth?
- Look Homeward, Spaceman; as Calvin M. Knox; *Amazing*; Aug. 1956; b&w illo: Llewellyn

  Fine thing! When a man spends six long years away from his hearthside – roaming the far reaches of outer space – and then returns home to find that even his mother didn't know he'd gone beyond the front gate!
- Macauley Circuit, The; *Fantastic Universe*; Aug. 1956
- Man of Many Bodies; as Ralph Burke *Fantastic*; Dec. 1956
- Man with Talent, The; *Future*, Win 1956 / *Science Fantasy*; Aug. 1957
- Mind for Business; *Astounding SF*; Sept. 1956
- Mummy Takes a Wife, The; as Clyde Mitchell (with Randall Garrett); *Fantastic*; Dec. 1956; ca: Ed Valigursky
- No Future in This; as Robert Randall; *SF Quarterly*; May56
- No Trap for the Keth; as Ralph Burke; *Imaginative Tales*; Nov. 1956
- O' Captain, My Captain!; as Ivar Jorgenson *Fantastic*; Aug. 1956; b&w illo Virgil Finlay / *SF Greats*; Winter 1969 (all RS issue of reprints)
- Promised Land, The; as Robert Randall; *Astounding SF*; Aug. 1956
- Revolt of the Synthetics; as Robert Burke; *Fantastic*;

Aug. 1956
- Rain of Luck; *Amazing Stories*; July 1956
- Rivals, The; *Amazing*; Nov. 1956; b&w illo: Virgil Finlay
- Run of Luck; as Calvin M. Knox; *Amazing Stories*; July 1956
- Secret of the Green Invaders; as Robert Randall; *SF Adventures*; Dec. 1956
- Secret Weapon of Titipu; as Ralph Spencer; *Original SF Stories*; July 1956
- Slow and the Dead, The; as Robert Randall; *Fantastic*; Aug. 1956
- Songs of Summer, The; *SF Stories*; Sept. 1956
- Sound Decision; (with Randall Garrett); *Astounding SF*; Oct. 1956
- Sourdough; *Astounding SF*; Nov. 1956
- To Be Continued; *Astounding SF*; May 1956
- Tools of the Trade; as Robert Randall; *Original SF Stories*; Nov. 1956
- Vault of the Ages; *Amazing Stories*; Aug. 1956
- Venus Trap; *Future SF* #30, 1956 (no month)

1957

- A Season for Remorse; *Future SF*, Sum 1957; b&w illo: Ed Emshwiller
- A Time for Revenge; as Calvin M. Knox; *Super SF*; Oct. 1957
- Age of Anxiety; *Infinity*; June 1957
- An Enemy of Peace; as Ralph Burke; *Fantastic*; Feb. 1957
- And the Walls Came Tumbling Down ("short novel"); *If, Worlds of SF*; Dec. 1957; b&w illo: Ed Emshwiller; alt. title: Invisible Barriers
- Android Kill, The; as Alexander Blade; *Imaginative Tales*; Nov. 1957
- Anything His Heart Desires; Dream World; Aug. 1957
- Artifact Business, The; *Fantastic Universe*; Apr. 1957
- Assassin, The; *Imaginative Tales*; July 1957
- Bitter Homecoming; *Amazing Stories*; Dec. 1957
- Blaze of Glory; *Galaxy*; Aug. 1957; b&w illo: Gaughan
- Blue Plague, The; *Amazing Stories*; July 1957
- Call Me Zombie!; *Fantastic*; August 1957
- Chalice of Death; as Calvin M. Knox *SF Adventures*
- Citadel of Darkness; as Ralph Burke; *Fantastic*; Mar. 1957
- Cosmic Kill; as Robert Arnette; *Amazing Stories* April 1957
- Critical Threshold; *New Worlds*; Dec. 1957
- Dead World, The; as Warren Kastel; *Imaginative Tales*; Sept. 1957
- Deadly Decoy; RS w. Randall Garrett writing as Clyde Mitchell; *Amazing Stories* Feb. 1957
- Death's Planet; *Super SF*; Oct. 1957
- Earth Shall Live Again!; as Calvin M. Knox; *SF Adventures*; Dec. 1957
- En Route to Earth; as Calvin M. Knox *SF Quarterly*; Aug. 1957
- Father Image; *Saturn*; March 1957
- Flame and the Hammer, The; *SF Adventures*; Sept. 1957
- Force of Mortality; *Future*, #23, Fall 1957; b&w illo: Freas

How could everyone on this planet have died, all at the same time, when they knew the secret of immortality?

- Forgotten World; *Fantastic*; Mar. 1957
- Freak Show; as Hall Thornton *Fantastic*; Mar. 1957
- Galactic Thrill Kids; *Super SF*; Apr. 1957
- Godling, Go Home!; *SF Stories*; Jan. 1957 / *Nebula* (Scotland); Apr. 1958
- Guest Rites, The; *Infinity*; Feb. 1957
- Happy Unfortunate, The; *Amazing*; Dec. 1957
- Harwood's Vortex; *Imagination*; Apr. 1957
- Hero from Yesterday; as Robert Randall; *Imagination*; Dec. 1957
- Hidden Talent; *Worlds of If*; Apr. 1957
- His Head in the Clouds; as Calvin M. Knox; *SF Stories*; Sept. 1957; cover & B&W illo: Ed Emshwiller
- Hot Trip for Venus; as Ralph Burke; *Imaginative Tales*; July 1957
- House Operator; as S.M. Tennshaw; *Imagination*; Dec. 1957
- Housemaid No. 103; as Ivar Jorgenson; *Imaginative Tales*; Nov. 1957
- Hunters of Cutwold, The; as Calvin M. Knox; *Super SF*; Dec. 1957
- Incomplete Theft, The; w Randall Garrett writing as Ralph Burke; *Imagination* Feb. 1957
- Lunatic Planet, The; as Ralph Burke *Amazing*; Nov. 1957 / *SF Greats* Win 1969
- Man Who Hated Noise, The; as S. M. Tennshaw; *Imaginative Tales*; Mar. 1957
- Middle-age Rookie; as Warren Kastel; *Fantastic* May 1957
- Misfit; *Super SF*; Dec. 1957
- Mystery of Deneb IV, The; *Fantastic*; Feb. 1957
- Neutral Planet; *SF Stories*; July 1957
- New Men for Mars; as Calvin M. Knox; *Super SF*; June 1957
- New Year's Eve – 2000 A. D.; as Ivar Jorgenson; *Imaginative Tales*; Feb. 1957
- Nudes of Quendar III, The; *Imaginative Tales*; Jan. 1957
- Old Man, The; as S. M. Tenneshaw; *Imagination*; Apr. 1957
- One-Way Journey; *Infinity*; Nov. 1957
- Outcast of the Stars; *Imagination*; Feb. 1957
- Outpost Peril; *Imaginative Tales*; Sept. 1957
- Overlord of Colony Eight; *Imagination*; Oct. 1957
- Pirates of the Void; as Ivar Jorgenson; *Imaginative Tales*; July 1957
- Postmark Ganymede; *Amazing Stories*; Sept. 1957
- Precedent; *Astounding SF*; Dec. 1957
- Quick Freeze; *SF Quarterly*; May 1957; *New Worlds*; May 1957
- Reality Unlimited; *Imagination*; Aug. 1957
- Rescue Mission; *Imagination*; Dec. 1957
- Run of the Mill; *Astounding SF*; July 1957
- Secret of the Shan, The; as Richard Greer (with Randall Garrett); *Fantastic*; June 1957
- Seed of Earth, The; *Super SF*; Apr. 1957
- Ship-Shape Pay-Off; w Harlan Ellison
- Shrines of Earth, The; *Astounding SF*; Nov. 1957

- Slaughter on Dornell IV; as Ivar Jorgenson; *Imagination*; Apr. 1957
- Slaves of the Star Giants; *SF Adventures*; Feb. 1957
- Solitary; *Future*, Spring 1957; *Nebula* (Scotland); Mar. 1958
- Spawn of the Deadly Sea; *SF Adventures*; Apr. 1957
- Starship Saboteur; *Imaginative Tales*; Mar. 1957
- Sunrise on Mercury; as Calvin M. Knox; *SF Stories*; May 1957; story written for ca: Ed Emshwiller
- Swords Against the Outworlders; as Calvin M. Knox; *Fantastic*; Mar. 1957
- This World Must Die!; As Ivar Jorgenson; *SF Adventures*; Aug. 1957
- Three Survived; *Super SF*; Aug. 1957
- Thunder Over Starhaven; As Ivar Jorgenson; *SF Adventures*; Oct. 1957
- Twelve Hours to Blow!; *Imaginative Tales*; May 1957
- Ultimate Weapon, The; as S. M. Tennshaw; *Imaginative Tales*; Jan. 1957
- Valley Beyond Time; *SF Adventures*, Vol. 2, No. 2; Dec. 1957; Cover by Ed Emshwiller / *Science Fantasy* (UK); Feb. 1958
- Warm Man; *Mag of Fantasy & SF*; May 1957
- Wednesday Morning Sermon; as Alexander Blade; *Imaginative Tales*; Jan. 1957
- Why?; *SF Stories*; Nov. 1957
- Winds of Siros, The; *Venture*; Sept. 1957
- Woman's World; *Imagination*; June 1957
- World of a Thousand Colors; *Super SF*; June 1957

1958

- 3117 Half-Credit Uncirculated; as Alexander Blade; *SF Adventures*; June 1958
- A Little Intelligence; as Robert Randall; *Future*, Oct. 1958
- A Madman on Board; *Imagination*; Feb. 1958
- A Planet All My Own; as Richard F. Watson; *Super SF*; Aug. 1958
- A World Called Sunrise; as Eric Rodman; *Super SF*; Aug. 1958
- Alaree; *Saturn: Magazine of SF & Fantasy*; Vol. 1, #5; Mar. 1958
- Aliens Were Haters, The: *Super SF*; Dec. 1958
- All the King's Horses; as Robert Randall *Astounding SF*; Jan. 1958
- Birds of a Feather; *Galaxy*; Nov. 1958; b&w art: Wally Wood
- Castaways of Space; as Dan Malcolm; *Super SF*; Oct. 1958
- Coffins Are for Corpses; as David Challon; *Monster Parade* Dec. 1958; titled Back from the Grave in *Mike Shayne's Mystery Mag* 1958
- Cold-Blooded Ones, The; as Calvin M. Knox; *Super SF*; Aug. 1958
- Constabulary Duty; as Calvin M. Knox; *SF Stories*; June 1958
- Crossroads of the Ghouls; as Ralph Burke; *Monster Parade* Dec. 1958

- Decision Final; as Robert Randall; *Imaginative Tales*; Mar. 1958
- Dig That Crazy Scientist; as Alex Merriman; *Monster Parade* Nov. 1958
- Eve and the Twenty-Three Adams; *Venture*; Mar. 1958
- Exiled From Earth; as Richard F. Watson; *Super SF*; Dec. 1958
- Fight with the Gorgon, The: *Super-SF;* Oct. 1958
- Fires Die Down, The; *Nebula* (Scotland); June 1958 / *Famous SF*, Sum 1968
- Four, The: as Calvin M. Knox *SF Stories*; Aug. 1958
- Frontier Planet; as Calvin M. Knox; *Super SF*; June 1958
- Gateway to Terror; Space Travel; Nov. 1958
- Happy Sleepers, The; as Calvin M. Knox *Super SF*; Feb. 1958
- Heir Reluctant; *Astounding SF*; June 1958
- Homecoming Horde; *Imagination*; Aug. 1958
- House Divided; *Nebula* (Scotland); Dec. 1958
- Hunt the Space-Witch!; As Ivar Jorgenson; *SF Adventures*; Jan. 1958
- Invasion Vanguard; as T. D. Bethlen; *SF Stories*; May 1958
- Iron Chancellor, The: *Galaxy*; May 1958; b&w art: Wally Wood
- Isolationists, The; as George Osborne; *SF Stories*; Nov. 1958
- Lure of Galaxy A, The: As Ivar Jorgenson; *Imaginative Tales*; Mar. 1958
- A Madman on Board; *Imagination*; Feb. 1958
- Man Who Believed in Werewolves, The; as Charles D. Hammer; *Monster Parade*, Nov. 1958
- Man Who Never Forgot, The; *Mag of Fantasy & SF*; Feb. 1958 / *Science Fantasy (British)*; Dec. 1958
- Menace from Vega; as Robert Randall; *Imagination*; #61, June 1958
- Moon of Death; as E. K. Jarvis; *Amazing Stories*, Jan. 1958 / *Great SF*; May 1966
- Never Trust a Thief!; As Ivar Jorgenson; *Imagination*; Feb. 1958
- No Way Out; *Astounding SF*; Feb. 1958; b&w illo: van Dongen
- Overlord's Thumb, The: *Infinity*; Mar. 1958
- Ozymandias; As Ivar Jorgenson; *Infinity*; Nov. 1958 / *New Worlds*; May 1960; as RS
- Passport to Sirius; *If, Worlds of SF*; Apr. 1958
- Planet of Parasites; as Calvin M. Knox; *Super SF*; Apr. 1958
- Point of Focus; *Astounding SF*; Aug. 1958
- Prime Commandment; as Calvin M. Knox; *SF Stories*; Jan. 1958; ca: Ed Emshwiller; b&w art: Freas
- Prison Planet; *Super SF*; Feb. 1958
- Reluctant Traitor, The: as Ralph Burke; *SF Adventures*; June 1958
- Road to Nightfall; *Fantastic Universe*; July 1958
- Secrets of the Torture Cult; as Hall Thornton; *Monster Parade* Dec. 1958
- Seed of Earth, The; original title Journey's End; *Super SF*; April 1958

- Shadow on the Stars; *SF Adventures*; Apr. 1958; alt title: Stepsons of Terra
- Silent Invaders, The; as Calvin M. Knox; *Infinity*, Oct. 1958
- Slaves of the Tree; as Eric Rodman *Super SF*; June 1958
- Slice of Life; as Calvin M. Knox *Infinity*; b&w illo: Richard Kluga; Apr. 1958 / *New Worlds*; Aug. 1958
- Spacerogue; as Webber Martin *Infinity*; Nov. 1958; ca: Ed Emshwiller
- There Was an Old Woman; *Infinity*; Nov. 1958
- Traitor Legion; *Imaginative Tales*; Jan. 1958
- Unique and Terrible Compulsion, The; as Calvin M. Knox; *Super SF*; Dec. 1958
- Unknown Soldier of Space; *Imaginative Tales*; May 1958
- Untouchables, The: as Calvin M. Knox *Super SF*; Oct. 1958
- Vanishing Act; as Robert Randall (collaboration w Randall Garrett); *Imaginative Tales*; Jan. 1958
- Vengeance of the Space Armadas; as Calvin M. Knox; *SF Adventures*; Mar. 1958; incorporated into LEST WE FORGET THEE, EARTH
- Voyage to Procyon; *Imagination*;#61, June 1958
- Wages of Death, The: *Worlds of If*; Aug. 1958; b&w illo: Virgil Finlay
- We, the Marauders; *SF Quarterly*; Feb. 1958
- Woman You Wanted, The: *Future*, #36, Apr. 1958; cover & b&w illo: Emshwiller

1959
- A Cry for Help; as Eric Rodman *Super SF*; Apr. 1959
- Appropriations; *Saturn*; May 1959 / *New Worlds*; Dec. 1959
- Beasts of Nightmare Horror; as Richard F. Watson; *Super SF*; June 1959
- Certainty; *Astounding SF*; Nov. 1959
- Collision Course; *Amazing Stories*; July 1959
- Company Store; STAR SF STORIES; Fred Pohl, Ballantine, 1959
- Counterpart;*Fantastic Universe*; Oct. 1959
- Day the Monsters Broke Loose, The; *Super SF*; June 1959
- Deadlock; *Astounding SF*; Jan. 1959
- Delivery Guaranteed; as Calvin M. Knox; *SF Stories*; Feb. 1959; ss written for cover art by Ed Emshwiller
- Demons of Cthulhu; as Charles D. Hammer; *Monster Parade*, Mar. 1959
- Earthman's Burden; *New Worlds*; Feb. 1959
- Eye of the Beholder; *SF Stories*; Sept. 1959
- Guardian Devil; *Fantastic*, May 1959
- Heap Big Medicine; see Strong Waters (1958)
- Hi Diddle Diddle!; as Calvin M. Knox *Astounding SF*; Feb. 1959
- His Brother's Weeper; *Fantastic Universe*; Mar. 1959
- Horror in the Attic, The; as Alex Merriman; *Super SF*; Aug. 1959
- Impossible Intelligence, The; *SF Stories*; Nov. 1959; ca: Ed Emshwiller
- In Gratitude; see There Was an Old Woman (1958)

- Insidious Invaders. The; as Eric Rodman; *Super SF*; October 1959
- Leisure Class; *Fantastic Universe*; July 1959
- Loathsome Beasts, The; as Dan Malcolm *Super SF*; October. 1959
- Malnutrition; *New Worlds*; July 1959; see Alaree (1958)
- Monsters Came by Night. The; as Charles D. Hammer; *Super SF*; Oct. 1959
- Monsters That Once Were Men; as Eric Rodman; *Super SF*; Aug. 1959
- Mournful Monster; as Dan Malcolm; *Super SF*; Apr. 1959; b&w art: Ed Emshwiller
- Mugwump Four; *Galaxy*; Aug. 1959; b&w art: Don Martin
- Outbreeders. The; as Calvin M. Knox *Fantastic Universe*; Sept. 1959
- Planet of the Angry Giants; as Dirk Clinton; *Super SF*; Aug. 1959
- Re-Conditioned Human; *Super SF*; Feb. 1959
- Strong Waters; *Nebula* (Scotland); Jan. 1958; *as* Heap Big
- There's No Place Like Space; *SF Stories*; May 1959; Emshwiller b&w art
- Thing Behind Hell's Door, The; as Alex Merriman; *Monster Parade* March 1959
- Translation Error; *Astounding SF*; Mar. 1959
- Undertaker's Sideline, The; as Richard F. Watson; *Monsters and Things* April 1959
- Vampires from Outer Space; as Richard F. Watson; *Super SF*; Apr. 1959; B&W art: Ed Emshwiller
- Waters of Forgetfulness; as Eric Rodman; *Super SF*; Feb. 1959
- Which Was the Monster?; as Dan Malcolm; *Super SF*; Aug. 1959
- World He Left Behind Him, The; *Nebula* (Scotland); Feb. 1959
- You Can't Cheat Death's Demon; as David Challon; *Monsters and Things*; April 1959
- You Do Something to Me; as Calvin M. Knox; *Future SF* #41; Feb. 1959; ca: Ed Emshwiller

1960
- Calibrated Alligator, The; as Calvin M. Knox; *Astounding SF*; Feb. 1960
- Still Small Voice, The; *Amazing*; May 1960
- Stress Pattern; *Astounding SF*; Jan. 1960
- Subterfuge; *Amazing Stories*; Mar. 1960

1961
- Dark Companion; *Amazing Stories* January 1961
- Man Who Came Back, The; *New Worlds*; #103, Mar. 1961
- Seed of Earth (novella); *Galaxy*, June 1961

1962.
- Nature of the Place, The; *Mag of Fantasy & SF*; Feb. 1963

1963
- The Nature of the Place; *Mag of Fantasy & SF* Feb. 1963

- Pain Peddlers, The; *Galaxy*; Aug. 1963
- Shadow of Wings, The; *Worlds of If*; July 1963
- To See the Invisible Man; *Worlds of Tomorrow*; Apr. 1963
- Unbeliever, The; *Magazine of Horror*; Aug. 1963

1964
- Neighbor; *Galaxy*; Aug. 1964

1965
- At the End of Days; *New Worlds*; Sept. 1965; *Magazine of Horror* #27; May 1969
- Blue Fire; *Galaxy*; June 1965; incorporated into TO OPEN THE SKY
- Sixth Palace, The; *Galaxy*; Feb. 1965
- Warriors of Light, The; *Galaxy*; Dec. 1965

1966
- Halfway House; *Worlds of If SF* #110; Nov. 1966
- Lazarus Come Forth; *Galaxy*; Apr. 1966
- Open the Sky; *Galaxy*; June 1966
- Where the Changed Ones Go; *Galaxy*; Feb. 1966

1967
- Bride 91; *Worlds of If*; Sept. 1967
- By the Seawall; *Worlds of If*; Jan. 1967
- Flies; DANGEROUS VISIONS; ed. by Harlan Ellison; Doubleday, NY; with afterword by RS; b&w illo: Leo. & Diane Dillon
- Hawksbill Station; *Galaxy*; Aug. 1967
- King of the Golden World; *Galaxy*; Dec. 1967; alt. titled The King of the Golden River

1968
- Among the Rememberers; re-titled Perris Way; *Galaxy* Nov. 1968; incorporated into NIGHTWINGS
- As Is; *Worlds of Fantasy*, Vol.1, #1 (no month) 1968; b&w illo: Jack Gaughan
- Going Down Smooth; *Galaxy*; Aug. 1968; story written for cover art by Vaughn Bodé
- Nightwings; *Galaxy*; Sept. 1968; cover /b&w art: Jack Gaughan
- *Passengers; ORBIT 4; anthology edited by Damon Knight, Putnam*
  No question that "Passengers" was first published in ORBIT 4, December, 1968. But it won a Nebula in 1970, and the trophy, which I just looked at, plainly says it's the Best Short Story of 1969. Under the Nebula rules then in effect, I now recall, stories published in December were considered to have been published in the following year, so that they would not be injured through having been available to readers (and voters) for just thirty days of the year of their publication. The 1970 Nebula anthology lists it with a 1968 copyright date; the other winners (Ellison, Le Guin, and one other) all have 1969 copyright dates. Somewhere along the way I must have forgotten that it actually came out in December of 1968, and started thinking of it as a 1969 story, because it won a Nebula for 1969 in April of 1970.
  Then we come to the Hugos of 1970. At the Heidelberg

Worldcon "Passengers" was on the ballot but lost to a Samuel R. Delany story, which I correctly recalled had been published in New Worlds *in 1968. And I have been saying ever since that my 1969 story was beaten by an ineligible 1968 story for the Hugo to be awarded in 1970, when the truth of the matter seems to be that both Delany's story and mine were ineligible for Hugos at the 1970 Worldcon. It's a very messy story, I now see, and it's too late for me to start retracting my statement, now that I've made it at least three times in introductions to "Passengers." I doubt that I'll be having any more Collected Stories series published, but if I ever do, I'll delete the offending claim then.* —RS

- Perris Way; *Galaxy*; Nov. 1968; incorporated into NIGHTWINGS
- Fangs of the Trees, The; *Mag of Fantasy & SF*, Oct. 1969
- To the Dark Star; THE FARTHEST REACHES; J. Elder, Trident

1969
- After the Myths Went Home; *Mag of Fantasy & SF*; Nov. 1969
- How It Was When the Past Went Away; THREE FOR TOMORROW; Meredith; 1969
- Sundance; *Mag of Fantasy & SF*, June 1969
- To Jorslem; *Galaxy*; Feb. 1969; incorporated into NIGHTWINGS

1970
- A Happy Day in 2381; NOVA; Harry Harrison; Delacorte;
- Black Is Beautiful; THE YEAR 2000; ed. Harry Harrison; Doubleday,
- In the Beginning; SCIENCE AGAINST MAN; ed. A. Cheetham; Avon
- Ishmael in Love; *Mag of Fantasy & SF*; July 1970
- Pleasure of Our Company, The; INFINITY, ONE; ed. R. Hoskins; Lancer;
- Reality Trip, The; World of *Worlds of If*; May 1970
- Ringing the Changes; ALCHEMY AND ACADEME; ed. A. McCaffrey; Doubleday
- Song the Zombie Sang, The; *Cosmopolitan*; Dec.; with Harlan Ellison
- Throwbacks, The; *Galaxy*; July 1970
- We Are Well Organized; *Galaxy*; Dec. 1970; incorporated into THE WORLD INSIDE
- We Know Who We Are; *Amazing*; July 1970
- World Outside, The; *Galaxy*; Oct. 1970; incorporated into THE WORLD INSIDE

1971
- All the Way Up, All the Way Down; *Galaxy*; July 1971; incorporated in THE WORLD INSIDE
- Caliban; INFINITY THREE. ed. R. Hoskins; Lancer; 1972
- Going; FOUR FEATURES/ Anon/Hawthorn
- Good News from the Vatican; UNIVERSE 1; ed. Terry Carr; Ace;
- In Entropy's Jaws; INFINITY 2; R.Hoskins; Lancer Books;
- Something Wild Is Loose; THE MANY WORLDS OF SCIENCE FICTION; ed. Ben Bova; Dutton

1972
- Caught in the Organ Draft; AND WALK NOW GENTLY THROUGH THE FIRE / Vertex April 1973
- Now + n, Now − n; NOVA 2; ed. Harry Harrison; Delacorte
- Thomas the Proclaimer; THE DAY THE SUN STOOD STILL, Thomas Nelson
- What We Learned from This Morning's Newspaper; INFINITY FOUR; ed. R. Hoskins; Lancer;
- When We Went to See the End of the World; UNIVERSE 2; ed. Terry Carr; Ace
- Push No More; STRANGE BEDFELLOWS: SEX AND SCIENCE FICTION; ed. Thomas N. Scortia; Random House

1973
- Breckenridge and the Continuum; SHOWCASE; ed. Roger Elwood; Harper & Row
- Getting Across; FUTURE CITY; ed. Roger Elwood; Simon & Schuster
- In the Group; EROS IN ORBIT; ed. J. Elder; Trident
- Many Mansions; UNIVERSE 3; ed. Terry Carr; Ace
- Ms. Found in an Abandoned Time Machine; TEN TOMORROWS; ed. Roger Elwood; Fawcett Publications, Inc.
- Ship-Sister, Star-Sister; FRONTIER: TOMORROW'S ALTERNATIVES; ed. Roger Elwood; Macmillan Pub.
- Some Notes on the Pre-Dynastic Epoch; BAD MOON RISING; ed. Thomas M. Disch
- The Feast of St. Dionysus
- The Mutant Season; ANDROIDS, TIME MACHINES AND BLUE GIRAFFES; ed. by RS; Follet Publishing Com.
- The Science Fiction Hall of Fame; INFINITY FIVE; ed. Roger Elwood; Lancer Books, Inc
- The Wind and the Rain; SAVING WORLDS; Roger Elwood & Virginia Kidd
- This Is the Road; NO MIND OF MAN

1974
- A Sea of Faces; UNIVERSE 4; ed. Terry Carr; Random House
- Born With the Dead; *Mag of Fantasy & SF*; Apr. 1974; special RS issue; ca: Ed Emshwiller
- Capricorn Games; THE FAR SIDE OF TIME; ed. Roger Elwood; Lancer Books, Inc
- In the House of Double Minds; Vertex April 1973
- Schwartz Between the Galaxies; STELLAR 1; edited by Theodore W. Hipple; Ballantine
- The Day the Founder Died; CRISIS, ed. by Roger Elwood; Thomas Nelson
- The Dybbuk of Mazel Tov IV; WANDERING STARS; ed. Jack Dann; Harper & Row
- Trips; FINAL STAGE: THE ULTIMATE SCIENCE FICTION ANTHOLOGY; eds. Edward Ferman & Barry N. Malzberg; Charterhouse

1975
- Silhouette; THE NEW ATLANTIS, ed. Robert Silverberg; Hawthorne

1977
- The Weight Watcher; A Readers' Digest condensed version of The Iron Chancellor; READER'S DIGEST SCIENCE FICTION TOP-PICKS; Reader's Digest Services; PB

1980
- Our Lady of the Sauropods; *Omni* Sept. 1980

1981
- A Thief in Ni-Moya; *Asimov's SF* December 21, 1981
- A Thousand Paces Along the Via Dolorosa; *Twilight Zone Magazine;* July 1981
- How They Pass the Time in Pelpel; *Twilight Zone Magazine,* May 1981
- In the Fifth Year of the Voyage; *Mag of Fantasy & SF*, Dec. 1981; ca: Barclay Shaw
- The Desert of Stolen Dreams; *Mag of Fantasy & SF*, June 1981
- The Palace at Midnight; *Omni;* July 1981
- The Regulars; *Asimov's SF;* May 1981
- The Soul-Painter and the Shapeshifter; *Omni;* Nov. 1981
- Waiting for the Earthquake; *Omni* BEST OF OMNI SCI-ENCE FICTION 2; PB, (Originally written for an antholo-gy edited by Harlan Ellison, MEDEA)

1982
- Among the Dream Speakers; *Asimov's SF;* January 18, 1982
- At the Conglomeroid Cocktail Party; *Playboy* magazine; August 1982
- Calintane Explains; *Asimov's SF;* February 1982 (Chapter 7); Arbor House
- Gianni; *Playboy;* February 1982
- Jennifer's Lover; *Penthouse;* May 1982
- Not Our Brother; *Twilight Zone;* July 1982
- The Changeling; *Amazing Stories;* November 1982
- The Far Side of the Bell-Shaped Curve; *Omni* Magazine
- The Man Who Floated in Time; SPECULATIONS; ed. I. Asimov & Alice Laurance
- The Pope of the Chimps; PERPETUAL LIGHT; ed. Alan Ryan
- The Time of the Burning; *Asimov's SF;* March 1982
- The Trouble with Sempoanga; BEYOND 2

1983
- Amanda and the Alien; *Omni;* May 1983
- Basileus; BEST OF OMNI SCIENCE FICTION 5; maga-zine size PB; *Omni*
- Dancer's in the Time-Flux; LANDS OF NEVER ED. Maxim Jakubowski; HEROIC VISIONS; PB; Ace
- Homefaring; *Amazing Stories;* Nov. 1983; b&w art: Artfact
- Multiples; *Omni;* October 1983
- Needle in a Timestack; *Playboy;* June 1983

- The Election; *Analog* March 1983

1984
- Gate of Horn, Gate of Ivory; UNIVERSE 14; ed. Terry Carr; PB
- The Affair; *Playboy* June 1984; alt title: Snake and Ocean, Ocean and Snake
- Tourist Trade; *Playboy* December 1984
- Lord of Darkness(Excerpt)
- Valentine Pontifex(Excerpt)

1985
- Sailing to Byzantium; *Asimov's SF;* Feb. 1985
- Sunrise on Pluto; THE PLANETS; PB

1986
- Against Babylon; *Omni;* May 1986; incorporated into novel THE ALIEN YEARS
- Blindsight; *Playboy* December 1986; incorporated into novel HOT SKY AT MIDNIGHT
- Gilgamesh in the Outback; *Asimov's SF;* July 1986; Chapter 1-5 of the novel TO THE LAND OF THE LIVING; Winner of Hugo Award for best novella, 1987. Nominated for Nebula Award for best novella, 1986.
- Watchdogs; *Twilight Zone;* Aug. 1986; b&w illo: Robert Pizzo

1987
- Hardware; *Omni;* October 1987
- The Fascination of the Abomination; *Asimov's SF;* July 1987; cover art: Joe Bergeron; b&w illo: Gary Freeman; The title is from Conrad's HEART OF DARKNESS
- The Iron Star; THE UNIVERSE; ed. Byron Preiss; 1987; Bantam
- The Secret Sharer; *Asimov's SF;* Sept. 1987; nominated for Nebula Award for best novella 1987; cover & b&w illo: Bob Eggleton
- The Pardoner's Tale; *Playboy;* June 1987

1988
- At Winter's End, (excerp) *Asimov's SF;* Jan1988; ca: Hisaki Yasuda
- Gilgamesh in Uruk; *Asimov's SF;* June 1988
- Hannibal's Elephants; *Omni;* Oct. 1988
- House of Bones; TERRY'S UNIVERSE; ed. by Beth Meacham; Tor, PB
- The Dead Man's Eyes; *Playboy;* August 1988
- We Are for the Dark; *Asimov's SF;* Oct. 1988; cover & b&w illo: Hisaki Yasuda

1989
- Batman in Nighttown; (with Karen Haber); THE FURTHER ADVENTURES OF BATMAN; ed. Martin H. Greenberg; PB; Bantam
- Chip Runner; MICROVERSE; PB
- Enter a Soldier. Later: Enter Another; *Asimov's SF;* June 1989; Nominated for Nebula Award for best novelette, 1989.

Winner of Hugo Award for best novella, 1990.
- In Another Country; *Asimov's SF,* March 1989
- Tales From the Venia Woods; *Mag of Fantasy & SF,* October 1989
- The Asenion Solution; FOUNDATION'S FRIENDS; PB; Tor
- To the Promised Land; *Omni,* May 1989; a Roma Eterna story
- A Sleep and a Forgetting; *Playboy,* July 1989

1990
- Hot Sky; *Playboy;* Feb.1990
- Interludes; TIME GATE: DANGEROUS INTERFACES;1990; ed. RS; Baen
- Lion Time in Timbuctoo; *Asimov's SF,* October 1990
- The Catch; *Omni* August 1990
- They Hide, We See; ISAAC ASIMOV'S UNIVERSE Vol. 1: The Diplomacy Guild; w introduction by RS

1991
- A Tip on a Turtle; *Amazing Stories;* May 1991
- An Outpost of the Empire; *Asimov's SF,* November 1991
- Hunters in the Forest; *Omni;* Oct. 1991
- The Face of The Waters; *Amazing Stories;* Aug. 1991
- The Last Surviving Veteran of the War of San Francisco; *Omni;* March 1991

1992
- It Comes and Goes; *Playboy;* Jan. 1992
  The only censorship I can recall involved this story for Playboy *in which the protagonist was a member of Alcoholics Anonymous. The editor pointed out that* Playboy *didn't want to offend the liquor manufacturers that advertised in the magazine, so I made him a drug addict instead. Didn't change the story in any important way, just substituted one addiction for another and collected my five thousand bucks. When I reprinted it in some story collection of mine, I used my version, not* Playboy's*! —RS*
- A Long Night's Vigil at the Temple; AFTER THE KING ed. by Martin H. Greenberg
- The Perfect Host; OMNI BEST SF 1; PB
- Thebes of the Hundred Gates
- Looking for the Fountain; *Asimov's SF;* May 1992
- Kingdoms of the Wall (Excerpt)

1993
- The Sri Lanka Position; *Playboy;* Dec. 1993

1994
- Via Roma; *Asimov's SF,* April 1994

1995
- Hot Times in Magma City; *Asimov SF,* Mid-December, 1995; ca: John Maggard
- The Dragon on the Bookshelf; THE ULTIMATE DRAG-ON; Dell; PB; w Harlan Ellison
- The Red Blaze Is the Morning; NEW LEGENDS; Tor; PB
- The Second Shield; *Playboy;* December 1995

1996
- Death Do Us Part; *Omni* Online, ed. by Ellen Datlow / *Asimov's SF;* August 1997
- Diana of the Hundred Breasts; *Realms of Fantasy,* Feb. 1996
- The Martian Invasion Journals of Henry James; IN WAR OF THE WORLDS: GLOBAL DISPATCHES; ed. Kevin J. Anderson; Bantam/Spectra
- The Tree That Grew from the Sky; *Science Fiction Age* September 1996

1997
- Beauty in the Night; *Science Fiction Age;* Sept. 1997
- Call Me Titan; *Asimov SF,* February, 1997; ca: Jael
- On the Inside; *Science Fiction Age;* Nov. 1997
- The Church at Monte Saturno; *Realms of Fantasy* April 1997

1998
- The Colonel in Autumn; SF Age; March 1998; section of THE ALIEN YEARS
- Waiting for the End; *Asimov's SF,* Oct/Nov. 1998

1999
- A Hero of the Empire; *Magazine of Fantasy & SF;* Oct/Nov 1999; a Roma Eterna story
- A Killing Light; w Karen Haber; STARDRIVE: STARFALL; TSR/Wizards of the Coast,; PB
- Travelers; *Amazing Stories;* Summer 1999
- Getting to Know the Dragon; FAR HORIZONS: The Great Worlds of Science Fiction (ed. RS), Avon

2000
- The Millennial Express; *Playboy;* Jan. 2000

2002
- The Second Wave; *Asimov's SF,* August 2002; a Roma Eterna story
- With Caesar in the Underworld; *Asimov's SF,* October/November 2002; a Roma Eterna story

2003
- The Reign of Terror; *Asimov's SF,* April 2003
- Crossing Into the Empire; *Realms of Fantasy;* June 2003
- The Book of Changes; LEGENDS II; ed. by RS

2005
- A Piece of the Great World; ONE MILLION A.D.; ed Gardner Dozois; SF Book Club

2006
- Hanosz Prime Goes to Old Earth; *Asimov's SF,* April/May, 2006
  Both "Hanosz Prime" and "The Emperor and the Maula" [see 2007] use material from an abandoned novel of mine — the only one I've ever given up on — which I began writing around 1986. After 160 pages or so I realized that the story I had in mind was impossible to manage successfully — it was a vast unwieldy thing

likely to collapse of its own weight — but it had some very nice set-pieces in it and I've used them in various stories since. "Hanosz Prime" is an outright extract,only slightly edited, from the abandoned book. "The Emperor and the Maula"'s material is unrelated to that book, but I used a few descriptive passages from it in the later story.— RS

2007
- Against the Current; *Mag of Fantasy & SF*; Oct/Nov
- The Eater of Dreams; *Asimov's SF*, April/May 2007
- The Emperor and the Maula; (see Hanosz Prime, 2006); THE NEW SPACE OPERA; eds: Gardner Dozois and Jonathan Strahan; HarperCollins Eo

In the case of "Emperor" Gardner Dozois asked me to write a story for a book called THE NEW SPACE OPERA. I asked him what the new space opera was, because the term meant nothing to me and I didn't want to appear like a fossil of an earlier age amid the newer writers in the book, and he said it's just like the old space opera, only better written. So I used the old Scheherazade plot and decorated it with some space-operatic frills and furbelows, nodding affectionately at the old PLANET STORIES school of writing without in any way trying to imitate it. After nearly sixty years of writing sf I can't take the old tropes seriously any more, but I certainly do feel affection for them…. I haven't forgotten how to write the standard pulp story but I don't see much reason for doing so at this late date.— RS

2009
- The Way they Wove the Spells in Sippulgar; *Magazine of Fantasy & SF,* Oct/Nov, 2009 (60th anniversary issue); *I had stories in the 30th, 40th, and 50th anniversary issues, so I felt it behooved me to do one for the 60th. (I did one for the 20th, too, but it got crowded out and appeared a month later.) I doubt that anyone else has had stories in four consecutive decade-marking anniversary issues of the magazine, and I do like establishing little longevity records of that sort.— RS*

RADIO SCRIPTS

EXPLORING TOMORROW
Broadcast history: December 4, 1957 to June 13, 1958. Mutual Radio Network. 25 mins.; Cast: New York radio personnel: Mandel Kramer, Bryna Raeburn, Lawson Zerbe, Lon Clarke; Host: John W. Campbell, Jr.; Announcers: Bill Mahr, Guy Wallace; Producer-Director: Sanford Marshall

My records show that I had eleven scripts aired on Exploring Tomorrow (radio series) from the winter of 1957-8 through the spring of 1958, when I guess the show was canceled. I was paid $100 a script. —RS

COUNTRY BOY – Aired 12/18/1957
THE MIMIC – Aired 03/19/1958
THE MOON IS NEW – (original title: The Moon is Red) – Aired 01/22/1958/
DESTINATION: ARCTURUS (originally written for Exploring Tomorrow)
HIS HEAD IN THE CLOUDS – (From *Original SF Stories* cover ss)
THE OLD MAN – (Adaptation of ss from *Imagination.*)
COLLECTING TEAM – (Adaptation of 1956 ss from *Super SF*)
THE SOURDOUGH – (Adaptation of *Astounding SF* ss)
PRECEDENT – (Adaptation of *Astounding SF* story)
SOUND DECISION; w. Randall Garrett; Air Date: 04/02/1958
OVERPOPULATION – Air Date: 04/09/1958; (Adaptation of *Astounding SF* ss No Way Out)

FANZINES

SPACESHIP #1; 1949; 28 issues thru May 1955

GRAPHIC/COMIC ADAPTATIONS

- THE FURTHER ADVENTURES OF BATMAN; Bantam; 1989; ed. Martin H. Greenberg; PB, anth; ss Batman in Nighttown by Karen Haber and RS; 401 pp; ca: Kyle Baker

- ADVENTURES OF THE BATMAN; MJF Books/DC Comics; 1995; HC; ed. Martin H. Greenberg; ss Batman in Nighttown by Karen Haber & RS; 553 pp; ca: Steve Stanley *…mostly the work of my wife Karen. I did a few touchups here and there.— RS*

STARSTREAM: ADVENTURES IN SCIENCE FICTION
- Whitman Publishing; series began 1976; #2; adapts ss Collecting Team; art by Giorgio Cambiotti; adaptation: Steve Skeates

QUESTAR: Illustrated SF Classics
- Golden Press/Western Pub; 1979; reprints Collecting Team with art by Cambiotti

UNKNOWN WORLDS OF SF
- Curtis/Marvel Comics; July, 1975; issue #4; ss Good News From The Vatican adapted by Gerry Conway & A. Gonzales,

NIGHTWINGS
- DC Comics (DC Science Fiction Series); Jan. 1985; Trade PB; adapted by writer: Cary Bates, artists: Gene Colan & Neal McPheeters; ca: Bill Sienkiwicz

SEVENTH SHRINE
- Marvel Comics; June 2007; PB; 144 pp; full color art by European artist Anders Finer

FAPA (Fantasy Amateur Press Association)
Founded in 1937 by sf author and editor Donald Wollheim.
Members are expected to produce a certain amount of mate-
rial per year for inclusion in a collected periodical mailed to
the entire group.
• RS began membership Aug. 1949
I'm still a member of FAPA, 59 years later. I'm its current
president, in fact.

LIST OF ILLUSTRATIONS

List of illustrations (by page number) and photographic acknowl-
edgements. Every effort has been made to contact all copyright
holders. The publisher will be happy to correct in future editions
any errors or omissions brought to their attention.

Emshwiller. © Columbia Publications, Inc.

66. THE MASKS OF TIME, ©Ballantine Books, 1968; cover art by Robert Foster.

67. RS with John W. Campbell Jr. c. 1969.

68. Baycon banquet, 1968, Berkeley, California. Harlan Ellison helping RS, as toastmaster, present the Hugos. Philip Jose Farmer, to RS's right, is guest of honor. (courtesy of RS)

70. RS with Harlan Ellison and Barbara Silverberg.

71. RS holding Nebula Award for "Passengers," 1968. Photo © by Jay Kay Klein, used with permission.

72. Photo courtesy & © Andrew I. Porter

75. NIGHTWINGS 1970 edition with Jack Gaughan jacket artwork.

76. Ballantine paperback edition of NEEDLE IN A TIMESTACK, Nov. 1966; cover art by Richard Powers.

77. A photo of the Riverdale, NY house taken by Moshe Feder (courtesy of RS)

78. THORNS, ballantine paperback. THOSE WHO WATCH, Signet paperback.

79. Panter paperback edition of THE WORLD INSIDE.

80. (top) RS with Roger Zelazny, 1967, (Photo courtesy & © Andrew I. Porter).

80. (bottom) Signet paperback edition of NEW DIMEN-SIONS IV.

81. Cover art by Jack Gaughan for "Nightwings" in *Galaxy* Magazine (© Jack Gaughan Estate, used with permission)

82. *Magazine of Fantasy & Science Fiction* special RS issue, April, 1974, © Spilogale, Inc.

83. Photo by Bill Rotsler.

85. Photo courtesy & © Andrew I. Porter

88. RS with Samuel R. Delany. Photo © by Jay Kay Klein, used with permission.

91. *New Worlds Science Fictio*, May 1960.

93. RS at Brian Aldiss home in the UK, (Photo courtesy & © Andrew I. Porter).

95. INFINITE JESTS, hardcover published by Chilton, 1974.

96. RS c. 1970s. Photo © Jay Kay Klein.

98. FIRST AMERICAN INTO SPACE, © Monarch Books paperback, 1961.

101. TOWER OF GLASS paperback, Bantam Books, 1971

103. Ledger page from 1956 (courtesy of RS).

104. Photo © by Jay Kay Klein, used with permission.

105. Philip K. Dick with RS at the 1968 Worldcon (Photo by David A. Kyle)

106. THE SEED OF EARTH Ace paperbeck edition, 1977. Cover art by Don Ivan Punchatz.

107. EARTHMAN & STRANGERS, © Dell 1966 paper-back edtion.

108. SON OF MAN, ballantine paperback.

109. Two separate Ace Double PB editions: NEXT STOP THE STARS and INVADERS FROM EARTH.

110. THE 13th IMMORTAL and THE SEED OF EARTH, Ace Double.

112. *Astounding Science Fiction* magazine. © Street & Smith

113. DYING INSIDE, 1972; © Scribner's Sons

114. THE SILENT INVADERS and INVADERS FROM EARTH, Avon paperbacks

117. Art by Wally Wood for "Birds of a Feather" *Galaxy*, Nov. 1958. © Galaxy Publishing Corp.

118. Photo courtesy & © Andrew I. Porter

121. NIGHTWINGS, Avon paperback 1969; TO OPEN THE SKY, Ballantine paperback 1967.

122. Art by Tim White for THOSE WHO WATCH. ©Tim White, used with permission.

123. DYING INSIDE, Ballantine paperback 1973. DOWN TO THE EARTH Signet paperback 1971.

124. THE BEST OF ROBERT SILVERBERG, Pocket Books. Danish edtion of ALIENS FROM SPACE 1960.

125. Art by Tim White for THORNS, © Tim White, used with permission.

126. LORD VALENTINE'S CASTLE, Harpeet & Row, 1980.

127. NEW DIMENSIONS III, Signet paperback 1973.

128. Original idea for LORD VALENTINE'S CASTLE, (courtesy of RS)

130. Dust jacket author's photo from 1983. Photo by Susanne Lee Houfek.

131. Majipoor map drawn by RS, (courtesy of RS).

133. PARSECS AND PARABLES, Doubleday, 1970.

135. STARSTREAM: Adventure in Science Fiction #2, art by Cambiotti, ©1977 Whiman Publishing.

137. Cover illustration by John Picacio for SON OF MAN (Pyr) ©2008 John Picacio. Used with permission.

138. *Terra* German magazine reprinting THE 13TH IMMORTAL.

139. (top) Persian edtion of STEPSONS OF TERRA. (Bottom) WORLDS'S FAIR 1992.

140. (top) RS at the 1982 Nebula Awards.

140. Page spread 1997 NONSTOP SF MAGAZINE; art © L. Ortiz.

141. (top) Burmese edition of LIGHT FOR THE WORLD. (bottom) AT WINTER'S END, Warner Books, 1988.

142. Art by Bob Eggleton for THE ALIEN YEARS. © Bob Eggleton, used with permission.

143. (top) THE SF BESTIARY, Dell, 1974. (bottom) CAPRICORN GAMES, Pan Books, 1979.

144. THE TIME HOPPERS (Avon PB) and THE BOOK OF SKULLS (Signet PB)

145. STARSTREAM: Adventure in Science Fiction, (Unpublished art by Joe Brozowski), ©1977 Whiman Publishing.

146. 149. 150. 153. 159. Photos © Andrew I. Porter

151. 155. ASIMOV SF © Davis Publications, Inc.

152. A TIME OF CHANGES, Doubleday, 1971.

153. RS with H. Ellison & Larry Shaw. Photo © by Jay Kay Klein, used with permission.

154. TO LIVE AGAIN, Doubleday, 1969.

162. RS and Joe Halderman (courtesy of RS).

166. RS and Karen Haber (courtesy of RS).